Sustained SOX

A practical guide for implementing a sustainable Sarbanes Oxley process
Volume I of III

MICHAEL S. HUGH

Bloomington, IN Milton Keynes, UK
authorHOUSE

AuthorHouse™
1663 Liberty Drive, Suite 200
Bloomington, IN 47403
www.authorhouse.com
Phone: 1-800-839-8640

AuthorHouse™ UK Ltd.
500 Avebury Boulevard
Central Milton Keynes, MK9 2BE
www.authorhouse.co.uk
Phone: 08001974150

©2006 Michael S. Hugh. All rights reserved.

No part of this book may be reproduced, stored in a retrieval system, or transmitted by any means without the written permission of the author.

First published by AuthorHouse 3/30/2006

ISBN: 1-4259-2482-4 (dj)
ISBN: 1-4259-2483-2 (sc)

Library of Congress Control Number: 2006902570

Printed in the United States of America
Bloomington, Indiana

This book is printed on acid-free paper.

INTRODUCTION

This is Volume I of a three-part series on Sarbanes Oxley (SOX) processes. It provides a wide perspective of the internal control policies, procedures and guidelines that need to be developed for SOX compliance. In each volume, you are provided with detailed information on every step of the Sarbanes Oxley certification process.

The subject matter is *extensive* and could not all be covered in the first volume; which introduces you to the main processes and the supporting details necessary to implement and maintain these processes on an ongoing basis.

The series was originally written to assist our clients in the implementation of an Internal Control Framework for Financial Reporting ("ICFFR")[1] that complied with the requirements of the Sarbanes Oxley Act of 2002 (SOX).

During 2003 and 2004, SOX was in an evolutionary stage which caused many companies to meet this challenging environment on a reactive basis. Under these circumstances, many companies achieved their initial certifications with processes that they soon discovered could not be sustained in the following years with the reduced costs and related resources that they had originally planned in 2003/4.

In 2005, these companies attempted to reengineer their initial processes so that they could achieve their goals on an ongoing basis. These attempts achieved mixed results and several companies have been forced to repeat this reengineering process in 2006.

The contents of entire series are based on our work in the design, implementation and assessment of these frameworks for both the *initial* certifications and for the *subsequent, ongoing* certifications.

Other elements in this series are the results of our design and implementation of a successful series of SOX Management Systems. These systems have been used to achieve both the initial and the subsequent certifications for our clients and have been employed in both the Entity Level and Process/Transaction level assessments of their internal control frameworks.

INTENT OF THIS VOLUME

This volume is the introductory volume that introduces you to several key, critical processes required to sustain Sarbanes Oxley process for the long term.

From the initial SOX 404 certifications of late 2004 to now, many companies have struggled to build and maintain an ongoing, sustainable SOX process. The intent of this volume is to assist you and your company to build and maintain the processes that will enable you to achieve your initial certification (*if you have not already done so*) and, simultaneously, to

---

[1] INTERNAL CONTROL OVER FINANCIAL REPORTING is defined by Rules 13a 15(f) and 15d 15(f) of the U.S. Securities and Exchange Act of 1934 to mean a process designed by, or under the supervision of, the CEO and CFO, and effected by the board of directors, management and other personnel, to provide reasonable assurance regarding the reliability of financial reporting and the preparation of financial statements for external purposes in accordance with generally accepted accounting principles and includes those policies and procedures that: I) Pertain to the maintenance of records that in reasonable detail accurately and fairly reflect the transactions and dispositions of the assets of your company; ii) Provide reasonable assurance that transactions are recorded as necessary to permit preparation of financial statements in accordance with generally accepted accounting principles, and that receipts and expenditures are being made only in accordance with authorizations of management and directors; and iii) Provide reasonable assurance regarding prevention or timely detection of unauthorized acquisition, use or disposition of your company's assets that could have a material effect on the financial statements.

construct processes that are sustainable in subsequent years as the SOX regulatory environment further evolves.

NOTE CAREFULLY

Our intent is to provide you with *sound, practical processes* that can be used in any company – regardless of size or location. It is not intended to be a legal or accounting treatise. Its intent is to provide you with a recommended series of *field proven* processes that you can review, modify and implement within your company in a relatively short time frame.

The material in this volume is designed to provide information in regard to the subject matter covered and is distributed with the understanding that the publisher, authors, and editors are not rendering legal, accounting, or other professional services within this volume. If legal advice or other expert assistance is required, the services of a competent professional should be sought.

INTENDED AUDIENCE FOR THIS SERIES

This volume is written and organized to assist anyone engaged in your company's SOX activities to understand the required processes.

We recommend that Volume I should be used by the general internal controls population in your company. Volumes II & III should be used by the management of the internal control processes and specialized practitioners in the internal controls governance team.

These processes are provided from multiple organizational perspectives. These views will assist all managers to better understand their roles and responsibilities.

ORGANIZATION OF VOLUME

The first two chapters provide the required SOX environmental information. Each chapter thereafter is self contained and is designed to address a specific process in the certification cycle.

CHAPTER 1 – ORGANIZING FOR SARBANES OXLEY

The focus is on organizing on a company wide basis for SOX and provides a comprehensive view from two perspectives.

- PERSONNEL ORGANIZATION - the roles and responsibilities, including external vendors that are involved in the assessment of internal control framework.

- PROCESS ORGANIZATION - the development and implementation of the internal control policies, procedures and guidelines that will be used to manage the internal control framework.

The organization of the responsible personnel is critical to ensuring the efficiencies required for a sustained certification process. This chapter highlights the key roles and responsibilities (at all organizational levels), reporting hierarchy, etc. that must be in place to ensure compliance and to achieve these efficiencies from both the initial and sustained processes.

It also serves as an introduction to the subsequent chapters that elaborate on the detail steps required for each of the high level processes introduced in this chapter.

By the end of this chapter, you will have the necessary background information to:

- implement and modify your company's organization chart, roles and responsibilities, and
- begin the design/modification of your internal control policies and procedures in order to develop a sustainable series of processes.

CHAPTER 2 – PREREQUISITES FOR SARBANES OXLEY

The focus is on the prerequisites required for a stable, cost efficient infrastructure necessary to support and maintain your initial and ongoing assessment/certification processes:

The subjects covered in this chapter are:

- SOX POLICIES, PROCEDURES AND GUIDELINES – further elaborates on Chapter 1 by providing you with the additional content that should be incorporated into these critical documents,

- SOX REPOSITORY – provides the introduction to the Repository and its primary roles and responsibilities in the SOX environment. It reviews the validation, storage, analysis, reporting and other critical functions that will be use within the repository for SOX documentation and evidence,

- SOX MASTER FILES – explains how these files are used to ensure a unified, consistent method of documenting the internal control framework,

- SOX PLANS & CALENDAR – developing and establishing a timeline for both the initial effort and the subsequent, ongoing efforts is critical,

- SOX COMMUNICATIONS INFRASTRUCTURE – you may already be aware of the complexity and diversity of SOX communications from your initial efforts. Without a comprehensive, communications architecture and related processes to coordinate your company wide efforts, the communications for SOX can become onerous and unfocused – ultimately leading to resource and timing bottlenecks.,

- SOX TRAINING PROGRAMS - - provides an overview of the training programs required for the entire internal control framework

CHAPTER 3 – THE ENTITY LEVEL CONTROL PROGRAM

Using the COSO framework for illustrative purposes, this chapter reviews the construction of the entity level control program beginning at the:

- COSO COMPONENT level,
- Through the POINTS OF FOCUS and
- Subsequently, to the design, implementation and assessment of the required CONTROLS.

The chapter provides examples by COSO component and point of focus which will assist you in designing/modifying your present program. It also provides an overview of the methods used to assess, analyze and report on these controls. Detailed assessment procedures are provided in Chapter 9.

Chapter 4 – Communications Infrastructure

The entire communications infrastructure, data requirements and other key elements are reviewed. Some of the subjects included are:

- SOURCES from which communication information originate – the SOX reference Library, the Plans & Calendar function, the Repository Analyses and Reports function, etc. The necessary procedures and formats are reviewed in detail,

- CHANNELS or paths that should be developed for delivering the information – the development of library distribution, training, presentation, etc. channels is provided,

- The INFORMATION REQUIREMENTS of the SOX Audience and how communications should be formatted for presentation – since each constituent will have defined roles and responsibilities, the communications flow should be customized to meet the requirements of these roles.,

- The information requirements should be formatted into STANDARD ANALYSES AND REPORTS. Chapter 7 further expands on this section and provides examples of the analyses and reports.

Chapter 5 – Plans & Calendars

This chapter focuses on timing and the sequence of events – and not the details of processes which are covered in subsequent chapters.

It starts with a complete fiscal year calendar example and decomposes this into quarterly or monthly calendars. For each quarter, you are provided with standard planning templates for the main sections of the calendar e.g.

- FINANCIAL STATEMENTS RISK ASSESSMENT – provides the required steps through the final assignment of significant accounts and processes,

- PROCESS AND CONTROL DOCUMENTATION SUBMISSION TIMELINES – the recommended sequence of these activities throughout the entire fiscal year,

- ASSESSMENT (Testing timelines) – for both the Entity and Transaction Level control testing sequence and timelines,

- DEFICIENCY MANAGEMENT PROCESSES – reviews the collection, combination, duplicate elimination and aggregation timelines,

- SUB CERTIFICATION PROCESS – the sequence of this process, and

- EXTERNAL AUDITOR COORDINATION – coordinating with the External Auditor to ensure that Business Units have a complete calendar that covers all SOX activities.

By the end of the chapter, you should have completed a skeleton of your future fiscal year calendar subdivided by quarter.

Chapter 6 – SOX Repository

These are the steps necessary to establish the Repository with detailed checklists for the required tasks e.g.

- Constructing the INVENTORY of documents that should be submitted to and maintained within the library,

- Defining the required FORMAT for each document,

- Defining the BUSINESS RULES that will be used in the validation process for each type of document submitted to the Repository,

- Defining the ANALYSIS AND REPORTING REQUIREMENTS, and

- AUDIT PREPARATION requirements.

Upon completing the chapter, and with the aid of the checklists, you should be ready to implement/modify your Repository to meet your ongoing requirements on a sustainable basis.

CHAPTER 7 – FINANCIAL STATEMENTS RISK ASSESSMENT

The results of this process are the assignment of the Significant Accounts and Processes coverage responsibilities to the Business Unit/Location. Business Units are required to design, implement and assess the processes and controls for each significant/process assigned to them as a result of this risk assessment.

This chapter and its worksheets provide you with the processes and methods to:

- Perform the preliminary financial statement risk assessment process,

- The assignment of default financial assertions to each financial statement line,

- Decompose each financial statement line into its significant accounts,

- Assign the significant processes for each financial statement line and significant accounts, and

- Assign the responsibility to each business unit.

The second section of this chapter deals with the reconciliation of all documentation received by the repository to the list of assigned Significant Accounts and Processes from the first section of this chapter. This ensures that Business Units have met their coverage assignments. In the event that a significant account's coverage does not meet guidelines, this chapter illustrates the escalation and reporting processes.

CHAPTER 8 – REPORTING AND METRICS

The reports and metrics that should be produced by the SOX Department for the internal control framework are provided in detail. This includes:

- The PREREQUISITES required for the efficient operation of these processes,

- The DATA / INFORMATION required for basic, advanced and exception reporting,

- The INVENTORY OF REPORTS AND METRICS that we recommend,

- The GUIDELINES AND COMPARISON PROCESSes that should be used for exception reporting and metrics, and

- The LAYOUT (format) of reports by SOX function (e.g. senior management reports vs. business unit reports).

The advanced reports should be gradually modified and implemented within your company, based on their complexity and the maturity of your company's SOX processes.

More advanced Reports and Metrics are provided in Volume II.

CHAPTER 9 – ASSESSMENT (TEST) PROCESSES

These are the processes that should be used to assess the entire internal control framework. The chapter is subdivided into the following sections:

- AN OVERVIEW of the complete assessment process,

- The GROUND RULES that should be implemented prior to any activities commencing,

- ASSESSMENT PROCESSES for the Entity Level controls,

- ASSESSMENT PROCESSES for the Transaction Level controls, and

- SUMMARIZATION AND CONCLUSION processes that should be employed for Management Reporting.

IT Assessment processes are covered in Volume II.

CHAPTER 10 – THE DEFICIENCY MANAGEMENT PROCESS

This chapter provides the details for the key processes required for a robust deficiency management process. In this chapter, we review:

- IDENTIFICATION AND COMPILATION of deficiencies from all sources e.g. entity level program, transaction level program, external auditors, internal auditors, etc.

- COMBINATION AND ELIMINATION of duplicate deficiencies

- AGGREGATION of deficiencies based on the aggregation factors outlines in this chapter,

- Deficiency ANALYSIS AND REPORTS

- REMEDIATION PLANS and status reporting,

CHAPTER 11 – OTHER KEY SOX PROCESSES

This chapter focuses on five major subjects:

- DISCLOSURE COMMITTEE – the purpose, role, responsibilities and processes for the Disclosure Committee,

- SEGREGATION OF DUTIES – an overview of the concept of Segregation of Duties and the procedures that should be employed within your company,

- SUB CERTIFICATION PROCESS – the process by which the various organization levels certify to the design, implementation and assessment of their portion of the internal control framework,

- EXTERNAL AUDITOR COORDINATION – the coordination required to ensure that your internal control framework audit is conducted as expeditiously as possible, and

- SPECIAL YEAR END PROCESSES – the 13th month and other special processes required in the fiscal year post closing cycle for SOX assessment.

VOLUME II

Volume II provides more advanced, but cost effective, procedures that focus on the following key subjects

INFORMATION TECHNOLOGY

The IT Environment and its related processes and controls that should be developed - focusing on the following major subject areas:

- Security Access,
- Applications – change management, End User Application Testing, etc.,
- Data,
- Infrastructure, and
- Interfaces.

It includes the processes and controls for the General Computing Controls and application controls. An introduction is provided in Volume I.

PROCESSES AND CONTROLS

Volume II provides additional information on subjects that are introduced in Volume I.

- STANDARDIZED PROCESSES AND CONTROLS– when adopted, the use of these standardized processes can reduce the overhead for ongoing SOX certifications. Volume I introduces you to this subject,

- PROCESS AND CONTROL CONNECTORS AND END TO END PROCESSES – the design, implementation and assessment of complex processes and controls, and

- SYNCHRONIZED PROCESSES AND CONTROLS – these require coordination across multiple business units e.g. Human Resources, Accounts Payable, Accounts Receivable, etc.

SOX MANAGEMENT SYSTEM REQUIREMENTS

In Volume I, we introduced you to the analyses and reports required to support the SOX effort. In Volume II, we provide you with the information on how to *automate* these processes.

It includes the recommended data structures; the validation processes that should be employed (Volume I provides you with the initial validation requirements); the analyses and queries that you should execute on this validated data; etc.

One of the primary focal points in this volume is the design of the data base necessary to achieve the highest level of automation possible.

ADDITIONAL VOLUME II CONTENTS

The additional subjects included in Volume II are

- Advanced Repository Management and period archiving
- Deficiency Management,
- Entity Level Controls, etc.

VOLUME III

Volume III focuses on the following subjects:

TRAINING AND PRESENTATION MATERIAL

The recommended training materials including Senior Management presentation formats, Audit Committee presentations, Fiscal Year End conclusion presentation formats, Deficiency Management presentations, etc.

TRAINING MATERIALS

Training Kits include Assessment training kits, Sub certifications, Entity Level Control training kits, etc.

ADVANCED WORKSHEETS

Volume III provides you with advanced, specialized worksheets for all processes, advanced report formats, special processes for IT and synchronized controls.

INTERVIEWS AND SURVEYS

The entire suite of interview and survey forms is included in this volume.

ASSESSMENT WORKSHEETS AND TOOLS

The entire of Assessment Worksheets and tools is included in this volume.

ADDITIONAL INFORMATION ON THIS SERIES

This series was written at a specific point in time (June through August 2005). Anticipating future changes (regulatory, etc.) and questions from our readers, we have provided you with the ability to access more current information on Sarbanes Oxley, additional recommended processes, reports, etc., and an on-line Q&A/FAQ section for registered members at www.sustainedsox.com.

In the event, you have any specific questions, or would like to contact me with your specific questions or comments; I can be reached at mshugh@hughenterprises.com or mshugh@sustainedsox.com.

Michael S. Hugh

TABLE OF CONTENTS

INTRODUCTION I
- INTENT OF THIS VOLUME I
- NOTE CAREFULLY II
- INTENDED AUDIENCE FOR THIS SERIES II
- ORGANIZATION OF VOLUME II
  - Chapter 1 – Organizing for Sarbanes Oxley ii
  - Chapter 2 – Prerequisites for Sarbanes Oxley iii
  - Chapter 3 – The Entity Level Control Program iii
  - Chapter 4 – Communications Infrastructure iv
  - Chapter 5 – Plans & Calendars iv
  - Chapter 6 – SOX Repository iv
  - Chapter 7 – Financial Statements Risk Assessment v
  - Chapter 8 – Reporting and Metrics v
  - Chapter 9 – Assessment (Test) Processes vi
  - Chapter 10 – the Deficiency Management Process vi
  - Chapter 11 – Other Key SOX Processes vi
- VOLUME II VII
  - Information Technology vii
  - Processes and Controls vii
  - SOX Management System requirements vii
  - Additional Volume II contents viii
- VOLUME III VIII
  - Training and Presentation Material viii
  - Training Materials viii
  - Advanced Worksheets viii
  - Interviews and Surveys viii
  - Assessment Worksheets and Tools viii
- ADDITIONAL INFORMATION ON THIS SERIES VIII

CHAPTER 1 - ORGANIZING FOR SARBANES OXLEY 1
- INTENT OF THIS CHAPTER: 1
- THE KEY INDIVIDUALS OR DEPARTMENTS 1
  - Business Unit Responsibilities 3
  - Business Unit Personnel roles 5
  - SOX Department Responsibilities 6
  - SOX Department Personnel Roles/Functions 8
  - The Internal Audit Department 11
  - External Vendors 12
  - The Board and Audit Committee 12
  - The External Auditors 13
- THE KEY SOX PROCESSES 13
  - SOX Preparatory processes 15
  - Initial Financial Statements Risk assessment 17
  - Entity Level Risk Assessment 17
  - Documentation of the internal control framework 18
  - Assessment of the design and operational effectiveness of the transaction level framework 18
  - Submission of all documentation 19
  - Analysis of the coverage of the Financial Statements 19
  - Deficiency Management processes 20
  - SOX Management Analyses and Reporting 20
  - External Auditor Coordination and Reporting processes 21
- SUB CERTIFICATION PROCESS 21
- SUMMARY 22
  - Organization Charts 22
  - Qualifications Reconciliation 23
  - Example of Roles / Responsibilities Chart 23

CHAPTER 2 – PREREQUISITES FOR SARBANES OXLEY 25
- INTENT OF THIS CHAPTER 25

OVERVIEW..25
SELECTION ON AN INTERNAL CONTROL FRAMEWORK...26
   COSO Framework...27
DEVELOPMENT AND IMPLEMENTATION OF SOX POLICIES AND PROCEDURES 27
   Development Cycle 27
   Check list of Policies and Procedures 28
   Use of standardized processes 30
   Process Implementation / Documentation Procedures................................31
   Standardized Controls 33
   Control Implementation / Documentation Processes 33
   Other Documentation Standards...34
THE SOX REPOSITORY 35
MASTER FILES AND CODING STANDARDS 36
SOX CALENDAR 36
   Fiscal Year Calendar...37
   Quarterly calendars 37
   Calendar Contents 37
COMMUNICATIONS INFRASTRUCTURE..38
TRAINING PROGRAMS 38
SUMMARY 39
   Next Steps...40

CHAPTER 3 - ENTITY LEVEL CONTROL PROGRAM 41
INTENT OF THIS CHAPTER: 41
OVERVIEW..41
ESTABLISHING THE ENTITY LEVEL CONTROL PROGRAM 42
   Control Framework – COSO 42
   Development of the Internal Control Framework..42
   Defining the Entity Level Control Components / Controls...........................42
   Assignment of Control Owners for the Entity Level Control Program.........43
   Interviews/ Surveys 44
   Relationship between Control Owners and SOX Department 45
COSO - CONTROL ENVIRONMENT 46
   What is the Control Environment?..46
   The points of focus in the Control Environment 46
COSO – RISK ASSESSMENT 57
   The Points of focus in the Risk Assessment 57
COSO – INFORMATION AND COMMUNICATION 59
   The Points of Focus for Information and Communication...........................60
COSO – MONITORING 65
   The Points of focus for Monitoring 66
SUMMARY 69
   Example of Entity Level Control Map 69
   Typical Anonymous Employee Survey questions.......................................70
   Typical CEO Interview Questionnaire...72

CHAPTER 4 - COMMUNICATIONS REQUIREMENTS FOR SARBANES OXLEY 79
INTENT OF THIS CHAPTER 79
OVERVIEW..79
COMMUNICATIONS OVERVIEW 80
   Communications Material / Sources..80
   Channels..80
   Security Classifications 81
   SOX Audience...81
COMMUNICATION SOURCES AND MATERIALS 81
   Reference Libraries...81
   Reference Library Contents 82
   Plans & Calendars 83
   Messages (Emails)..84
   Analyses & Reports 84
THE SOX COMMUNICATIONS AUDIENCE... 85

    Sox Audience Members 85
  COMMUNICATIONS & PUBLICATIONS CONTENT 85
    Description of Content Tables 86
    Tools required to support Communications Strategy 87
    SOX Quarterly Bulletins 87
    Financial Statement Risk Assessment Results 88
    SOX Internal Documentation and Publications for SOX processes 89
    Calendar & Plans 89
    Regulatory and External Publications 90
    Library Listing 90
    Sub Certifications 90
    SOX Department Reports 91
    Ad Hoc Requests / Communications 92
    Training 93
  SOX AUDIENCE COMMUNICATIONS REQUIREMENTS 93
  MESSAGE FORMATS 96
  SUMMARY 96
    Next Steps 96

CHAPTER 5 - SARBANES OXLEY PLANS & CALENDARS 99

  INTENT OF CHAPTER 99
  OVERVIEW 99
  INITIAL PHASE PLANS & CALENDARS 100
  ONGOING PHASE PLANS & CALENDARS 101
  NORMAL CALENDAR PREPARATION ASSUMPTIONS 101
    Calendar Input Sources 102
  STANDARD CALENDAR PRACTICES OF SOX DEPARTMENT 103
    Meetings and Conferences 103
    Communications and Publications 103
    Standard SOX planning template 103
    Maintenance of Task and Issue Lists 104
  CALENDAR PUBLICATION DATES 104
  STANDARD TEMPLATE 104
  METHODOLOGY FINALIZATION AND UPDATE CALENDAR ACTIVITIES 105
    Annual Review of Methodology 105
  RISK ASSESSMENT OF FINANCIAL STATEMENTS (SCOPING) CALENDAR 107
    Assumptions used in the preparation of this section 107
    Calendar Scoping Activities 107
    Recommended Calendar Template 108
  PROCESS AND CONTROL DOCUMENTATION CALENDAR 109
    Timing for submission of documentation 109
    Repository 110
    Q1 / Q2 / Q3 Recommended Calendar Template 110
    Q4 Recommended Calendar Template 111
  ASSESSMENT (TESTING) CALENDAR 112
    Recommended Calendar Template 112
  DEFICIENCY MANAGEMENT (INCLUDING REMEDIATION PLANS) CALENDAR 112
    Quarterly Deficiency Calendar Template 112
  SENIOR MANAGEMENT AND COMMITTEE REPORTING CALENDAR 113
    Example of Normal Corporate Calendar 114
  SUB CERTIFICATION PROCESSES CALENDAR 114
    Sub certification Timetable 115
  EXTERNAL AUDIT COORDINATION CALENDAR 115
  TRAINING CALENDARS 115
  SUMMARY 116
    Next Steps 116

CHAPTER 6 – THE SOX REPOSITORY 117

  BACKGROUND 117
  IMPLEMENTATION STEPS 117
    Initial Setup 117

- Ongoing Repository Operations 118
- Reporting and Analysis functions 118
- Special Functions 118
- DEFINITION OF THE SOX REPOSITORY 118
  - Functions performed by the Repository Department 118
  - Prerequisites for the Repository 119
- PROCESSES, METHODS AND TOOLS 119
  - Step 1 – Establish the Repository Storage medium 120
  - Step 2 – Develop / Establish inventory of required SOX documents 120
  - Step 3 – Develop / Establish Document formats - Content / Elements 121
  - Step 3a – Define Supporting Documentation requirements 122
  - Step 4 – Define Data Management and Validation rules 123
  - Step 5 – Define Initial Analysis and Reporting requirements 125
- ESTABLISHING THE REPOSITORY 125
- REPOSITORY DOCUMENTS 126
  - Reference Library - SOX Policies, Processes, Guidelines and instructions 126
  - Finance Statement Risk Assessment work Sheets and supporting documents 126
  - Transaction Process/ Control Documentation 127
  - Entity Level Program Documentation 127
  - Assessment (Test) Results 127
  - Deficiency Listings 128
  - Sub certifications 128
  - Significant Changes 128
  - Finance Division Error Logs 128
- REPOSITORY ACCEPTANCE OF SOX DOCUMENTS 129
  - Initial receipt 129
  - Documentation Inventory Process 130
  - Rejection Analysis 130
- ANALYSIS FUNCTIONS 130
  - Test Analyses 130
  - Transaction Deficiency Distribution Report 130
  - External Auditor Issue Report 131
  - Other Deficiency Distribution Report 131
  - Tests (Assessment) Exceptions 131
  - Sub Certification Exceptions 131
  - Remediation Plans Distribution 131
  - Remediation Plan Exceptions 132
- REPORTING FUNCTIONS 132
  - Board Committee reporting 132
  - Senior Management Reports 133
- PREPARATION FOR AUDITS 133
  - Security Accesses 134
  - Completeness Checks 134
  - Audit Trails 134
  - Evidence of Reports to Audit Committee 134
- AUTOMATION ALTERNATIVES FOR THE REPOSITORY 134
  - Potential Tools 134
  - User Perspective on SOX Tools 135
- SUMMARY 138

CHAPTER 7 – THE FINANCIAL STATEMENTS RISK ASSESSMENT PROCESS 139
- INTENT OF THIS CHAPTER 139
- FINANCIAL STATEMENT COVERAGE OVERVIEW 139
- SECTION I - FINANCIAL STATEMENT RISK ASSESSMENT (THE INITIAL PROCESS) 140
  - Prerequisites 140
  - PCAOB Requirements 140
  - Input required for this process 140
  - Process Steps 141
  - Output 141
  - Risk Assessment Team composition 142
- WORKSHEETS 142

STEP 1 - INITIAL ASSESSMENT PROCESS 144
   Size and Composition 144
   Loss Susceptibility 144
   Account Volume 144
   Nature of Account 145
   Accounting and Reporting Complexity 145
   Exposure to Losses 145
   Contingent Liabilities 145
   3rd Party transactions 145
   Changes from Prior Periods 145
   Deficiencies 146
   Errors 146
   Significant Changes 146
   Significant Account 146
   Additional Information 146
   Process output 146
   Archival Information 147
STEP 2 – ASSIGNMENT OF DEFAULT FINANCIAL ASSERTIONS 147
   PCAOB References 147
   Assignment Process 147
   Output of this Section 148
STEP 3- DECOMPOSITION INTO SIGNIFICANT ACCOUNTS 149
   Format of decomposition map 150
   Process Steps 150
   Reconciliation capabilities 150
   Significant Account Process Output 151
   Identification of Significant Business Units 152
   Management Judgment 153
STEP 4 - COMMUNICATION OF BUSINESS UNIT RESPONSIBILITIES 153
   Quantitative Account Listing 153
   France Quantitative Account Listing 153
   USA Quantitative Account Listing 154
   Qualitative Account Listing 154
NOTES AND DISCLOSURE LISTINGS 154
SECTION II - RECONCILIATION OF FINANCIAL STATEMENT COVERAGE 155
STEP 5 - REPOSITORY DOCUMENTATION AND EXTRACTION 155
   Significant Account Extraction Report 156
STEP 6 - COMPARISON TO SIGNIFICANT ACCOUNT REQUIREMENTS 156
   Business Unit Coverage Exception Report 157
   Corporate Management Exception Report 157
APPENDIX A– FINANCIAL STATEMENT NOTES / DISCLOSURES WORKING PAPERS 158
SUMMARY 159

CHAPTER 8 – REPORTING AND METRICS FOR SOX 161

INTENT OF THIS CHAPTER 161
IMPORTANCE OF VALID, ACCURATE DATA 161
PREREQUISITES FOR REPORTING AND METRICS 161
   Basic Prerequisites 161
   Common Keys (threads) throughout documentation 162
   Critical Information Prerequisites 162
REPORTING AND METRICS OVERVIEW 163
REPORT LEVELS 163
   Basic Reporting 164
   Class reporting 164
   Advanced Reporting 165
   Assessment Reporting 165
   Exception Reporting 165
METRICS 165
BASIC REPORTS 166
   Process / Control Reports 166
   Test (Assessment) Reports 168

  Deficiency Reports 169
  Remediation Plans 170
  Other Documentation 171
 ADVANCED / COMPOUND REPORTING 173
  Controls, Test and Deficiency Perspective 173
  Time Line Perspectives 174
 EXCEPTION REPORTING 175
  Basic Standards required for exception reporting 175
  Data Standards Exception Reporting 176
  Rules 177
  Completeness 177
  Detailed Metrics 178
 SUMMARY 180

CHAPTER 9 – SARBANES OXLEY ASSESSMENT (TEST) PROCESSES 181
 INTENT OF THIS CHAPTER 181
 OBJECTIVES OF THE ASSESSMENT/EVALUATION PROCESSES 181
 OVERVIEW 181
 GROUND RULES 182
  Assessors / Testers 182
  Evidence Maintenance 183
  Objectivity Level 183
  Sample Sizes 183
  Test Methods - Entity Level Controls 184
  Test Methods - Transaction Level Controls 184
  Timetables - Transaction Level Controls 185
 ENTITY CONTROLS 185
  Interviews 185
  Anonymous Employee Survey 186
  Supporting Evidence 186
  Assessment check list for the Control Environment 187
 TRANSACTION LEVEL CONTROLS 189
  Walkthroughs 189
  Process Testing 190
  Transaction Level Control Testing 192
  End User Computing Application form 196
  Test Result Form Review 196
  Cross checks of test results 197
 IT CONTROL ASSESSMENTS 198
 TEST RESULTS ANALYSIS 199
 SUMMARY 200

CHAPTER 10 – SARBANES OXLEY DEFICIENCY MANAGEMENT PROCESSES 201
 INTENT OF THIS CHAPTER 201
 OVERVIEW 201
 DEFICIENCY IDENTIFICATION / SOURCES 202
 REPOSITORY DEFICIENCY PROCESSES 204
  Submission processes 204
  Validation processes 208
  Normal Repository processes 208
  Communication Processes 208
 DEFICIENCY PROCESSES 209
  Business Unit Communication Process 209
  Deficiency Combination / Aggregation Process 209
  Remediation Plans 211
  Closing of a deficiency 211
  Analysis / Reporting 211
  Business Unit Deficiency Reports 212
 REPORT SAMPLES 212

CHAPTER 11 – OTHER SOX SUBJECTS 215
 INTENT OF THIS CHAPTER 215

DISCLOSURE COMMITTEE OVERVIEW 215
   Roles and Responsibilities 215
   Disclosure documents: 216
   Membership 216
SEGREGATION OF DUTIES 217
   Roles and Responsibilities 217
   Timing 217
   Segregation of Duties Guidelines 217
   Exemptions 218
SUB CERTIFICATION PROCESS 219
   Prerequisites 219
   Sub Certification Organization 219
   Sub certification process 220
   Sample Sub Certification Form 222
   Schedule A – Identified Deficiencies 223
   Schedule B – Significant Changes 223
   Schedule C – Errors and Exceptions 223
EXTERNAL AUDIT COORDINATION 224
   Basic Information exchange 224
   Scheduling and protocols 225
   Assessment (test) guidelines for the fiscal year 225
   Issue and Deficiency Management 225
   Management Escalation processes 226
SPECIAL YEAREND PROCESSES 226
   Issue cutoff dates 226
   Annual / Yearend Controls 226
   Sub certifications 226
   Repository data 227

GLOSSARY 229

Chapter 1 - Organizing for Sarbanes Oxley

Intent of this chapter:

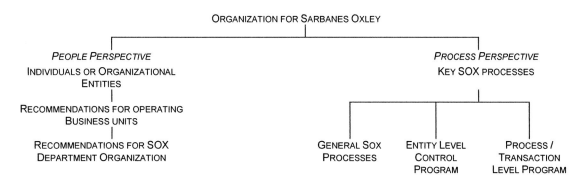

As illustrated above, this chapter concentrates on providing you with two perspectives for organizing the SOX.

- The ORGANIZATION OF ALL PERSONNEL (including external vendors) that are responsible for the design, implementation and assessment of the internal control framework. The focus is to define the roles and responsibilities of these individuals within your company. This perspective is *people* oriented., and

- The second is the DEVELOPMENT AND IMPLEMENTATION OF THE SOX POLICIES, PROCEDURES AND GUIDELINES that will be used to manage the internal control framework. This perspective is more *process* oriented.

This subjects covered in this chapter provide an introduction to the subsequent chapters which elaborate on the detail steps required for each of the processes.

The key individuals or departments

The Board, CEO and CFO (CEO and CFO - hereinafter referred to as Senior Company Management) have a direct responsibility for designing, implementing and assessing the internal control framework. They customarily delegate many of these activities to a separate unit within the company which we have titled the "*SOX Department*" for ease of reference. Regardless of this assignment, the accountability for these responsibilities still remains with the CEO and CFO.

These activities are usually centered on the following units within the company:

1. The operating BUSINESS UNITS are responsible for implementing and assessing the internal control framework within their units.

   Business Units are defined as all units within the company that have a direct or indirect impact on the financial reporting results or processes within the company.

   They may also be centralized units performing a specific function within the company head office (e.g. Central Finance Department) or distributed units (e.g. Regional or Country Finance Departments),

2. The INTERNAL AUDIT DEPARTMENT - depending on your company and the judgment of your External Auditors, the Internal Audit department may be directly involved in the review and assessment on the design and operational effectiveness of the internal control framework.

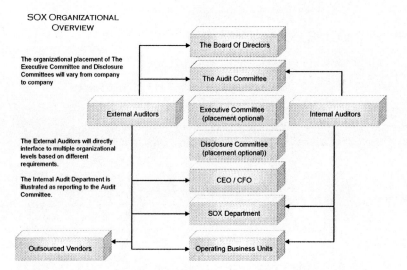

SOX ORGANIZATIONAL OVERVIEW

The organizational placement of The Executive Committee and Disclosure Committees will vary from company to company

The External Auditors will directly interface to multiple organizational levels based on different requirements.

The Internal Audit Department is illustrated as reporting to the Audit Committee.

External Auditors may rely on Internal Audit's assessments of routine controls.

The Internal Audit Department may also identify financial reporting issues or deficiencies in the course of their normal audit activities within the company. These are combined with other deficiencies to provide some of the deficiency management data used in the aggregation processes (refer to Chapter 9 for additional detail on this process).

Their role and responsibilities are customarily defined by the Audit Committee. In the chapter on Entity Level Controls, we highlight several of their roles and responsibilities.

3. LEGAL/COMPLIANCE DEPARTMENTS – The Legal and Compliance Departments are responsible, like any other business unit, to document their departments' processes and controls that have an impact on Financial Reporting. However, it should be noted that these departments are also responsible for the assembly/compilation of deficiencies received from external regulators for inclusion into the deficiency data used in the aggregation process (similar to the deficiencies by the Internal Audit Department).

In some companies, the Legal and Compliance Departments have the responsibility for reviewing and approving all SOX Management reports prior to publication,

4. The CEO and CFO usually rely on the SOX Department to ensure that all Business Units meet the company's policies, procedures and guidelines for designing, implementing and assessing (testing) the internal control framework.

The CEO and CFO also rely on the sub certification process by which the business units will certify that the internal control framework, under their direct control, is operating effectively. These sub certifications are usually supported by an audit or examination process executed by the Internal Audit or SOX Department periodically.

Both the CEO and CFO should provide written assurances to the Board and the Audit Committee, on a regular, periodic basis, that the internal control framework is operating effectively; or where there are deficiencies, to report on the status of remediation efforts.,

5. EXTERNAL VENDORS, who are responsible for performing various processes and services on an outsourced basis, may have an impact on the Financial Reporting processes within the company. These vendors, through contractual arrangements, will have to assess and evaluate their internal control frameworks and provide your company with the evidence of this assessment e.g. SAS 70[2], etc.

---

[2] STATEMENT ON AUDITING STANDARDS (SAS) NO. 70, Service Organizations, is an internationally recognized auditing standard developed by the American Institute of Certified Public Accountants (AICPA). A SAS 70 examination signifies that a service organization has had its control objectives and control activities examined by an independent accounting and auditing firm. A formal report including the auditor's opinion is issued to the service organization at the conclusion of a

In some cases, your company may request the right to directly audit certain critical processes based on specific contractual provisions. In some instances, your Auditor may advise you to include special provision provisions in your contract due to timing or other differences between the issuance of the SAS 70 and your fiscal yearend.

For example, your vendor may issue an annual SAS 70 in February of each year, but your fiscal yearend is December 31, you may need to include special audit or other provisions in your contract to cover this 10 month timing difference.

6. EXTERNAL AUDITORS - who will review, assess and determine whether your company has an effective internal control framework. The auditors will also provide your management with written documentation of any concerns or deficiencies. Auditors are required to meet various obligations under Auditing Standard 2 (AU2) of the Public Company Accounting Oversight Board (PCAOB)[3],

7. THE BOARD OR DIRECTORS AND BOARD COMMITTEES. If no Audit Committee exists within your company, then all responsibilities and requirements required of the Audit Committee will default to the entire Board. The same applies to the Disclosure Committee - refer to Chapter 11 for more information on the Disclosure Committee.

   The Board and its Committees are required to meet various obligations under Auditing Standard 2 (AU2) of the Public Company Accounting Oversight Board (PCAOB) and the applicable SEC rules, and

8. THE SOX DEPARTMENT – All company-wide SOX activities are usually planned, communicated and coordinated by the SOX Department.

   The Department is required to provide analyses, reports and recommendations to Company Management and the Board from the information compiled in the Repository.

   In some companies, the SOX Department may report to the Audit Committee, in others, it may report to company management who, in turn, report to the Board and Audit Committees.

BUSINESS UNIT RESPONSIBILITIES

Within the operating Business Units, there are usually two separate tracks of activities that are performed simultaneously. The Entity Level Control Program and the Process / Transaction Level program both require the active participation of the operating Business Units.

The Entity Level Control Program is usually centrally controlled and conducted by the SOX Department. Business Units assist by providing personnel for interviews, responding to questionnaires or workbooks, and providing supporting documentary evidence. They are usually not directly responsible for activities in other business units since this is a company-wide program requiring most activities to be assessed at the company wide level and not usually at the individual business unit level.

SAS 70 examination. The report enables service organizations to demonstrate that they have adequate controls and safeguards when they host or process data belonging to their customers.

[3] PUBLIC COMPANY ACCOUNTING OVERSIGHT BOARD (PCAOB) - The PCAOB is an a regulatory body created by the Sarbanes-Oxley Act of 2002, which regulates audits of SEC registrants. Operating under the U.S. Securities and Exchange Commission, the PCAOB has the authority for registration, inspection, and discipline of firms auditing SEC registrants, and sets standards for public company audits.

The design, implementation and assessment of the Process / Transaction level processes and controls usually are the *primary focus* within the individual business units.

The results of all Business Units' transaction level control activities are summarized by the SOX Department for Senior Management and Board reports. The SOX Department usually provides a summary report of the Entity Level program at the same time.

Business Units are usually responsible for the following:

1. Implementation of an Internal Control framework over Financial Reporting as directed by the company's policies, procedures and guidelines *within their specific Business Unit*. This includes certifying to management, after a thorough assessment by Unit Management, the operating status of the framework and its critical components within the unit,

2. Assisting in the assessment of the company's Entity Level Control Program by providing the assessors with all material (including accessibility to key personnel, supporting documentation, etc.), as required,

3. Documenting and evidencing the existence of the internal control framework within their unit. In the event, processes are "*handed off*" to other departments' processes for completion, the originating business units are responsible for ensuring (together with the receiving unit) that the entire "*end-to-end*" process is correctly designed and is operating effectively within both the originating and receiving business units,

4. Assessment (test) the design and operational effectiveness of the control framework within the operating business unit based on the company's testing guidelines on a regular, periodic basis,

5. Reporting on any design or operational deficiencies for the controls within the business unit's area of responsibility. For *end-to-end* processes, the Business Unit must also report deficiencies in any downstream processes/controls (those within the receiving business unit),

6. Ensuring that the process / transaction level controls cover all significant processes and accounts as assigned by the SOX Department to the unit based on the Financial Statement Risk Assessment process,

7. Ensuring that all significant changes that impact financial reporting or results are identified, documented and submitted to the SOX Department in the prescribed format at the end of each fiscal quarter or as mandated by the SOX Department or company management,

8. Ensuring that remediation plans for correcting any deficiencies, attributed to the Business Unit, are developed and executed on a timely basis for all deficiencies.

    Deficiencies may originate from non business unit sources (e.g. Internal Audit, External Audit, Regulators, etc.) and will be communicated by the SOX Department to the Business Unit.

    In the event of a disagreement with the assignment of a non-business unit identified deficiency, the Business Unit should advise the SOX Department promptly,

9. Coordinating all internal and external audit activities within their respective departments. Depending on the size, complexity and geographic dispersion of your company, Internal and External Auditors may have time and travel constraints that require a high level of

coordination within the individual business units. Unit management should be cognizant of these and should be required to make every reasonable effort to facilitate these audit activities,

10. Business Unit managers must provide a written representation of the existence and operation of the internal control framework.

    These representation (hereinafter referred to as *sub certifications*), based on company and regulatory guidelines, should be supported by the documentation and other evidentiary material that is required to be submitted to the SOX Department and its repository on a quarterly basis.

BUSINESS UNIT PERSONNEL ROLES

Operating Business Units should be organized in a control / governance hierarchy as follows:

1. CONTROL RESPONSIBILITY OFFICER/MANAGER - This individual is

   - The first level manager to whom the person performing the control activity reports,

   - The primary owner of specific controls with accountability for updates to documents, testing of control activities and the remediation of identified deficiencies, and is

   - Required to certify that the design and operating effectiveness of their respective internal controls meet the company and regulatory guidelines after performing necessary assessments.

2. BUSINESS UNIT SOX MANAGER – These are usually the Organizational Managers of the business units or the Finance Managers for the Business Unit. This individual is:

   - Responsible for monitoring/correcting all financial control activities within their respective Units,

   - The owner of the balances of each significant account and related significant processes within their units

   - Responsible for two levels of control sub certifications.

     First, the manager must sign-off on specific control activities under their ownership as well as the entire end-to-end process and controls including transaction initiation, authorization, recording, processing and reporting which may require the participation of another business unit.

     Secondly, *in rare instances*, the manager may also be a Control Responsibility Office and required to sign off on those controls. *These should be reviewed and approved by a superior in accordance with your Segregation of Duties guidelines.*

   - Responsible for ensuring the execution of sub certifications by all their subordinate Control Responsibility Officers,

   - Responsible for ensuring that all *end-to-end* processes are assessed and may need to receive sub certifications from Control Responsibility Officers from receiving Business Units in order to assess the entire *end-to-end* process. These sub certifications from other Business Units do not replace the need for this manager to have an objective understanding and evaluation of the design and operating effectiveness of the controls included in the *end-to-end* process.

- In some instances, the manager may also be responsible for the account mapping of legal entity accounts to business unit accounts, for each account balance within the organizational unit.

3. OTHER BUSINESS LEVEL MANAGERS – In some companies, Business Units may "*roll up*" or report to higher levels within the organization. For example, Business Units within various States may *roll up* into a Regional Manager, who in turn *rolls up* into a Country Manager. These Managers inherit the same responsibilities as the Business Unit SOX Managers for the collection of their subordinate Business Units.

   Therefore, the Regional Manager is responsible for the internal control framework in all subordinate states.

4. LEGAL ENTITY SOX MANAGERS – This manager owns the balances of each account within the legal entity and has the additional responsibility for ensuring the integrity of all balances reported by the legal entity, as well as the controls over the integrity of financial information. This should be supported by sub certifications received from Control Responsibility Officers within the respective Legal Entities.

SOX DEPARTMENT RESPONSIBILITIES

The SOX Department is the hub which organizes, coordinates, analyzes and reports on all SOX activities and information within your company. The Department, acts on behalf of company management and the Board (and its Internal Audit Committee), and is usually authorized to:

1. Ensure that all departments within the company and the company, as an entity, complies with all internal control requirements,

2. Prepare (or commission the preparation of) all internal control guidelines, policies and procedures for Board, Board Committees and the company management's review and approval,

3. Coordinate all related activities based on policies and directives that have been issued and approved by the Board and company management from the previous step,

4. Assist and train all business units (and external vendors, where required) to:

   - Design and implement the internal control framework,
   - Prepare all required documentation and evidence required to support the existence of the framework and its operating effectiveness,
   - Assess (test) that the framework has been designed correctly and is operating effectively, and
   - Submit all required documentation to the SOX Department for review, analysis and reporting purposes.

5. Develop/Implement the Entity Level Control program within your company. Several elements of this program may already exist within your company and may require the department to coordinate/assemble these components into a comprehensive Entity Level Control Program.

In very large and complex companies, this may be assigned to a specialized unit that operates within the SOX Department or reports directly to the Audit Committee. Regardless of the organizational assignment, the responsibility for ensuring that the section of the framework operates effectively should still be assigned to the SOX Department,

6. Perform the assessment of the Entity Level Control program and its related controls as outlined in the chapter 3 and 9. This assessment may have a direct impact on the process/transaction level assessments,

7. Perform the risk assessment of the Financial Statements (including notes and disclosures). From this assessment, the department must establish:

    - The significant accounts and processes that must be covered by the framework,

    - The Business Units that are responsible for ensuring that their sections of the framework address the significant accounts / processes that are assigned to them,

    - Coverage of these significant accounts and processes requires the operating business units to execute all relevant design, implementation, documentation and assessment procedures required by the company's internal control policies, procedures and guidelines,

8. Ensure that all SOX activities are performed based on the company's plan/timetable and that all necessary documentation and evidence are filed with the SOX Department (Repository Unit) in the company's prescribed format at the required time,

9. Analyze the SOX documentation and results submitted by the Business Units, all other Company departments and the external auditors to ensure compliance with company guidelines,

10. Acquire all deficiencies from all sources including business unit assessments, external audit assessments, internal audit findings, regulatory findings, etc. and securely store in the Repository in the prescribed format,

11. Validate all data received from all sources to ensure accuracy, compliance with internal control policies and guidelines.

    All non-compliant data should be returned to originators with a listing of corrections required and a return date by which these corrections should be made.

    Where online or real time systems are used, this should be a built in feature of the system to provide system users with instant feedback,

12. Aggregate all identified deficiencies to determine whether a significant deficiency or material weakness exists in the company's internal control framework,

13. Report to company management, operating business unit management and the Board regularly on the state of the internal control framework, all SOX activities, all deficiencies and all other items that may require management and board attention,

14. Coordinate all External Auditor SOX activities within the company as part of the communications and planning processes,

15. Jointly organize and cooperate with other Control (it is usually prudent for larger companies to combine all control activities in one department for process and cost efficiency purposes) and other Corporate Governance Departments within the company on Financial Reporting controls and activities.

The primary focus of the SOX Department is the financial reporting element of the COSO framework. The other elements (Strategic, Operations, and Compliance elements of the COSO framework) are usually the responsibility of other control departments.

SOX DEPARTMENT PERSONNEL ROLES/FUNCTIONS

The department's organization is dependent on the size and complexity of your company. This section defines all the personnel roles - these can be combined or further separated to define specific jobs based on your company's requirements. For example, the communications and plans & calendars roles could be combined in smaller companies.

1. SOX DEPARTMENT MANAGER – this individual has direct responsibility for managing this department and its responsibilities. The manager usually reports directly to the CFO with additional reporting responsibilities to the CEO, Board and Audit Committees as directed.

2. SOX REPOSITORY MANAGER – the individual responsible for managing the acceptance, validation, analysis, security and storage functions for all SOX data. This individual ensures that all documentation complies with Corporate and SOX standards and that all non-compliant items are promptly returned to their originators with rejection reasons together with instructions for their correction and resubmission.

    The individual is also responsible for ensuring that operating Business Units submit all required documents and evidence on a *timely* basis. Any missing documentation or related assessment evidence or sub certifications must be promptly identified and followed up with the Business Unit.

    All documentation and evidence received is to be stored in a secure Repository that meets your company highest security standards for confidential information. This information must be available, on demand, for External Auditors and employees with the necessary clearance.

    Only information that has been validated against the company's documentation standards should be used in any internal control related analyses and reporting.

3. SOX BUSINESS UNIT COORDINATION MANAGER – This individual is responsible for coordinating and assisting the Business Units in executing their roles. This manager may also be responsible for the preparation of all analyses and reports originating from the SOX Department.

    The manager's primary responsibility is to ensure that the operating Business Units

    - Comply with the internal control framework policies, procedures and guidelines,

    - Are coordinated in their SOX activities – with specific emphasis on the assessment processes which may require coordination with IT, External Vendors or other business units when processes span more than one business unit,

    - Meet the timelines prescribed by the company as detailed in the Plans & Calendars as published by the department quarterly,

- Assign qualified, trained personnel to execute their internal control responsibilities,

- Identify deficiencies promptly,

- Provide accurate remediation plans for any deficiencies, and

- Resolve any Internal or External Audit Issues promptly

These objectives are usually achieved by employing individuals who are familiar with the financial reporting and operations elements within the specific Business Units for which they are responsible.

These individuals assist the Business Unit Managers to achieve their control objectives and will assist in training or any other task required for SOX certification with the exception of assessments – *unless the SOX Department and the External Auditor provide an exemption for this activity.*

The Business Coordination Unit members provide vital information to the SOX Department Management through their progress reports on the state of the Business Unit activities. They also provide feedback on the implementation of policies, procedures etc. on a regular basis thereby assisting the SOX Department to make allowable adjustments wherever possible.

4. POLICY / PROCEDURES (METHODOLOGY) MANAGER – this manager is responsible for the development, administration and maintenance of all internal control policies, procedures, guidelines, etc. The role is also responsible for

    - Providing advisory support to the operating Business Units in interpreting any regulations, etc.,

    - Assisting in the preparation of all training material, when requested by the Training Manager. This assistance function should include the review of training material for accuracy and compliance with internal and external rules, and

    - In some companies, because of their intimate knowledge of the rules and regulations, this manager is also responsible for the entire Entity Level Program assessment process,

5. SOX CALENDARS / PLANS MANAGER –Chapter 5 reviews the details for the development of the calendar and related plans.

    This manager should be responsible for:

    - Developing and modifying of all Calendars & Plans for the Fiscal Year and Quarters. They will also develop and publish special fiscal yearend plans covering the post closing period (the 13th month),

    - Ensuring the inclusion of all External Auditor and Internal Audit Department activities in these plans and calendars, and

    - Developing and maintaining all SOX Task, Issue and Decision Lists for publication and resolution, and

- May also be responsible for ensuring that all deliverables and dates are achieved with the assistance of the Business Unit Coordination Manager.

6. TRAINING / COMMUNICATIONS MANAGER –The development of the communications protocols and processes and the ongoing management of the communications flow are essential to an efficient SOX effort. Chapter 4 focuses on the development of the communications infrastructure.

    This manager is responsible for ensuring that all responsible company personnel are trained for all internal control related activities for process/transaction control activities.

    The training on the Code of Conduct, Anti Fraud programs, Whistle Blower program etc. (Entity Control requirements) is usually the responsibility of the Human Resources and Corporate Training departments and is not usually considered to be this manager's responsibility.

    In some companies, this individual is also responsible for *monitoring* of these Entity Level Control training programs to ensure they achieve the necessary standard. For example, this manager would monitor the progress of the Anti Fraud training program and report on any training gaps or improvements to the SOX Department Manager and the department responsible for the training.

    This manager may *outsource* the actual SOX training to the company's Training Department but still is held responsible for the quality and delivery of the program.

    This Manager is responsible for:

    - Developing and maintaining all training materials pertaining to the regulations, policies, procedures, guidelines, etc,

    - Maintaining an attendance log of all participants who successfully complete internal control training programs,

    - Ensuring that all training participants' HR files are updates with the results of these training programs,

    - Delivery of the training classes for the operating Business Units. Depending on your company's training methods, this may be done physically, computer based training, outsourced to your company's training department or outsourced to an external consulting organization,

    - Developing and maintaining all standard message formats to be used as outlined in Chapter 4,

    - Developing and maintaining the Communications infrastructure as outlined in Chapter 4, and

    - Developing and publishing a Quarterly SOX bulletin that provides the latest information on the SOX Life Cycle. This bulletin may be published as a part of a larger company publication.

7. DEFICIENCY MANAGEMENT MANAGER – This individual is responsible for

- The assembly of all Entity Level and Transaction Level control deficiencies identified by the Business Units and the Entity Level program,

- The collection of all deficiencies from all non Business Unit sources e.g. Internal Auditors, Regulators, etc.,

- Ensuring that remediation plans have been filed with the repository and are effective in addressing the deficiencies,

- The management and reporting of deficiencies on both an entity level and transaction level, and

- The Deficiency Combination and Aggregation processes.

All of these are further reviewed in detail in Chapter 10,

8. EXTERNAL AUDIT COORDINATION MANAGER – Based on the size and complexity of your company, this role may be a stand alone function or may be combined with any of the previous roles. The decision usually hinges on the number and complexity of issues raised by your External Auditors.

During the course of the SOX Audit, the coordination of the External Auditor activities *and* the resolution of any issues raised by the External Auditors are the responsibility of this manager with the assistance of the Plans & Calendar Manager.

The primary responsibility of this role is to ensure that External Auditor issues are addressed and closed promptly to the Auditor's satisfaction. Depending on the type of issue raised by the External Auditor, (e.g. missing control in a process, etc.) some of these may graduate to deficiencies if they are not resolved within the Auditor's deadlines.

THE INTERNAL AUDIT DEPARTMENT

In chapter 3 on Entity Level controls, we have detailed several of Internal Audit's roles and responsibilities and their applicability to the Entity Level Control Program. We have assumed that these have been adopted within your company and that the Internal Audit Department has the following mandate:

1. Meet or exceed the requirements established by the company's Entity Level Control program for the Internal Audit Department,

2. The Internal Audit Department may be the focal point which is responsible for the collection of all identified deficiencies from non Business Unit sources e.g. Regulatory Authorities. In this volume, we have assumed that this responsibility has been assigned to the Legal / Compliance Departments – but provide this option for your consideration,

3. The department, in the performance of its normal duties may identify design and operating deficiencies or, more importantly missing controls, in its periodic review of the

   - business units and their processes and controls, and

   - the company's Entity Level Control Program

4. The Department should also audit the processes and data utilized by the SOX Department in order to ensure that the Board and company management receive the most accurate, validated information on a timely basis about the state of the company's

internal control framework.

5. The Internal Audit Department may be "*relied upon*" by the External Audit based on the auditor's assessment of the department's capabilities to assess the framework objectively. This reliance is usually limited to processes and their related controls that are classified as routine[4],

EXTERNAL VENDORS

Most organizations contract with an external vendor to provide various services and products that may be too expensive, complicated, or time-consuming for the company to perform internally.

These arrangements are usually referred to as "*outsourcing contracts*". Depending on the contractual arrangements between your company and the external vendor, the SOX requirements may vary.

In most outsourcing contracts, the service or product provided by the external vendor is a part of the external vendor's standard business model. In these circumstances, your company should receive a Statement on Auditing Standards (SAS) No. 70 (hereinafter referred to as a SAS70) at or near to your company's fiscal yearend. The timing of this report may be critical depending on your external auditor's opinion.

If the contractual arrangements between your company and the external vendor are customized, whereby the external vendor's SAS 70 does not meet your internal control requirements, then special contractual provisions will need to be negotiated to ensure that your company has special audit and other review privileges over the external vendor's internal control framework.

THE BOARD AND AUDIT COMMITTEE

The Board and its Audit Committee have special responsibilities defined within the Public Company Account Oversight Board Auditing Standard 2.

Depending on your company's Board of Directors structure, your company may or may not have an Audit Committee or Disclosure Committee. If these committees do not exist, then the Board is required to assume their responsibilities.

The Board, under PCAOB Auditing Standard 2, is responsible for:

1. Evaluating the performance and effectiveness of the Audit Committee[5] on a regular and periodic basis (please refer to the most current copy of PCAOB – Auditing Standard 2 for

---

[4] PCAOB AS 2 Paragraph 72 classifies transaction types as follows

ROUTINE TRANSACTIONS are recurring financial activities reflected in the accounting records in the normal course of business (for example, sales, purchases, cash receipts, cash disbursements).

NON ROUTINE TRANSACTIONS are activities that occur only periodically (for example, taking physical inventory, calculating depreciation expense, adjusting for foreign currencies). A distinguishing feature of non routine transactions is that data involved are generally not part of the routine flow of transactions.

ESTIMATION TRANSACTIONS are activities that involve management judgments or assumptions in formulating account balances in the absence of a precise means of measurement (for example, determining the allowance for doubtful accounts, establishing warranty reserves, assessing assets for impairment).

[5] Public Company Accounting Oversight Board (PCAOB) – Auditing Standard 2 – Paragraph 56

specific requirements),

2. Performing their responsibilities on a timely basis as outlined in the chapter on Entity Level controls an in PCAOB Auditing Standard 2,

3. Employing an effective oversight process for understanding and evaluating the period end financial process. The Board and the Audit Committee must be capable of demonstrating the existence and effectiveness of this process to the External Auditors,

4. In the event that the External Auditor uses the work of internal personnel in their evaluation of the internal control framework, the Board may be required to oversee the work of these testing personnel and their employment, and

5. Receiving and evaluating any significant deficiencies or material weaknesses identified in the course of the assessment of the control environment,

The Audit Committee also is charged with specific responsibilities under the PCAOB Auditing Standard 2 and applicable SEC rules.

KEY SOX PROCESSES

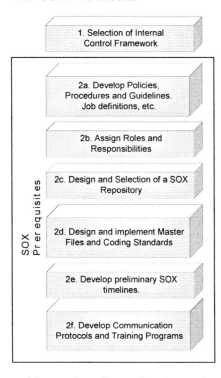

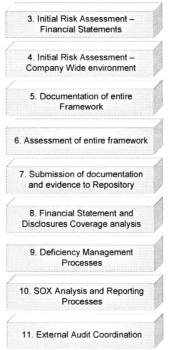

THE EXTERNAL AUDITORS

The Auditor's roles and responsibilities are clearly defined within the Public Company Accounting Oversight Board's Auditing Standard 2 and should be referenced as required.

THE KEY SOX PROCESSES

This section provides the perspective from a *process oriented* point of view.

The previous section provided an organizational hierarchy perspective with its applicable personnel roles.

Both sections should be reviewed in order to achieve a two dimensional overview of the SOX organization model.

The key processes are subdivided into the following sections as illustrated in the diagram. The SOX Management Analyses and Reporting section, together with the External Audit Section, are performed through the entire SOX life cycle *but for illustrative purposes, they are displayed at the end of the diagram* (items 10 and 11).

1. SELECTION OF AN INTERNAL CONTROL FRAMEWORK MODEL. The company should (or already has selected) select the control framework model it intends to implement. Most companies have selected the COSO model based on the work of the Committee of Sponsoring Organizations of the Treadway Commission. There are other models that are also available for use (e.g. Coco, CSA, King, Cadbury, etc.) Throughout this volume, we

have used the COSO model to illustrate the various examples because of the extensive use of this model amongst most companies.

Companies usually engage in two activity tracks – the Entity Level Control Program and the Process/Transaction Level Program.

These tracks are integrated within different company functions. Both these tracks follow similar paths. However, the Entity Level program, because of its centralized nature, is usually designed, documented and assessed from a central, company wide unit with support provided, as required, by the operating business units.

The Process / Transaction Level program requires the business units to be directly responsible for the design, implementation, documentation and assessment of internal controls, based on company guidelines and time tables, within their units,

2. PREPARATORY PROCESSES required prior to the initial SOX certification or at the beginning of each subsequent fiscal year. These include the preparation of management guidelines, communications protocols, calendars/plans, establishing/maintaining a Repository, archiving of previous year's files, developing and implementing Department processes, data formats, workbooks etc. This is covered in detail in Chapter 2.

3. INITIAL RISK ASSESSMENT based on the analysis of the prior fiscal yearend's financial statements. The results of this assessment should be the identification and communication of the responsibility to implement controls to cover all identified significant accounts and processes to the business units and locations (including external vendors),

4. RISK ASSESSMENT based on the entity level control framework. This assessment may have a direct impact on the process/transaction level controls assessments. For example, if a control fails in the Entity Control program, it may invalidate related controls in the process/transaction level program. The Entity Level control program is reviewed in greater detail in Chapter 3 with its assessment processes in Chapter 9,

5. DOCUMENTATION OF THE INTERNAL CONTROL FRAMEWORK for transaction level processes over financial reporting. Your company should require all operating business units to submit documentation to support their implementation and assessment of the transaction level processes and controls within your company. This documentation should be in a form and format defined and approved by company management and the Audit Committee and submitted to the Repository as outlined in Step 7.

    Simultaneously, the documentation for the Entity Level program should also be completed as defined in Chapter 3,

6. ASSESSMENT OF THE DESIGN AND OPERATIONAL EFFECTIVENESS OF THE FRAMEWORK throughout the company (and external vendors, as required). The assessment should be performed based on internal company approved guidelines that meet or exceed those established by the regulatory authorities as reviewed in Chapter 9. This applies to the Entity Level Controls and the Transaction / Process Level Controls. Results of these tests should be submitted to the Repository promptly.

7. SUBMISSION OF ALL OTHER SUPPORTING DOCUMENTATION and other framework information to the Repository for storage, review, analysis, reporting and communication to Company Management and your External Auditor. The information should be collected and compiled in a central Repository in an approved format for review and analysis by the SOX Department and the external auditors,

8. ANALYSIS OF THE COVERAGE OF THE FINANCIAL STATEMENTS AND DISCLOSURES provided by the framework. In order to ensure completeness, the SOX Department must ensure that the internal control framework covers the financial statements and disclosures to the level prescribed by management and regulatory guidelines and to demonstrate to the External Auditors the effectiveness of the internal control framework over these financial statements and disclosures.

   Your company must be in a position to evidence this to the external auditors by using the procedures outlined in Chapter 7,

9. DEFICIENCY MANAGEMENT PROCESSES are critical in ensuring that all identified deficiencies are acquired from all sources, duplicate deficiencies reconciled and eliminated and finally, that the deficiencies are aggregated to provide company management, the Board of Directors, the Audit Committee and External Auditors with a comprehensive analysis of state of the internal control framework.

10. SOX MANAGEMENT ANALYSES AND REPORTING. The need for accurate, validated and regular periodic reporting on the status of the internal control activities and its related processes should be self explanatory, and

11. EXTERNAL AUDITOR COORDINATION AND REPORTING processes - these include the planning, agreement on audit protocols and guidelines, documentation requirements, etc.

SOX PREPARATORY PROCESSES

The certification process requires careful planning and preparation for both the initial and ongoing efforts. If properly planned and implemented in the initial phase, the ongoing effort will require less time and effort when compared to the initial effort.

Therefore, the effort expended in the first year must include the steps necessary to ensure that the SOX life cycle can be sustained, on an ongoing basis, with reduced costs and resource requirements in subsequent years.

Throughout this volume, we emphasize the need for forward planning and execution in order to reduce the effort required for subsequent fiscal periods.

The basic preparation requires the following minimum preparation steps (these are reviewed in more detail in Chapter 2):

1. SELECTION OF AN INTERNAL CONTROL FRAMEWORK – most organizations are implementing the COSO framework. However, there are alternative frameworks that can be implemented. Your company should select the appropriate model for its proposed internal control framework (e.g. CoCo, CSA, Cadbury, King, etc.).

2. DEVELOPMENT, APPROVAL AND IMPLEMENTATION OF THE SOX POLICIES AND PROCEDURES that will be used within the company (and based on its outsourcing contracts, may be required to be used by some of your external vendors). These policies and procedures should include, at a minimum, the following:

   - COMPANY INTERNAL CONTROL OVERVIEW AND GUIDELINES – This should be your company's guidelines issued to all operating Business Units for the design and implementation of internal control framework. This should provide your SOX community with the company's proposed framework, implementation plans and process steps. The manual should define clearly all design principles, implementation standards, assessment methods for both the entity level and transaction level programs,

- DOCUMENTATION STANDARDS – for preparation of the documents required to evidence the existence and operational effectiveness of the internal control processes, controls, test results, deficiencies, remediation plans, etc.,

- ASSESSMENT STANDARDS – the minimum guidelines established by management for assessing the internal control framework,

- COMMUNICATIONS PROTOCOLS including escalation procedures,

- TRAINING MATERIALS AND SCHEDULES – this is critical to ensuring that your SOX community has the skills and knowledge necessary to perform their roles and responsibilities,

- SOX PLANS & CALENDAR detailing all submission dates, reporting dates, etc., and

- INTERNAL SOX DEPARTMENT PROCEDURES e.g. Deficiency Management, procedures, Repository procedures, etc.

3. Establishing MASTER FILES for use in the documentation of the framework, assessments, etc. The use of these master tables ensures that the data from which SOX analyses and reports are prepared is *consistent* on a company wide basis.

   Depending on the level of automation used, these lists must be distributed to your operating Business Units to ensure that their documentation is maintained at the current version of these master files. For real time or on line systems, these should be a part of all online or validation system processes.

4. DEFINITION OF ALL SOX ROLES AND RESPONSIBILITIES throughout the organization has been clearly defined and documented and submitted to the Board and company management for their review and approval.

   Immediately following this initial step, individuals should be appointed to their roles and approved by company management and the board (where required).

   All appointments should be formally communicated to the Internal Audit Department and the External Auditors. For company wide appointments, these appointments should be communicated to your entire company.

   All job definitions must include the minimum experience, qualification and skill requirements.

5. SELECTION OF A SECURE REPOSITORY for all documentation of the internal control framework evidence, procedures, library of regulations and rules, internal company guidelines, working papers, etc.

   The Repository will be the central storage point into which all SOX related information is submitted, validated, analyzed and stored. It must be the central source for all company wide policies, procedures, guidelines, communications, data and information. *From this data source, all company management and Board/Audit Committee reporting must originate.*

   The repository must also be the central point from which the Auditors (both internal and external) will receive the data, information and any evidentiary material necessary to perform their assessments.

The repository is usually maintained in a digital format, but in some instances it may be maintained in a physical format because of the type of documentation.

INITIAL FINANCIAL STATEMENTS RISK ASSESSMENT

An initial risk assessment of the Financial Statements and its disclosures should be performed by a specialized team comprising of personnel from the SOX Department, Finance Division and appropriate Business Units

The results from this initial risk assessment for process/transaction level controls (*not the entity level controls*) is a listing of the financial statement lines, their related significant accounts, the business units/significant account control coverage[6] requirements which must be supported by the internal control framework and evidenced by documentation filed by these Business Units in the Repository.

This team should also establish the guidelines for identifying *qualitative* accounts to be used by the operating business units.

Finally, the team should also develop a *Financial Statement Notes and Disclosures responsibility matrix*. This matrix should establish which of the operating Business Units are responsible for providing data and information to the Finance Division for the financial statements notes and disclosure preparation processes.

ENTITY LEVEL RISK ASSESSMENT

The Entity Level Risk assessment is usually performed by a specialized team, within the SOX Department or other central risk/controls department. The unit must have access to all organizational levels (including the CEO, CFO, Board, Audit Committee, etc.), company policies, evidentiary materials, company procedures etc.

They are required to assess the overall entity level control environment. This is usually addressed by assessing several key items that may have a pervasive impact on the overall environment. Typical examples of these are (this is a limited list for illustrative purposes):

- The CONTROL ENVIRONMENT,
- RISK ASSESSMENT processes,
- INFORMATION AND COMMUNICATION processes,
- MONITORING controls,
- CENTRALIZED PROCESSING AND CONTROLS, including shared service environments,
- CONTROLS TO MONITOR RESULTS of operations, and to monitor other controls, and
- PERIOD-END FINANCIAL REPORTING process

Each Entity Level control must be owned by a senior manager/officer within the company. In rare instances, a control may be owned by a Board Committee (or one of its members). The

---

[6] SIGNIFICANT ACCOUNT CONTROL COVERAGE – in this instance, we are referring to the Business Unit transaction level controls which should document the Significant Account and Process to which they apply. The controls receive from a Business Unit are usually compared to the list assigned by the SOX Department at the end of each fiscal period. If the Business Unit did not "cover" or meet the requirement to implement a control(s) for specific significant accounts, the unit is usually required to correct this deficiency promptly.

entity level assessment requires *active* Board, Management and company personnel participation via questionnaires, interviews, evidence gathering, etc.

It also requires an extensive review of key documentation within the company including policies, procedures, personnel records, compensation records, Board and Committee minutes and other supporting material.

Therefore, the composition of this team is usually *restricted to individuals who have a high security clearance and who have executed the necessary confidentiality (non disclosure) agreements.*

DOCUMENTATION OF THE INTERNAL CONTROL FRAMEWORK

It is critical to understand that documentation on its own does not prove the existence and operating effectiveness of the internal control framework. It should be viewed as the *proof* that the necessary work has been performed within/by the respective units.

The actual work of designing, implementing and assessing the framework is essential. Documentation is the *result* of this work and should not be viewed as the requirement.

In other words, preparing the documentation is not a substitute for the actual implementation and assessment work that needs to be performed.

The documentation of the internal control framework requires an extensive effort in the initial year of SOX certification. Subsequent years should require a reduced effort, if the initial phase is properly performed.

The documentation should include the following basic information:

1. ENTITY LEVEL CONTROLS – these are outlined in detail in Chapter 3,

2. PROCESSES AND THE PROJECT STEPS FOR TRANSACTION LEVEL CONTROLS process maps and/or narratives,

3. The CONTROLS within these processes – these should be documented in a specific format that permits automated validation, detailed analysis and reporting by the Repository,

4. ASSESSMENT DOCUMENTATION (TEST RESULTS) – this should document the steps taken to assess the specific process and its related controls. The assessment results should be submitted to the Repository for storage, analysis and reporting, etc.

5. IDENTIFIED DEFICIENCIES – detailing the type of deficiency, the current status of deficiency, etc,

6. REMEDIATION PLANS – these should outline the remedial steps (for transaction level controls) that will be taken by the Business Unit's management (or company management if it is an entity level control) within a specific time frame.

It is important that the documentation standards, guidelines and all other assessment policies and procedures be developed and implemented *prior* to this section commencing.

ASSESSMENT OF THE DESIGN AND OPERATIONAL EFFECTIVENESS OF THE TRANSACTION LEVEL FRAMEWORK

The assessment process usually comprises of two elements:

- An EVALUATION process in which a "walkthrough" process is executed to ensure correctness and completeness.

- A TEST process in which the process or control provides the anticipated result and does not provide a false or incorrect result

SUBMISSION OF ALL DOCUMENTATION

All documentation should be submitted to the Repository for validation, analysis and safekeeping on a regular, periodic basis.

Upon submission, Business Units and the Entity Level Control Unit are normally required to confirm the status of the internal control framework (evidenced by the documentation and evidentiary material submitted) with an *explicit* assertion statement to company management of the effectiveness of the internal control framework by executing a sub certification form (refer to chapter 11 – Sub Certifications).

This sub certification form is usually designed by the SOX and Legal Departments and is intended to provide assurances to the CEO, CFO and Board that the Business Unit management have complied with internal control guidelines and that these units have provided complete, accurate and timely documentation, results and evidence supporting their sub certifications.

Upon receipt of the documentation, the Repository is required to:

- VALIDATE the documentation received complies with the company's internal control documentation guidelines,

- ACCEPT or REJECT the documentation based on these guidelines and apprise the business unit and company management of any discrepancies so that corrective action can be taken promptly before the fiscal period end,

- EXAMINE the documentation by business unit and for the entire company to ensure that there is no missing documentation on a company wide basis,

- ORGANIZE the documentation within the Repository based on the fiscal period and document types e.g. processes, controls, test results, etc.,

- SECURE the information from further changes. Changes are only permitted via the SOX Department Change Management process.

    Documentation should only be changed by the originator and should require that the change management process be followed in order to ensure the data integrity of the Repository.

ANALYSIS OF THE COVERAGE OF THE FINANCIAL STATEMENTS

At the end of a submission period, the SOX Department must ensure that the internal control framework covers all the required financial statement lines and their respective significant accounts identified in the Financial Statement risk assessment process at the beginning of the submission period.

This critical process is required to assure company management, the Board, Audit Committee and External Auditors that the framework covers the appropriate financial statement lines and disclosures identified in the risk assessment.

Any gaps must be immediately identified and the responsible Business Units must be required to correct their internal control frameworks within their business units by a specified deadline.

DEFICIENCY MANAGEMENT PROCESSES

Deficiency Managements Processes throughout this volume emphasize the need to identify deficiencies *as early as possible in the initial or ongoing SOX cycles.* The rationale for this is simple – *the earlier a deficiency can be identified, the earlier the necessary remediation actions can be taken to correct the deficiency.*

Under specific circumstances, not correcting a significant deficiency on a timely basis can result in the deficiency being promoted into a material weakness.

Deficiencies can be identified at both the Entity Level and the Transaction level. Both types of deficiencies can originate from multiple sources (e.g. Business Unit, Internal Audit, etc).

Some of these may be duplicates. For example, the Internal Audit in the course of an audit may identify a deficiency in Q1. The Business Unit (that was audited) may also identify the *same* deficiency in its framework assessment process.

Both departments will submit these identified deficiencies to the Repository during the deficiency submission cycle. The SOX Department has to review these deficiencies and identify them as duplicates before proceeding to the deficiency aggregation process.

In addition, because the deficiencies that are submitted to the SOX Department may *not* have been communicated to the responsible department (e.g. Regulatory deficiencies may have been sent to the Legal Department and not to the specific Business Unit), the department must ensure that all identified deficiencies are formally communicated to each Department periodically for both their review/comment and for the submission of a remediation plan outlining the corrective steps for the deficiency.

Deficiencies must be tracked on a monthly basis. Remediation plan updates should be required to be filed by the responsible business unit monthly.

After the elimination of duplicates, deficiencies should be aggregated, based on the company's and regulatory guidelines, and all significant deficiencies and material weaknesses must be promptly reported to company management, the Board and the Audit Committees.

The External Auditor's aggregation process may produce a different set of significant deficiencies and material weaknesses. These should be reviewed with the External Auditor to resolve any differences. Differences between the two lists should be provided to the Board and its committees with relevant explanations and SOX Department recommendations.

The Board and Audit Committee should review these lists with both the External Auditor and SOX Department present. Based on this review, the Board and/or Audit Committee will direct company management (and the SOX Department) to take the steps that the Board or Audit Committee deems necessary.

SOX MANAGEMENT ANALYSES AND REPORTING

The Analyses and Reporting should comprise of the following minimum classes:

1. PLAN / CALENDAR ANALYSES AND REPORTING – these should detail the progress based on the established time line, the exceptions (e.g. delayed tasks, missed tasks, etc.), new tasks, unplanned activities, etc.,

2. FRAMEWORK METRICS – these should detail the status of the construction, assessment and other key activities for the internal control framework,

3. FRAMEWORK EXCEPTION ANALYSES – these should detail gaps in documentation or activities, activities or documentation not meeting company or regulatory standards, etc.

4. FRAMEWORK ASSESSMENT REPORTS – these should provide company management with an assessment of the state of the internal control framework,

5. DEFICIENCY MANAGEMENT REPORTS, and

6. EXTERNAL AUDIT ISSUES – all issues identified by the external auditors.

EXTERNAL AUDITOR COORDINATION AND REPORTING PROCESSES

The External Auditor Coordination processes should be designed to ensure that:

1. The Auditors are supplied with all necessary documentation and framework evidence on a mutually agreed timetable. The importance of this activity in both the initial and ongoing phases cannot be overemphasized as there may be a direct impact on the auditor's review and assessment processes. Tardiness or miscues may lead to delays and cost increases,

2. External Audit issues are identified and resolved promptly in order to ensure that they do not evolve into deficiencies,

3. Reconciliations are performed between internally identified deficiencies and external audit identified deficiencies promptly,

4. The External Auditor's activities within the Business Units are coordinated with the Business Unit Managers on a timely basis, and

5. External Auditors receive copies of all company management, Board and Audit Committee reports necessary for their assessment.

SUB CERTIFICATION PROCESS

The Sub certification process, outlined in Chapter 11, is executed at the end of each submission cycle (or at your discretion) to achieve three objectives:

1. To ensure that all individuals responsible understand and agree to their responsibilities,

2. All responsible personnel certify in a prescribed format that they have executed these responsibilities as per your company's guidelines within the prescribed timeframes; any exceptions are identified and forwarded to the SOX Department.

3. The certifications provide the CEO and CFO with reasonable assurances that the company's internal control framework is well designed, implemented and operating effectively.

These sub certifications are filed in the Repository and are reconciled to the SOX Master list of individuals (that are required to certify) to ensure that there are no missing sub certifications.

SUMMARY

In this chapter, we have provided you with an overview of the organizational requirements for the SOX Certification process. The intent has been to introduce you gradually to the key elements required to achieve a successful SOX Life Cycle.

Later chapters provide additional detail on each of the items covered in this chapter and should be reviewed in detail before starting to develop the initial phase of SOX or modifying your existing SOX processes.

ORGANIZATION CHARTS

At this stage, you should start the following items that you will expand and modify as you proceed through this volume.

1. ORGANIZATION CHART – Draw your proposed organization chart at a high level. The organization chart should comprise of three components:

    - The SOX Corporate Organization Chart – modify the chart provided,

    - A typical Business Unit organization chart outlining the roles and responsibilities, and

    - The SOX Department Chart – modify the chart provided.

2. SOX PROCESSES – Adopt or modify the processes we have outlined in the second section of this chapter. As you proceed through each chapter, you will expand this framework into detail process steps,

3. SOX DEPARTMENT – Adopt or modify the SOX Department Organization Hierarchy in the third section of this chapter. Assign the roles and responsibilities outlined in the SOX Department worksheet,

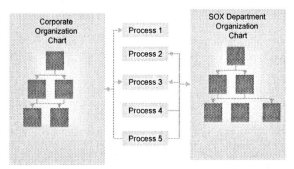

- ROLES AND RESPONSIBILITIES – match the processes to the organization charts in order to establish the preliminary roles and responsibilities. Refer to the diagram for assistance.

    In this diagram, we illustrate the processes in the center. The Corporate and the SOX Department Organization structures are on either side of these processes.

    1. Map each process to either the Corporate Organization and/or the SOX Department structure – some processes will reside solely in the Corporate Structure, some only in the SOX Department Structure and some will be shared. Wherever possible, try to reduce the number of shared processes, and

2. This initial mapping will assist you to identify the roles and responsibilities that you will need to focus on.

QUALIFICATIONS RECONCILIATION

1. For each role that you have defined in the preliminary chart, you should then define the minimum qualifications for the role,

2. After completing the organization chart, perform a preliminary assignment of the roles,

3. Determine if each candidate meets the minimum requirements. If the candidate does not meet the requirements, prepare a "*request for exemption*" memo to be forwarded to the CEO and CFO for their approval.

EXAMPLE OF ROLES / RESPONSIBILITIES CHART

This is an example of a typical Roles and Responsibilities Chart – this illustrates several of the key roles and responsibilities.

This is intended to assist you to design the high level table which i is used as the master control document to develop the company's entire roles and responsibilities.

TYPICAL ROLES AND RESPONSIBILITIES CHART					
ROLE / RESPONSIBILITY	BOARD COMMITTEES	CEO / CFO	SOX DEPARTMENT	BUSINESS UNIT SOX MANAGER	CONTROL RESPONSIBILITY OFFICER
POLICY/ PROCEDURE CREATION, UPDATE & APPROVAL PROCESS	• Review and approve high level policies	• Overall responsibility for design, development, and implementation of all policies	• Develop and submit high level policies to CEO / CFO for review and approval • Establishing Training and Communication protocols for all policies • Administration of policy execution and monitoring of compliance.	• Review all draft policies received from SOX Department • Departmental oversight of compliance with policy within own unit.	• Execution and compliance with policies
DELEGATION OF AUTHORITY / RESPONSIBILITIES	• Ensure delegation of Authorities and Responsibilities depending on company's guidelines for senior positions above a specific rank	• Ensure all delegated authorities and responsibilities are properly documented (task usually assigned to Personnel Department)	• Based on Entity Level program assessments, SOX Department should monitor compliance of this role	• Implement as directed	• Implement as directed
SEGREGATION OF DUTIES	• Review all Segregation of Duties exceptions and approve for limited period of time. • Review all exemptions at end of time period	• Receive summarized certifications on segregation of duties from SOX Department. • Engage Internal Audit to review periodically throughout company • Review all exemptions at end of time period	• Require all Business Unit SOX Managers and Control Responsibility Officers to certify compliance with Segregation of Duties guidelines	• Design, implement and monitor segregation of duties • Communicate to all Control Responsibility Officers	• Comply with Segregation of Duties guidelines
ANTI FRAUD PROGRAM (AS PART OF ENTITY CONTROL PROGRAM)	• Review of all Anti Fraud Exceptions and disciplinary actions with Company	• Final responsibility for all Anti Fraud Policies and Controls • Delegates	• Review results of assessment activities within Business Units and	• Design and implement programs/ controls to prevent, deter and detect fraud	• Implements as directed

Typical Roles and Responsibilities Chart					
Role / Responsibility	Board Committees	CEO / CFO	SOX Department	Business Unit SOX Manager	Control Responsibility Officer
	Management and external Auditors on a quarterly basis	certain authorities and responsibilities to Internal Audit and Business Unit Management	summarize for CEO/CFO	• Evaluate and monitor the anti-fraud program and procedures. • Asses anti fraud controls quarterly	
SOX Documentation and Process/Control Assessments	• Periodically review policy and management corrective actions	• Reviews and takes corrective disciplinary action based on exceptions escalated by SOX Department •	• Responsible for ensuring all Business Units Document and complete their assessments of the pertinent sections of the internal control framework • Review and validate all documentation received into the Repository	• Responsible for ensuring that the Business Unit meets or exceeds the SOX Documentation and Assessment Guidelines • Design and implement documentation and assessment processes within the Business Unit • Adheres to the SOX Department Plans & Calendar	• Meets company guidelines for controls and other responsibilities assigned by the Business Unit SOX Manager
Deficiency Management	• Review all Significant Deficiencies / Material Weaknesses and their respective remediation plans with External Auditors and Company Management on a quarterly basis.	• Review and take corrective action, when necessary, for all deficiencies analyzed and reported by SOX Department. • Review with Board and External Auditors at least quarterly	• Collect all identified deficiencies from all sources. • Validate all deficiencies and eliminate duplicates • Combine and aggregate and present to CEO and CFO on a quarterly basis, • Reconcile to External Auditor's list	• Responsible for ensuring that all Business Unit's deficiencies are forwarded to SOX Department on a quarterly basis, • Responsible for ensuring that all deficiencies have an active remediation plan • Responsible for managing remediation plan in order to eliminate deficiency	• Responsible for assessing controls as per company guidelines and identifying any deficiencies • Reporting of deficiency to Business Unit SOX Manager • Preparation and supervision of Remediation Plan.
Sub Certification	• Review of CEO/CFO certifications with CEO, CFO and External Auditors on a quarterly basis	• Receive all subordinate sub certifications based on SOX and Company Guidelines • Review all significant changes and exceptions with SOX Department on a quarterly basis • Direct Internal Audit to periodically review and audit critical Business Units for assessment of their certifications	• Acquire all sub certifications on a quarterly basis for summarization to CEO and CFO. • All Significant Changes and exceptions are identified for CEO and CFO review	• Responsible for providing sub certification for entire Business Unit • Summaries and reviews all Control Responsibility officers' sub certifications on a quarterly basis	• Provides sub certification for specific processes and controls to Business Unit SOX Manager

CHAPTER 2 – PREREQUISITES FOR SARBANES OXLEY

INTENT OF THIS CHAPTER

This chapter focuses on the prerequisites for a successful SOX certification. These build the foundation required for both the initial and ongoing certifications.

If properly constructed and implemented, these prerequisites will also ensure that the ongoing processes are sustainable on a long term basis. This chapter, similar to Chapter 1, serves as an introduction to the subsequent chapters that elaborate on the required process steps for each of the concepts or subjects introduced in this chapter.

OVERVIEW

If you have already achieved your initial SOX certification, then this chapter should be used as a checklist to ensure that your company has implemented the recommendations within this chapter during your initial effort.

This period of development must be carefully managed by the SOX Department and Senior Company Management. These items may need to be modified several times during the course of both the initial and subsequent certifications because of environment or regulatory changes, or based on feedback from your internal SOX community.

Many companies already have a preexisting internal control framework with related processes which should be modified to achieve the objectives. These companies should review the prerequisites outlined in this chapter in order to determine which elements of the preexisting framework can be modified to meet these requirements.

SOX PREREQUISITES

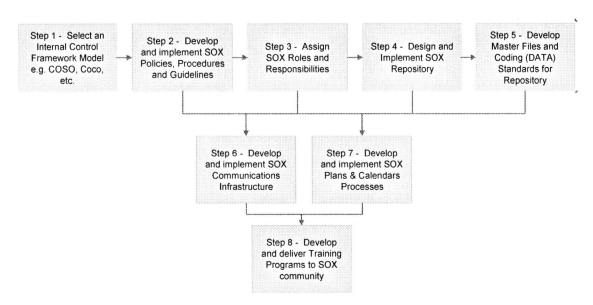

As illustrated in the diagram above, we have subdivided these prerequisites into the following primary steps:

1. SELECTION OF AN INTERNAL CONTROL FRAMEWORK MODEL – your company will select the best model for an internal control framework (this is usually only required for the initial

SOX certification),

2. DEVELOPMENT AND IMPLEMENTATION OF SOX POLICIES[7] AND PROCEDURES[8] - including applicable guidelines[9], job definitions, etc. This applies to both the Entity Level Control Program and the Transaction (Process) Level program.

3. Assignment of SOX ROLES AND RESPONSIBILITIES throughout the organization,

4. Design and implementation of the REPOSITORY,

5. Development of MASTER FILES AND CODING STANDARDS that will be used in the documentation of the internal control framework,

6. Design and implementation of the PLANS & CALENDAR,

7. Design and implementation of the COMMUNICATIONS INFRASTRUCTURE, and

8. Design and deliver TRAINING PROGRAMS to the SOX Community.

SELECTION ON AN INTERNAL CONTROL FRAMEWORK

Public Company Accounting Oversight Board's (PCAOB) Auditing Standard No. 2 (AU2) requires management to base its assessment of the effectiveness of controls over financial reporting using a suitable, recognized control framework, established by a body of experts that followed due-process procedures to develop the framework.

In the United States, the Committee of Sponsoring Organizations ("COSO") of the Treadway Commission has published the Internal Control – Integrated Framework (otherwise know as the COSO Report). This provides an appropriate framework for purposes of management's assessment because it

- Is free from bias,
- permits reasonably consistent qualitative and quantitative measurements of your company's internal controls,
- is sufficiently complete so that those relevant factors that would alter a conclusion about the effectiveness of your internal controls are not omitted, and
- is relevant to an evaluation of internal control over financial reporting.

The COSO framework consists of the following five interrelated components:

- Control Environment,
- Risk Assessment,
- Information and Communication,
- Monitoring, and
- Control Activities

---

[7] POLICY - A guiding principle designed to influence decisions, actions, etc. Typically, a policy designates a required processor procedure within an organization.
[8] PROCEDURE - a particular way of accomplishing an objective; generally refers to the method rather than the result. Procedures are usually developed to describe the methods for implementing policy.
[9] GUIDELINES - A written statement or policy statement that may be issued by any organizational entity for the purpose of providing future direction, clarification, or other necessary or useful information or direction as it relates to the particular work activity and process affected

The "*Control Activities*" component is used as the basis for the process/transaction level program and its assessment. The remaining components are used as the basis for the entity level control program and its assessment that are reviewed in more detail in chapters 3 and 9.

COSO FRAMEWORK

The framework should be viewed as a three dimensional model that provides the basis upon which to construct an internal control framework.

The first axis comprises of the operating business units and departments of your company.

The second axis, as referenced in the previous section, comprises of the control environment, risk assessment, information and communication, monitoring and control activities components.

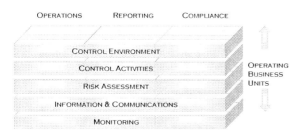

The third axis identifies the three primary objectives of internal control namely the efficiency and effectiveness of operations; financial reporting; and compliance with laws and regulations.

Sarbanes Oxley focuses primarily on Financial Reporting. However, various aspects of the operations and compliance with laws and regulations objectives may be directly related to the presentation and required disclosures in financial statements and should be encompassed in your internal control over financial reporting.

DEVELOPMENT AND IMPLEMENTATION OF SOX POLICIES AND PROCEDURES

The SOX Policies and Procedures should provide its audience with the operating rules under which the internal control framework will be designed, implemented, assessed and managed on an ongoing basis.

The development of these policies and procedures should be the direct responsibility of the SOX Department. Senior Company Management, the Board and Audit Committee should review and approve these policies and procedures and receive regular updates on their implementation on an ongoing basis.

The initial effort will require the expertise of several internal departments and may also require the assistance of qualified external consultants. The ongoing effort should require less resources and time if maintained on a consistent basis – *barring any unforeseen regulatory changes*.

DEVELOPMENT CYCLE

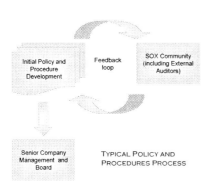

The SOX Department has the responsibility for the development of all SOX Policies and Procedures. This is usually done with the assistance of the Finance Division, Legal and Compliance Departments, Internal Auditors and, in some instances, external consultants. External Auditors are included in the feedback loop, depending on the subject area.

On the left is a representation of a typical development cycle.

It is important that the SOX Department provide its community with the ability to provide feedback *during* the development stages. Upon completion, the policies and procedures should be presented to the Senior Company Management and Board for review and approval.

In some instances, the Senior Management and the Board may require Internal Audit, Legal and Compliance Department reviews prior to granting their approval.

CHECK LIST OF POLICIES AND PROCEDURES

The SOX Department should develop a list of all planned policies and procedures. This list, together with the actual policies and procedures, should be stored in the Library component of the Repository.

This is a list of the basic manuals that should be produced:

BASIC MANUAL LIST		
TITLE	SAMPLE CONTENTS	DESCRIPTION
GENERAL CORPORATE MANUAL ON THE COMPANY INTERNAL CONTROLS (EMPLOYEES HANDBOOK)	<ul><li>Management's commitment to accurate Financial Reporting and Disclosure,</li><li>Discussion on why participation of all employees is required,</li><li>Overview of company's objectives for<ul><li>Control environment</li><li>Control activities</li><li>Information and communications</li><li>Monitoring</li><li>Risk assessment</li></ul></li><li>Explanation of Whistle Blower program – with emphasis on the anonymity of the program,</li><li>Anti fraud overview, and</li><li>Feedback communication channels to Company Management and Board including Governance Committee, Audit Committee, etc.</li></ul>	This is a general "all employees" manual explaining management's objectives, the duties and responsibilities of all employees, etc. for the internal control framework The whistle blower and anti fraud controls should be emphasized within this manual. In some companies, employees are required to acknowledge receipt of the manual and their understanding and commitment to the general principles.
SOX FINANCIAL REPORTING FRAMEWORK MANUAL	<ul><li>Company Objectives,</li><li>SOX 404 Environment within company,</li><li>Company Organizational Model,</li><li>Key Roles and Responsibilities – with emphasis on the SOX Department's and Business Units' roles,</li><li>Key Company Financial Control Principles,</li><li>Related documentation e.g.<ul><li>Entity Level Program</li><li>Finance Division Policy Manual</li><li>IT Security Manuals</li><li>HR Manuals, etc.,</li></ul></li><li>SOX Communications infrastructure and the roles of all participants,</li><li>Sample SOX Plans and Calendars,</li><li>Repository roles and responsibilities – including reader's responsibility, and</li><li>Key SOX Processes - some of these will be reviewed at a high level and then reference the more detailed manuals below</li></ul>	The intent of this initial manual is to provide any SOX participant with <ul><li>an introduction to the framework that the company has implemented,</li><li>the company management's objectives,</li><li>the key principles, and</li><li>references for further information</li></ul>
ENTITY LEVEL PROGRAM	<ul><li>Objective of Entity Level Program,</li><li>How company program is designed,</li><li>How assessments will be performed,</li><li>Role and responsibilities of various participants,</li><li>Processes that will be use in development and assessment of the program,</li><li>Checklist of Entity Controls organized by COSO component, Point of focus or other similar hierarchy,</li><li>Listing of controls and control owners (titles only), and</li></ul>	This manual is targeted at Company Management and any Entity Control owner (refer to Chapter 3 for more details). It provides them with an overview of the <ul><li>Entire Program,</li><li>Processes that will be</li></ul>

BASIC MANUAL LIST		
TITLE	SAMPLE CONTENTS	DESCRIPTION
	• Assessment processes	employed for development, implementation and assessment, • Their roles and responsibilities in this program, • SOX Department role in the program, and • External Auditor coordination
FINANCIAL STATEMENTS RISK ASSESSMENT MANUAL	Describes the Financial Statements Risk Assessment process with specific emphasis on the Business Units' roles and responsibilities. This manual is usually only distributed to • Business Unit Management, • Internal Audit Department, • External Auditor, • SOX Department personnel, and • Legal and Compliance Departments.	This manual will be reviewed by your External Auditors in order to perform an assessment of your company's methods.
PROCESS / CONTROL DEVELOPMENT AND IMPLEMENTATION MANUAL	This manual is described in more detail in this chapter. Contents should include: • How to design process (or use a standardized process), • How to document implementation of process, • How to document implementation of controls, • Achieving control objectives, • Identifying key Financial Controls, • Overview of assessment process guidelines, processes and reporting (usually this is in a separate manual which is why this manual only provides an overview with reference point to the more detailed manual), • How to identify and report deficiencies, and • How to prepare remediation plans The manual should also outline: • The Repository processes, • The Submission requirements, and • The Validation responses and the Business Units' responsibility to correct any errors,	This is the "how to" manual for designing, implementing and documenting the process / transaction level control framework.
COMPANY ASSESSMENT GUIDELINES	These are the company guidelines that define: • Detailed description of how a walkthrough is to be performed, • Detailed steps on how tests are to be performed, • Segregation of duties test (control performer cannot be tester), • Level of Testing requirements based on type of control, • Sample Sizes required for tests, • Frequency of tests, and • Format for reporting tests to Repository.	This manual governs the entire assessment process for transaction level controls. It should be issued annually with quarterly updates on sampling sizes, frequencies and assessment priorities.
DEFICIENCY MANAGEMENT MANUAL	Outlines the company policies for deficiencies. Provides detailed processes for (refer to Chapter 10 for details): • Identification and reporting of deficiencies to SOX Department, • SOX Department's role in collecting deficiencies from non Business Unit , • Business unit roles in confirming deficiencies, • Standard SOX Management and Escalation processes, • Deficiency Combination process,	This manual outlines the entire Deficiency Management process from two perspectives: • The SOX Department and its internal Deficiency Management processes, and • The responsibilities of the operating Business Units

BASIC MANUAL LIST		
TITLE	SAMPLE CONTENTS	DESCRIPTION
	• Aggregation Process, and • External Audit reconciliation processes	
OTHER SOX PROCESSES	This manual can be published as a single manual or a set of manuals and its contents should cover: • Sub Certification processes for all organization levels, • Remediation Plan Process Updates, • External Auditor Coordination, and • Finance Error Log Processes (refer to Chapter 9 for details)	Depending on the size of your organization, this manual should encompass all other SOX processes.

USE OF STANDARDIZED PROCESSES

Standardized processes are designed centrally within your company but operated and assessed within the operating business units. You may elect not to use standardized processes within your company, but you should carefully review the inherent advantages derived from using these processes.

All processes are usually linked to Significant Accounts that are identified in the Financial Statements Risk Assessment process (the Financial Statements Risk Assessment is reviewed in detail in Chapter 7).

Some organizations have developed standard processes that are implemented on a company wide basis. These standard processes are usually developed in conjunction with central Finance or IT divisions' personnel who are responsible for the governance functions of their respective functions.

A typical example would be a bank reconciliation process that can be published as a standard process for use by all operating business units. The process may only be customized based on overriding banking regulations or other unusual circumstances required by specific legal jurisdictions. Customization must be approved by a central SOX committee which usually comprises of representatives of the Senior Company Management, SOX Department Management and Finance Division / IT representatives.

This standardization of processes provides significant advantages to companies because they reduce the overhead costs and times in the development of test and walkthrough materials etc. In addition, they provide the foundation for

- *consistent, tangible* comparisons between the various operating business units and their internal control frameworks,

- standardization of SOX procedures,

- because of the standardization, management assessment analysis time and costs are usually reduced,

Simply put, it is simpler to compare like (similar) processes and the performance of the various departments if your processes are standardized.

In addition, process standardization imposes a management standard across the organization, which if complied with, provides you with assurances of a *consistent* approach to internal control throughout the entire organization that can be monitored centrally based on your risk assessment standards.

Without standardization, the assessment of the internal control framework becomes very in larger organizations, because of the unique elements that may be incorporated into each process by independent business units.

PROCESS IMPLEMENTATION / DOCUMENTATION PROCEDURES

Process implementation/documentation standards are developed to guide the operating Business Units in

- The design, implementation and assessment of a process within their business unit, and

- The preparation of the documentation that evidences the above activities.

If a standardized process is used, the Business Units is required to review the standard process documentation (that is maintained in a library in the Repository) and complete the required standard forms. Standardized processes have standard forms that need to be completed; *non standardized processes have documentation formats that must be adhered to in preparation for their documentation.* Therefore non standardized processes require an increased effort with accompanying increases in resource requirements and costs.

If the Business Unit does not use a standardized process, the documentation procedures should include the following:

1. DESIGN/IMPLEMENT THE PROCESS – a tutorial on how to process designs should be provided together with an implementation guide for the Business Unit.

2. A PROCESS MAP – Instructions on how to develop a process map, which is a graphical depiction of the flow of the transactions in the process, helps Process Owners, SOX Team members and the External Auditors understand the Significant Process detail steps and identify the types of errors that can occur in the process – thereby identifying the required controls objectives and controls,.

3. REQUIRED DOCUMENTATION PROCESS ELEMENTS – Each process document should contain a header that contains the following – these items should all be documented in your master files:

    - Business Unit ID,
    - Process Owner,
    - Process Type,
    - Process Classification,
    - Process Frequency,
    - Process ID or Name (the combination of the Business Unit ID and the Process ID should provide a unique compound process ID key for use in automating the analysis of processes),
    - Control objective(s)[10] for this specific process, etc.

4. PROCESS STEP DESCRIPTIONS (THE PROCESS NARRATIVE) – Each Process should be described in a step-by-step narrative which includes:

    - Information on the flow of the transaction including how transactions are initiated, authorized, recorded, processed, and reported,

---

[10] CONTROL OBJECTIVES – are usually defined within the master files by the Finance and SOX Departments. The objective of a control is to eliminate the risk a misstatement or non disclosure in the company's financial statements and disclosures. It may require several controls within a process to eliminate this risk or to reduce the risk to an inconsequential level. A process may have one or more control objective.

- All activities within the process regardless of the responsible party (including third parties),
- All the controls performed in the process including Key and non-Key Controls that are designed to prevent or detect fraud, and
- Data inputs and outputs to and from other organizations outside your company.

The period-end financial reporting process, specifically, should include the following:

- The procedures used to enter transaction totals into the general ledger,
- The procedures used to initiate, authorize, record, and process journal entries in the general ledger,
- Other procedures used to record recurring and non-recurring,
- adjustments to the annual and quarterly financial statements, such as consolidating adjustments, report combinations, and classifications, and
- Procedures for drafting annual and quarterly financial statements and related disclosures.

In preparing the process narrative or any other documentation, the preparer should take into account that external parties, who are not aware of your company's acronyms or other abbreviations, will be reviewing these documents. Therefore, the use of company specific acronyms and other terms should be excluded from this documentation.

When referencing individuals, the names of the individuals should not be used – instead the job title and business unit name should be used.

For each individual process step, the narrative must also contain, at a minimum, the following:

- Unique process step ID (within each process this step ID should be unique. For example, if you have two processes – PROC1 and PROC2 - within the Organization, they can each have a PROCSTEP1. For automation purposes, a unique compound key can be created from a combination of the Business ID, the Process ID and the Process Step ID),
- indicator whether this step is a control step (some companies document controls separately from process steps),
- individual responsible for performing the process step (*remember title – not name*),
- the type of process step e.g. decision step, etc.,
- the preceding process step, and
- the subsequent process step, etc.

5. CROSS REFERENCE LIST of the controls used within the process – if they are not identified as process steps and the process step that they control,

6. PROCESS TO PROCESS JUMP INDICATORS – within some processes, there are decisions points that determine the next step of the process based on a condition (usually an error indicator or flag).

The next step may be resident in a different process and requires the transaction to *jump* from one process to a different process.

The linkage between these two processes must be identified and documented in order that end-to end walkthroughs can be performed during the assessment process.

7. END TO END PROCESS CONNECTORS ("HAND OFFS") – this is a type of "*process to process jump indicator*", these occur at the *end* of a process and signify that the process will pass the transaction over to another process for conclusion.

    These are used usually in processes where the operating Business Unit *"hands offs"* a transaction to a centralized corporate department or an outsourced process for further processing.

    Typical examples usually occur in Accounts Payable transactions with the approval process starting in an operating Business Unit but ending in a centralized Accounts Payable Department.

8. PROCESS ASSESSMENT RESULTS – the results of process walkthroughs and tests must be filed with the Repository in the prescribed format detailed..

STANDARDIZED CONTROLS

The use of *standardized* controls is also recommended, wherever possible. The use of these standardized controls permits the use of standard assessment processes and should reduce the final SOX related costs within your company.

These controls, similar to the standardized processes in the previous section, should be jointly developed by the Finance, IT and SOX Departments and communicated to the operating Business Units. The resulting standardized control should be maintained in a Controls Library within the Repository for retrieval by the operating Business Units and Testers.

Operating Business Units should be requested to use standardized controls, wherever possible. Customization of standardized controls must be approved by a central SOX committee which usually comprises of representatives of the Senior Company Management, SOX Department Management and Finance Division representatives.

CONTROL IMPLEMENTATION / DOCUMENTATION PROCESSES

Controls must be implemented, documented and assessed based on your guidelines. The documentation required to evidence the existence and operating effectiveness of these controls should be documented in your company's standard format that permits automated validation, secure digital storage, analysis and reporting by the Repository.

If a standardized control is implemented, the documentation process uses a standard form from the library section in the Repository. If a non standardized control is used, the Business Unit has to prepare the required documentation using the prescribed format.

The documentation of controls should require, at a minimum, the following information:

1. REQUIRED CONTROL ELEMENTS – Each control should contain a header that contains the following (most elements should be acquired from master file lists that are included in any on line systems or as a standard part of your documentation):

    - Business Unit ID,
    - Process ID or Name,

- Control ID,
- Control Performer – individual responsible for performing the control,
- Control Tester – individual responsible for testing and evaluating the control,
- Control Type (e.g. estimation, routine, etc.),
- Control Classification (from master file list),
- Control Frequency (e.g. many times per day, daily, etc.),
- Control Objective,
- Control Method (from master file list e.g. manual, automated, etc.),
- Systems upon which this control relies (from a master list of systems),
- Indicator if system is an End User Computing Application (EUCA) (e.g. spreadsheet, etc.),
- Related control(s) – list any reliance factors – with references to control objectives,
- Significant Account(s) that this control covers, and
- Financial Assertions for *each* of the Significant Accounts that this control covers.

2. CONTROL DESCRIPTIONS – each description should contain, at a minimum, the following:

- Control Objective – should clearly define the control objective – most companies maintain master lists of control objectives. We would recommend this approach because of the ease of maintenance,
- Detail description of the control and its individual control steps, and
- Some organizations require individual control steps to be identified instead of a narrative,

3. CONTROL TO CONTROL JUMP INDICATORS – similar to processes, within some controls there are decision steps that determine whether a control passes a successful transaction to another control for further processing in order to achieve a specific control objective.

This next control must be indicated by the Business Unit ID, Process ID and Control ID (which together provide a unique compound key) within this documentation.

The linkage between these two controls must be identified and documented for end-to end walkthroughs during the assessment processes.

Typical examples usually occur in Accounts Payable transactions with the approval control starting in the Operating Business Unit but ending in a centralized Accounts Payable Department control for the actual disbursement.

4. CONTROL ASSESSMENT RESULTS – based on the performance of walkthroughs and tests performed within the Business Unit, the Repository should receive all results in a prescribed format. In the event of a deficiency, addition deficiency information will be required. Refer to Chapter 9 for example of form.

OTHER DOCUMENTATION STANDARDS

Documentation standards should also be established for (details are provided in later chapters):

1. ASSESSMENT STEPS AND RESULTS – form to be completed for every assessment performed by process and control,

2. DEFICIENCY REPORTING – form to be completed to report a deficiency (for both transaction and entity level deficiencies),

3. REMEDIATION PLANS – form to be completed with attachments, and

4. SUB CERTIFICATIONS – these would be centrally issued from the SOX Department for execution by the pertinent SOX participants e.g. Control Responsibility Officers will receive a sub certification form that is customized to their use (refer to Chapter 11 for additional details).

THE SOX REPOSITORY

The Repository is the secure central area in which all internal control framework documentation, working papers, policies, procedures, guidelines and evidence is stored, analyzed and maintained. Chapter 6 provides the detailed steps required to establish the Repository.

In this repository, all SOX data must be stored in archives by fiscal period. The security for this repository must be the highest level possible within your company.

The repository operates based on the following tenets:

1. The Repository cannot, under any circumstances, change documents or data received from any source. Documents can only be changed by the originator. Where the repository publishes reports based on derived data, the repository may only change the processes or methods used to *derive* the data and *not the underlying data itself*,

2. Data received from all sources must be validated versus company and regulatory guidelines. Items failing validation are to be returned to the originator for correction by a specified date,

3. Data must be archived/maintained by fiscal period (e.g. Q1 2006),

4. Data received in a post closing cycle must be maintained by the fiscal period and the cycle ID,

5. Data, because of its confidentiality, must be restricted to only security approved individuals. All individuals must be required to execute confidentiality agreements.

Depending on the automation available within your company this information may be stored in word processing documents, spreadsheets, relational database management systems, document management systems, imaging systems or specialized Control Management systems (refer to Chapter 11 for additional details).

Regardless of the level of automation, it is the responsibility of the SOX Department to select the methods and tools to be used in establishing and operating the Repository. Therefore, this selection process should use these qualification criteria in designing and selecting the Repository tools to be used.

1. SECURITY OF THE REPOSITORY – the security of the repository is paramount. Assuming that you will use some level of automation, your company's IT security guidelines

should be employed based on an agreement with your External and Internal Auditors,

2. VALIDATION CAPABILITIES – the capability to validate information received from the operating business units to ensure that they comply with your company's guidelines must be an integral part of any selected tool or method. Where possible, this should be executed on an automated basis.

Some companies attempt manual Quality Assurance processes that usually prove to be cost prohibitive or inconsistent in their results.

3. ANALYSIS – The Repository must be capable of supporting the analyses outlined in subsequent chapters. Therefore, we recommend the use, wherever possible, of a relational database management system or similar tool with analytical/query capabilities.

Several key analyses can be cumbersome to perform on a manual basis and require a high degree of automation e.g. the Financial Statement control coverage analysis where company management ensures that all significant accounts and units have been covered by the internal control framework can be costly and time consuming in larger companies if performed manually,

4. REPORTING – the tool selected should have extensive reporting capabilities as outlined in the chapter on Reporting and Metrics.

MASTER FILES AND CODING STANDARDS

In order to ensure consistency and integrity of all data/ information received from the various sources within your company, the SOX Department must mandate and impose coding standards that include the use of master files for specific fields within the various documents received.

Master files must be developed for all documentation elements that will be used later in the assessment analysis and reports.

If you are using specialized software for the repository, you should consult your IT Department or Software Vendor for their capabilities/requirements.

SOX CALENDAR

SOX Calendars can be published as stand alone entities or integrated into company wide calendars. The development of the SOX calendar should be the responsibility of the SOX Department with assistance from the Finance Division, IT and Internal Audit Departments.

External Auditors should be consulted for their input to the calendar in order to provide all details of External Auditor SOX activities.

The time period covered by the initial certification calendar usually takes more than 12 months in larger companies. The majority of this is due to the preparation time for the prerequisites identified in this chapter. These prerequisites are usually not as resource-intensive or time-intensive in subsequent years.

Fiscal Year Calendar

The calendar should be published in a preliminary format for a new fiscal year just prior to the end of the preceding fiscal year to allow the Business Units to provide feedback on scheduling conflicts.

After all necessary changes, the calendar is published in the first month of the new fiscal year. The target dates published within this calendar may have monthly or weekly targets instead of a specific date because many activities cannot be finalized until the preceding quarter.

Quarterly Calendars

Calendars are published on a quarterly basis with specific target dates for each quarter's activity. These calendars must be published at least two weeks prior to a fiscal quarter commencing and should include the External Auditor's planned activity dates within the Business Units.

Calendar Contents

The calendar should include the details of the following events. These events and their supporting information are explained in greater detail in the chapter on the SOX Plans & Calendar. This list is not in a priority or date sequence.

1. Risk Assessment activities (both Entity Level Control program and Financial Statements risk assessments) with planned target date for publications, interviews and collection of evidence,

2. Documentation events for Transaction Level Processes and Controls – provides guidelines to the Business Units of when they should engage in these activities within their units,

3. Assessment activities – provides test guidelines for Business Units to accomplish by specific dates e.g. High Risk Processes and controls must all be completed by Q2 in Year 2 and then be retested in Q4,

    For centralized/coordinated testing requirements for IT enabled and other IT controls, specific regional or application details are provided so that Business Units can determine their resource and timing requirements.

4. Repository Submission Activities – provides specific targets for dates by which process and control documentation, test results, deficiencies, remediation plans, etc. must be received by the Repository,

5. Deficiency Management Activities – Dates for submission / correction of deficiencies from all sources (e.g. Internal Audit, etc). The Business Units should be advised when to anticipate receiving the deficiencies assigned to them from external sources and their required confirmation dates,

6. Sub certification activities – the dates by which the Business Unit managers and other company management will be required to provide their certification forms for their assessment of the units' internal control framework,

7. PUBLICATION DATES FOR SOX ANALYSES AND REPORTS – these advise all Business Units of the publication dates for all information that will be produced by the SOX Department,

8. TRAINING SEMINARS AND OTHER MATERIAL – anticipated dates for training seminars etc.

9. KEY COMPANY WIDE DATES AND ACTIVITIES – timetable for Board, Audit and Disclosure committee meetings, and

10. SPECIAL FISCAL YEAREND PROCESSES – final submission of fiscal yearend control test results (for controls that are usually completed at the beginning of a new fiscal year but are based on the previous fiscal year).

COMMUNICATIONS INFRASTRUCTURE

Both the SOX initial and ongoing phases require extensive, targeted and organized communications. Unorganized communications usually leads to a high amount of unstructured communications which may, in turn, lead to increased costs and community apathy.

SOX communications are usually organized into five communications channels. A channel is defined for the purposes of this document as "The *path* along which communications are transmitted."

The following channels are usually required for SOX Communications:

1. LIBRARY CHANNEL – this is usually a unilateral path by which approved subscribers can access manuals, training material, regulations etc,

2. MESSAGE CHANNEL – a bi-lateral path used to transmit all dynamic electronic messages via a secure email facility. Wherever possible, email should originate and be received from/into a central SOX mailbox that is monitored and managed by specific personnel within the SOX Department,

3. REPORTING CHANNEL – path used to transmit all SOX periodic reports in electronic format,

4. TRAINING CHANNEL – delivery path for all SOX training programs, and

5. CONFERENCE / PRESENTATION CHANNEL – most companies use an annual (or more frequent) series of conferences to communicate with their SOX Audience their plans, procedure or policy changes, etc. and to receive feedback from the business units.

Additional detail information is provided in the chapter on Communications.

TRAINING PROGRAMS

The SOX Department is usually charged with the responsibility to provide three levels of training.

1. The CONCEPTS OF INTERNAL CONTROL and your company's internal control policies. In some companies, this is provided as a company wide program that is available to all employees employed in the financial reporting process. In others, it is limited to only the SOX community.

2. SOX PROCEDURES / ROLES AND RESPONSIBILITIES – these training classes are specifically targeted at the SOX Community. In larger companies, these training programs are

designed and delivered based on the attendees' roles and functions within the organization.

An attendance record is maintained of all attendees for the Entity Level Control program evidence. Attendees must attend Level 1 as a prerequisite.

3. SOX DEPARTMENT TRAINING – This training is usually limited to the SOX Department and external consultants employed within the SOX Department. Attendees must attend Levels 1 and 2 as prerequisites.

This is a representative list of the training programs that a medium size company should implement. Your External Auditors should be invited to participate in these sessions as a professional courtesy and in order for their staff to become familiar with your company's processes.

RECOMMENDED TRAINING MANUALS LIST			
TRAINING PROGRAM MODULE	USER GUIDE	LEVEL	RECOMMENDED AUDIENCE
General SOX and Internal Controls Training	Participants provided with listing of reference sources	1	All Employees
Executive SOX Training	No	1	All SOX Executive and Board Audience Members
Financial Statement Risk Assessment Training	Yes	2	SOX Department and Finance Division participants
Entity Level Control Assessment Training	Yes	2	SOX Department, Entity Control Owners, Entity Control Testers.
Process and Control Documentation Training	Yes	2	All Business Units SOX members
Walkthrough and Testing Training for process (transaction) level processes and controls which includes	Yes	2	All SOX Audience
Performing Validation and QA Reviews – Documentation and Testing	Yes	3	SOX Department
External Vendors Training Program	Yes	2	External Vendor Personnel with internal company liaison personnel
Segregation of Duties requirements	Yes	2	Business Unit Managers and SOX Managers
IT-General Controls Documentation and Testing	Yes	2	SOX Department. IT Process Owners and Testers
Repository Training for procedures and tools – must include all repository processes	Yes	3	SOX Department / External Auditors who will be using SOX Data
Deficiency Analysis and Aggregation	Yes	3	SOX Department and key Business Unit personnel. External Auditors should be invited as a courtesy.
PCAOB, Technical and Regulatory Requirements and Updates	PCAOB Rulings and Regulations to be provided	2/3	SOX Department, Internal Audit Department, Board and Committee members. External Auditors should be invited as a courtesy
Sub Certification Training based on SOX 302, 404 etc.	Yes	2/3	All sub certifiers and company certifiers (e.g. CEO, CFO) and the SOX Department

SUMMARY

In this chapter, we have provided you with the prerequisites required for the development of the internal control framework and the SOX Department processes that are necessary to support these activities..

Subsequent chapters provide additional detail on each of the items covered in this chapter and should be reviewed in detail before starting to develop the INITIAL phase of SOX or modifying your existing SOX processes.

NEXT STEPS

By the end of this chapter, you should be able to:

1. Review your present SOX POLICIES, PROCEDURES, AND GUIDELINES; compare these to the outlines provided in this chapter. If modifications are required, refer to the detail chapter and commence the modifications,

2. Review your existing REPOSITORY based on this chapter. Refer to the detailed chapter and commence the modifications required,

3. Review your COMMUNICATIONS INFRASTRUCTURE and make modifications as required after referring to the detailed chapter,

4. Review your PLANS & CALENDARS and make modifications as required after referring to the detailed chapter.

The detailed chapters should be reviewed in each instance for additional information.

Chapter 3 - Entity Level Control Program

Intent of this Chapter:

The intent of this chapter is to provide you with a fundamental understanding of the construction and components that normally comprise an Entity Level Control Program. It provides you with a recommended structure based on the COSO components, points of focus and examples for each class of controls that you should develop.

Examples of the assessment tools that should be used in designing, implementing and assessing the program are provided in more detail in Chapter 9.

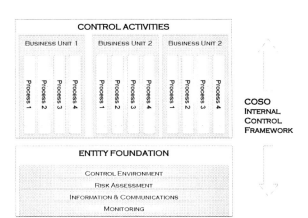

COSO INTERNAL CONTROL FRAMEWORK

Overview

The internal control framework should consist of two types of controls as illustrated on the left. Transaction/process controls (COSO component – Control Activities) require a foundation of the other four components of the COSO framework in order to provide a comprehensive internal control framework.

- ENTITY LEVEL CONTROLS – which are designed and implemented to ensure that sound management, corporate governance, risk management and financial reporting principles, are deployed and operating effectively throughout your company,

- TRANSACTION OR PROCESS LEVEL CONTROLS – these are designed and implemented to ensure the correct processing of all transactions within your organization.

Entity Level controls should be viewed as establishing the environment and behavior benchmarks to which all company personnel (and external vendors) must comply. They are also intended to ensure that there is oversight and supervision over your company's financial reporting.

Entity level controls should operate at all levels within your organization, depending on the specific control. They have a pervasive impact on the internal control framework at the process, transaction or application level.

The assessment of entity level controls is a fundamental and necessary component of management's assessment of internal control over financial reporting.

The diagram on the next page illustrates the steps that are used to implement an Entity Level Control program. Note the reference points to the transaction level controls program.

When designing the Entity Level and Transaction Level control programs, you should, at the same time, define the relationships between the two programs by COSO "*point of focus*". Establishing the relationships between the two streams ensures that you have a "*top down*" capability to perform a comprehensive, company wide risk assessment.

ESTABLISHING THE ENTITY LEVEL CONTROL PROGRAM

As discussed in Chapter 2, the first step is to select an Internal Control Framework model that is acceptable to your company, your auditors and regulators. In this example, we use the COSO model[11] to illustrate the rest of this chapter.

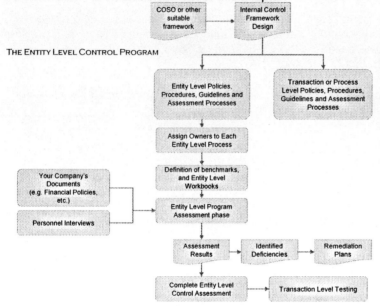

We would strongly recommend that you purchase and review the complete suite of COSO documents (including the Evaluation tools) from the COSO site (which links to the www.cpa2biz.com for all publications)

CONTROL FRAMEWORK – COSO

In most companies, COSO usually serves as the foundation upon which the entire entity level control program is based. Therefore, we have therefore used the COSO model for illustrative purposes.

DEVELOPMENT OF THE INTERNAL CONTROL FRAMEWORK

The design of the internal control framework is the first priority that has to be addressed by your company's Senior Management, the SOX Department and other key Finance Division and other personnel within your company.

The results of this design will be the policies, procedures, guidelines and other material necessary to implement the internal control framework. As illustrated in this diagram, we recommend that the team focus on developing and implementing two parallel tracks – the ENTITY LEVEL CONTROL PROGRAM and the TRANSACTION/PROCESS LEVEL CONTROL PROGRAM.

This chapter focuses only on the ENTITY LEVEL CONTROL PROGRAM.

DEFINING THE ENTITY LEVEL CONTROL COMPONENTS / CONTROLS

COSO publishes a well designed evaluation workbook that should be carefully reviewed and adapted to meet your company's requirements.

For each of the components (i.e. control environment, risk assessment, information and communication, and monitoring controls), you are assisted with various "*points of focus*" that should become the basis of developing your Entity Level Control program. For each point of focus, you should develop the control workbook that contains

- the description of the entity level control,
- the assessment steps,

---

[11] The Internal Control Integrated Framework Committee of Sponsoring Organizations of the Treadway Commission

- the evidence check list to support these assessments,
- interview sheets,
- the results of the assessment, and
- the final assessment

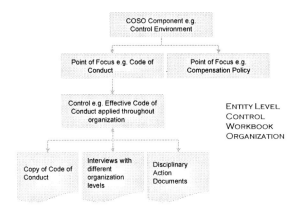

Depending on the tool (spreadsheet, database or customized system) that you use, this information should be linked together to provide a comprehensive view of the entire COSO component as outlined in the diagram on the left.

Upon developing a comprehensive list of the entity level controls that you will design and implement within your company, you should immediately confer with your External Auditors to provide them with an overview of the proposed program listing all components, their points of focus and, controls and the proposed assessment processes in order to receive their feedback on the proposed program.

Assuming that there is a tacit agreement between your company and your auditors, company management and the SOX Department should assign owners to each entity control.

ASSIGNMENT OF CONTROL OWNERS FOR THE ENTITY LEVEL CONTROL PROGRAM

For each Entity level control, a senior company manager should be appointed as the control (or point of focus) owner (in some circumstances, a board member may also act as a control owner).

The control owner is responsible for:

1. Internally championing and designing the entity level control and all its elements that have been assigned. The detail work can be assigned to qualified internal personnel or external consultants *but the final responsibility rests with the Control Owner*,

2. Developing an inventory of the entity level controls for the specific point of focus assigned,

3. Identify the regions or operating business units that are impacted or are responsible for implementation of these entity level controls – if the control is not company wide,

4. Development of the workbook that will be used to conduct the assessment of this entity level control. The workbook should provide interview Questions (which are subsequently compiled by the SOX Department into single comprehensive sections as outlined later in this chapter), listings of evidentiary material required, checklists of requirements etc.,

5. Performing an initial assessment of the design and existence of the elements of this control within your company. In many companies, several elements of the control usually already exist.

Therefore, this initial assessment is used to identify the additional steps required and to modify the design where required.

For future ongoing phases, the workbook should be reviewed at least once annually and necessary modifications made,

6. Developing a remediation/ implementation plan for any areas that require amendment, correction or modification. Assuming that some portion of the control was not present previously within your company, this becomes the final design and implementation phase of the control,

For subsequent ongoing phases, this section should be reviewed at least once annually and modifications made to controls and their respective workbooks,

7. Communicating the final requirements for the control, its supporting elements and evidentiary material are distributed to all Business Units within your company for implementation.

This communication activity is usually coordinated through the SOX Department and not conducted by individual control owners,

8. Developing a comprehensive assessment of the operational effectiveness of the control after the remediation / implementation steps as outlined in Chapter 9,

9. Summarizing the entire program's results at a corporate level. This summary should be filed with the CEO, CFO and SOX Department Manager promptly. The assessment must identify all deficiencies and remediation plans.

The results of this assessment may impact the transaction level assessments that are related to this entity level control, and

10. Control owners are required to submit all identified deficiencies and their remediation plans from the previous step with the Repository promptly.

INTERVIEWS/ SURVEYS

ENTITY CONTROL PROGRAM INTERVIEW AND SURVEY PREPARATION PROCESS

Entity Control Owners prepare questions for inclusion in Interviews and Surveys

SOX Department assembles Interviews and Surveys from points prepared by Entity Control Owners

Interviews and surveys are usually prepared centrally and are provided as a single, comprehensive interview to the individual being interviewed instead of individual interview sheets for each individual control.

The process for developing these comprehensive interviews is illustrated on the left.

The interviews and surveys are usually organized based on the following table. This table is a representative sample and should be modified as required.

INTERVIEW / SURVEYS MASTER CONTROL		
ORGANIZATIONAL ENTITY	SELECTION OF CANDIDATES	INTERVIEW SURVEY FORMAT
Board Members	Random Sample	Individual interview with each candidate
Board Committee Members	Random Cross Section – must include at least 50% of Audit Committee Members	Individual interview with each candidate
CEO	No Selection criteria required.	Individual Interview with CEO.
CFO	No Selection criteria required.	Individual Interview with CFO.
Finance Division Management	Must include Controller and	Individual interview with each candidate

INTERVIEW / SURVEYS MASTER CONTROL		
ORGANIZATIONAL ENTITY	SELECTION OF CANDIDATES	INTERVIEW SURVEY FORMAT
	Managers of at least 30% of Regional Finance Teams selected based on materiality of the region's contributions to the Financial Statements.	
Senior Company Management	At least 30% - must select regional managers and major contributors to Financial results (based on materiality)	Individual interview with each candidate
Internal Auditors	Chief Internal Auditor and representative sample of Auditors	Chief Internal Auditor – individual Interview. Other Auditors can be conducted jointly or via questionnaire
External Auditors	Senior Audit Team	Joint interview unless otherwise requested by Senior Partner
Other External Third Parties	Must include External Legal Counsel, Senior Consulting firms and critical outsourcers.	Individual interview with each candidate
Legal and Compliance Management	Senior Officers – Interview must cover all Regulatory issues	Individual interview with each candidate
HR Management	Senior HR Manager and any individuals responsible for Compensation Plans and disciplinary actions	
IT Management	Primary subjects are IT Strategy, Security and alignment to Business strategies	
IT Personnel	Primary subjects should be General Computing Controls	
Employees	Random Survey covering all operating Business Units	Anonymous survey assembled by SOX Department Entity Control Program.

RELATIONSHIP BETWEEN CONTROL OWNERS AND SOX DEPARTMENT

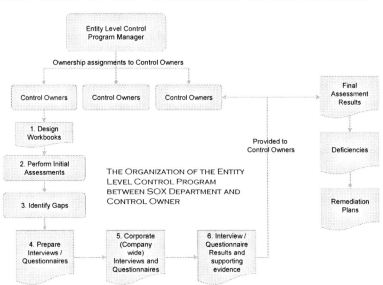

On the left, we illustrate the roles and responsibilities within the Entity Level Control Program.

The Control Owner has the responsibilities outlined in the previous section.

The SOX Department is responsible for coordinating the Control Owners' activities and results.

Upon completion of their control workbooks, the owners forward to the SOX Department all material. The Department, in turn, assembles the material into customized interviews, questionnaires and workbooks by respondent (e.g. CEO, CFO, etc.) and not by Control or Point of Focus (e.g. Code of Conduct/Ethics).

A special team, supervised by the SOX Department, conducts the interviews and other field work required for the assessment.

The results are assembled by the SOX Department and forwarded to the control's owners for final assessment.

COSO - CONTROL ENVIRONMENT

WHAT IS THE CONTROL ENVIRONMENT?

The control environment establishes the atmosphere within your company within which all personnel conduct their activities and carry out their control responsibilities.

It sets the tone by influencing the control consciousness of all personnel and by establishing the foundation for all other components of internal control, *thereby providing the necessary discipline and structure within the company.*

Control environment factors include the integrity, ethical values, and competence of the entity's people; management's philosophy and operating style; the way management assigns authority and responsibility; the way management organizes and develops its people; and the attention and direction provided by the Board of Directors and its Committees.

The objective of the control environment is to establish and promote a *collective* attitude toward achieving effective internal control over financial reporting and the provision of reliable financial statements.

THE POINTS OF FOCUS IN THE CONTROL ENVIRONMENT

In this COSO component, we have illustrated the major points of focus that should be included in your company's entity level control program.

1. **INTEGRITY AND ETHICAL VALUES (CODE OF CONDUCT)** – this class of entity level controls ensure the existence of a formal code of conduct/ ethics and other policies that define a set of rules regarding acceptable behavior practice, conflicts of interest, ethical standards etc. that will be used to govern the behavior of your employees, management and directors of your company.

   Additionally, it should include the processes by which these ethical values are cultivated, communicated and supported by all employees internally as well as externally in their interactions with the public, suppliers, clients and other parties with whom they interact..

COMPONENT: CONTROL ENVIRONMENT	POINT OF FOCUS: CODE OF CONDUCT	
CONTROL	CONTROL ASSESSMENT STEPS	CUSTOMARY OWNER / REFERENCES
CC 001 - A code of conduct and other policies regarding acceptable or permitted business practices, conflicts of interest, and expected standards of ethical behavior is developed and maintained on an ongoing basis in your company.	1. Obtain copy of latest code of conduct and ethics, 2. Review code for completeness, 3. Include in interviews questionnaires for all Senior Officers/managers of company, and 4. Summarize findings from all interviews, evidence and reviews and file with Repository promptly	Legal / Compliance Officer
CC 002 - The communications and training processes that your company employs to inform all employees of the policies regarding acceptable behavior and what they are required to do when they encounter improper or non	1. Obtain training and orientation material, 2. Determine when and how communications and training are provided, 3. Review / sample personnel records for completeness – ensure that a record is maintained	Senior HR Officer; Legal Compliance Officer

COMPONENT: CONTROL ENVIRONMENT	POINT OF FOCUS: CODE OF CONDUCT	
CONTROL	CONTROL ASSESSMENT STEPS	CUSTOMARY OWNER / REFERENCES
compliant behavior.	on personnel files, 4. Request evidence of Senior Management's communications on importance of ethics and code of conduct, 5 Sample interview personnel across several locations on Code of Conduct using pertinent questions on acceptable practices, etc., and 6. Summarize findings from all interviews, evidence and reviews and file with Repository promptly	
CC.003 – All new employees are informed of the importance of ethics and good internal control at their initial orientation into the company This is required to be delivered at the original orientation session and employees should be required to acknowledge receipt of this training.	1. Same as above – with focus on new employee orientation, and 2. Focus only on new hires in last six months of fiscal year..	Same as above
CC.004 - Company Management follows ethical guidelines in dealing with all parties. This must include employees, suppliers, investors, creditors, competitors, external counsel and auditors.	1. Obtain company guidelines, 2. Review for completeness – refer to Chapter 9 for checklist, 3. Determine whether company has a supplier Code of Conduct that is part of contractual arrangements (sample execution of agreement), 4. Interview sample of External Vendors (include outsourcers, auditors, etc.), and 5. Summarize findings from all interviews, evidence and reviews and file with Repository promptly.	Senior HR Officer; Legal Compliance Officer; Senior Administrative Officer
CC.005 - Management removes incentives or temptations that might cause personnel to engage in dishonest or unethical acts. Management reviews all incentives, etc. on a regular periodic basis.	1. Review all reward programs (including compensation programs), 2. Discuss plans, metrics of rewards, changes to plans, etc. with responsible Human Resource personnel, 4. Review compensation strategy to determine impact on fraud considerations, 5. Review if any complaints filed with Whistle Blower program, 6. Summarize findings from all interviews, evidence and reviews and file with Repository promptly	Senior HR Officer; Legal Compliance Officer
CC.006 - Compensation processes, such as bonuses, granting of options, stock ownership etc., are designed and implemented to promote an appropriate ethical tone (e.g. bonuses are not granted to those who circumvent established policies, procedures, or controls).	1.Review Executive Compensation Policy, 2. Discuss the executive compensation plans with the Executive Compensation HR committee, 3. Include as part of Senior Executives Interviews, and 4. Summarize findings from all interviews, evidence and reviews and file with Repository promptly	Senior HR Officer
CC.007 - When management becomes aware of non compliance with policies and procedures, they respond to such violations in an	1. Review HR records for disciplinary actions over last fiscal year, 2. Review Whistler Blower programs for complaints	

COMPONENT: CONTROL ENVIRONMENT	POINT OF FOCUS: CODE OF CONDUCT	
CONTROL	CONTROL ASSESSMENT STEPS	CUSTOMARY OWNER / REFERENCES
appropriate and timely manner based on established company guidelines. If there is a variation versus company guidelines that can be construed as favoritism, Management is obligated to explain any mitigating circumstances without violating any other company policies.	and resolutions to complaints, 3. If possible, conduct random survey of employees based on employee survey outlined later in this chapter,, 4. Include in Senior Company Management interviews, and 5. Summarize findings from all interviews, evidence and reviews and file with Repository promptly	
CC.009 - All changes to established relationships with external parties (e.g., attorneys, auditors, bankers) are approved at an appropriate level of management on a timely basis. If possible, all such changes should be subject to a 30 day review that is performed by Internal Audit or a qualified third party – that present their findings to management prior to approval.	1. Review any changes made in the last fiscal year, 2. Determine Review and Approval process and documentation used to evidence these processes, 3. Summarize findings from all interviews, evidence and reviews and file with Repository promptly	
CC.009 - Relationships with professional third parties are periodically reviewed to establish that the entity maintains associations only with reputable third parties.	1. Request relationship review documents for significant third party relationships, 2. Review findings for completeness.	

2. COMMITMENT TO COMPETENCE – This class usually focuses on ensuring that Management specifies the level of competence required for specific jobs.

COMPONENT: CONTROL ENVIRONMENT	POINT OF FOCUS: COMMITMENT TO COMPETENCE	
CONTROL	CONTROL ASSESSMENT STEPS	CUSTOMARY OWNER / REFERENCES
CTC.001 - Company personnel have the competence, experience and training necessary to perform their roles and responsibilities.	1. Obtain evidence of training sessions planned for high-risk or other key topics. This review should include the Agenda, Objectives and contents to ensure completeness, 2. Review and verify the strategy/plan for ensuring employees have the knowledge & skills for the job, 3. Survey a sample of representative high risk functions to review training provided to personnel by interview with specific personnel, and 4. Summarize findings from all interviews, evidence and reviews and file with Repository promptly	HR Department; Training Department
CTC.002 – The Management team possesses broad functional experience that is required for the company to achieve its objectives. The experience must encompass all critical functions of the company and should not focus or concentrate on any specific area.	1. Review background of the Senior Management team and verify that they have broad functional experience, 2. Review the Board of Directors election process and the nominees' credentials and biographies, 3. Based on above reviews determine whether present management team meets the established criteria,	CEO or CFO

COMPONENT: CONTROL ENVIRONMENT	POINT OF FOCUS: COMMITMENT TO COMPETENCE	
CONTROL	CONTROL ASSESSMENT STEPS	CUSTOMARY OWNER / REFERENCES
	4. Include as part of CEO and CFO interviews, and 5. Summarize findings from all interviews, evidence and reviews and file with Repository promptly.	
CTC.003 – Company Management consults with internal and external professionals on significant matters relating to internal control, accounting, and financial reporting issues.	1. Review current consulting projects relating to internal control, accounting and financial reporting issues, 2. Review with CEO and CFO how company determines whether use of external resources is appropriate and what are the selection criteria, 3. Summarize findings from all interviews, evidence and reviews and file with Repository promptly.	Same as above
CTC.004 – Management ensures that your company's personnel have access to appropriate training programs for all new accounting and financial reporting issues relevant to the company.	1. Obtain and review training programs for the year on accounting / financial reporting issues and the attendance records, 2. Review Internal Control training program and attendance records, 3. Review communication of program availability to staff, 4. In management interviews, review willingness of management to have personnel attend training sessions, 5. Determine management's opinion of quality of training programs, and 6. Summarize findings from all interviews, evidence and reviews and file with Repository promptly.	Senior HR Officer; Legal Compliance Officer; Senior Finance Officer, SOX Department Manager
CTC.005 – Formal job descriptions have been developed and implemented. These job descriptions include the experience, training and educational requirements required for the specific job. These job descriptions also provide clear supervisory lines and authorization levels.	1. Review job descriptions to verify that that job descriptions for key positions in the company exist. 2. Review sample of key job descriptions with the personnel in the jobs to determine currency and accuracy of job descriptions, 3. Determine linkage, if any, between job descriptions and performance evaluations with sample of employees, 4. Include as part of Senior Executives Interviews to determine importance and methods used to maintain these job descriptions, 5. Determine who in company management responsible for reviewing and approving job descriptions – interview and determine existing processes, and 6. Summarize findings from all interviews, evidence and reviews and file with Repository promptly.	Senior HR Officer, Senior Company Management
CTC.006 – When an error or deficiency is detected, the underlying cause is evaluated, and appropriate remedial actions are taken on a timely basis including training, reassignment, and additional resources.	1. Review Error logs for last fiscal year, 2. Select sample based on materiality, location and error type, 3. Review remediation plans to determine corrective action taken 4.Categorize remediation actions into training, reassignment, additional resources and dismissal	Senior Finance Officer; Senior HR Officer

COMPONENT: CONTROL ENVIRONMENT	POINT OF FOCUS: COMMITMENT TO COMPETENCE	
CONTROL	CONTROL ASSESSMENT STEPS	CUSTOMARY OWNER / REFERENCES
	categories, 5. Summarize findings from all interviews, evidence and reviews and file with Repository promptly.	
CTC.007 – When significant changes occur in the business or its immediate environment, Management reviews the competence of the accounting and financial reporting personnel to appropriately address new issues resulting from the changes.	1. Review restructuring plans, 2. Review personnel assignments (include individual's qualifications, training and experience) for key elements of plan 3. Review with CEO, CFO and Controller who determines assignments are made for key roles, and 4. Summarize findings from all interviews, evidence and reviews and file with Repository promptly	CEO / CFO

3. BOARD OF DIRECTORS / BOARD COMMITTEES AND THEIR MANDATES – this encompasses all the entity controls relating to the Board of Directors, which is the primary governance body responsible for the oversight of the business and ensuring effective internal control *(especially because of management's ability to override system controls).*

One of the key elements that should be assessed is whether your company has appointed a Disclosure committee[12] (as recommended by the SEC), to oversee the disclosure process on an ongoing basis.

Included in this committee's mandates (or other designated committee or manager within your company) should be to ensure that information to be disclosed to the SEC and other written information disclosed to the investment community is reported accurately and on a timely basis and that the information is collated and communicated to management, including senior officers, to allow timely decisions regarding required disclosure.

The Board and its responsible committees should also include monitoring and enforcing disciplinary actions where breaches of disclosure or insider trading rules are identified.

This component usually focuses on ensuring the following.

COMPONENT: CONTROL ENVIRONMENT	POINT OF FOCUS: BOARD / COMMITTEE MANDATES	
CONTROL	CONTROL ASSESSMENT STEPS	CUSTOMARY OWNER / REFERENCES
BOD.001 - The Board and/or Audit Committee are independent of management. The Board meets privately with the Internal and External Auditors, without management present, to discuss and challenge the reasonableness of the financial reporting and internal control process and systems.	1. Review the mandates of the Board of Directors and Committees, 2. Review minutes of Board and its Committees, 3. Interview cross section of Board and Audit Committee members, 4. Interview Internal and External Auditors,	CEO / CFO / Audit Committee Member

---

[12] Refer to Chapter 11 for additional details. Disclosure controls and procedures as defined in SEC Exchange Act Rule 13a-15(d) pertain to controls and procedures that are designed to ensure that information required to be disclosed in the reports that it files or submits under the Exchange Act is recorded, processed, summarized and reported, within the time periods specified in the Commission's rules and forms. Further, disclosure controls and procedures include, without limitation, controls and procedures designed to ensure that information required to be disclosed in the reports that it files or submits under the Exchange Act is accumulated and communicated to the management, including the CEO and the CFO, or persons performing similar functions, as appropriate to allow timely decisions regarding required disclosure.

COMPONENT: CONTROL ENVIRONMENT	POINT OF FOCUS: BOARD / COMMITTEE MANDATES	
CONTROL	CONTROL ASSESSMENT STEPS	CUSTOMARY OWNER / REFERENCES
	5. Summarize findings from all interviews, evidence and reviews and file with Repository promptly.	
BOD.002 – The Audit Committee raises challenging questions to management on a regular periodic basis. These questions that indicate an understanding of critical accounting policies.	Same as above.	Same as above
BOD.003 – Board and Committee members have sufficient knowledge and experience of accounting and regulatory requirements, industry experience, and the company's business operations. In addition, all members maintain their independence from company management.	1. Review background and expertise of Board and Committee members. Note all members with Financial and Accounting experience, 2. Interview cross section of members on expertise and board and committee independence, 4. Interview CEO and CFO on board independence and expertise, 3. Review minutes and mandates, 4. Summarize findings from all interviews, evidence and reviews and file with Repository promptly	Same as above
BOD.004 – The company, on a regular basis, communicates to its employees, suppliers and investors the Board's role, including self monitoring of its effectiveness and operating protocols.	1. Review Corporate communications on this subject, 2. Include as part of general employee survey, 3. Review Board minutes on evaluations conducted by itself or independent external parties, 4. Summarize findings from all interviews, evidence and reviews and file with Repository promptly	Same as above
BOD.005 – There are frequent and timely meetings with Chief Financial Officer, Internal Auditors, External Auditors and key members of the financial management team to review the internal control framework and its effectiveness, etc. These meetings should be performed at least on a semi annual basis (there is no specific frequency and you may adapt this frequency to meet your company's needs).	1. Review Board and Committee minutes pertaining to these subjects, 2. Include in Internal Auditor, External Auditor, Controller and key Financial officers' interviews, 3. Summarize findings from all interviews, evidence and reviews and file with Repository promptly.	Same as above
BOD.006 – There is timely and adequate reporting to ensure that the Board has the necessary information to monitor management's objectives and strategies, the company's financial position and operating results, and terms of significant agreements / contracts.	1. Review minutes to determine timing and currency of reports and information provided to Board and its committees by Management, 2. Determine sources of information received by Board to ascertain whether Board receives multiple perspectives, 3. Determine content of board presentations to ascertain whether all subject areas covered, 4. Summarize findings from all interviews, evidence and reviews and file with Repository promptly.	Same as above
BOD.007 – Timely, appropriate reporting on investigations of complaints, sensitive information, non compliance, and questionable activities is provided to the Board and its Committees. Based on this	1. Determine process for advising Board of these matters, 2. Review prior year to determine timing of reporting to Board and its adequacy,	Same as above

COMPONENT: CONTROL ENVIRONMENT	POINT OF FOCUS: BOARD / COMMITTEE MANDATES	
CONTROL	CONTROL ASSESSMENT STEPS	CUSTOMARY OWNER / REFERENCES
reporting the Board and its Committees monitor that management takes the necessary corrective or disciplinary action.	3. Review all minutes to determine Board and Committee monitoring actions, 4. Summarize findings from all interviews, evidence and reviews and file with Repository promptly.	
BOD.008 – The Board or its Committees regularly review Senior Company Management Compensation including incentive plans tied to performance.	1. Review Board and Committee minutes 2. Review Board and Committee mandates to ensure that this responsibility is included, 3. Review last Senior Compensation minutes, 4. Summarize findings from all interviews, evidence and reviews and file with Repository promptly	Same as above
BOD.009 – The Board and its Committees perform regular reviews and self appraisals to monitor their effectiveness.	1. Determine whether part of Board and Committees mandates, 2. Review method and results of self appraisal processes, 3. Summarize findings from all interviews, evidence and reviews and file with Repository promptly	Same as above
BOD.010 – The Audit Committee (or other committee) should specifically address/ensure management's adherence to the company's established code of conduct by regular reviews and evaluations.	1. Review of Board and Committee minutes for last year for any evidence of oversight, 2. Summarize findings from all interviews, evidence and reviews and file with Repository promptly	Same as above
BOD.011 – The Audit Committee constructively challenges management's decisions, major transactions, and explanations of past results at regular, periodic meetings.	1. Review of Board and Committee minutes for past year's review results, transactions etc. 2. Summarize findings from all interviews, evidence and reviews and file with Repository promptly.	Same as above
BOD.012 – The Board Committees' responsibilities are clearly delineated (e.g. an audit committee charter or mandate), and Management, the Board and committee members understand those responsibilities clearly.	1. Review Mandates (charters), 2. Interview Chairman and cross section of Board and Committees on this subject, 3. Summarize findings from all interviews, evidence and reviews and file with Repository promptly.	Same as above
BOD.013 – The Audit Committee reviews and approves the scope of activities and other engagement details pertaining to the internal and external auditor engagements.	1. Review minutes for scope discussions, 2. Review committee's role in overseeing key engagements, 3. Review reporting process from both Internal and External Auditors, 4. Summarize findings from all interviews, evidence and reviews and file with Repository promptly.	Same as above
BOD.014 – The Board and Audit Committee regularly receive information from company management related to key developments (regulatory, policy, procedural etc.) that may impact financial reporting.	1. Review minutes for this subject, 2. Summarize findings from all interviews, evidence and reviews and file with Repository promptly	Same as above
BOD.015 – The Audit Committee issues directives to management detailing specific actions to be taken as a result of its findings and follows up on all directives to determine that they have been properly addressed.	1. Review and validate The Audit Committee Mandates to ensure if the findings and follow up concerning financial statements, management's discussion and analyses of financial conditions and results of operations, as well as financial information and the earning guidance is provided is correct and	Same as above

COMPONENT: CONTROL ENVIRONMENT	POINT OF FOCUS: BOARD / COMMITTEE MANDATES	
CONTROL	CONTROL ASSESSMENT STEPS	CUSTOMARY OWNER / REFERENCES
	properly addressed, 2. Review the Audit Committee Minutes, and 3. Summarize findings from all interviews, evidence and reviews and file with Repository promptly	
BOD.016 – A process exists for the audit committee to be informed on a timely basis, and anonymously when appropriate, of significant issues.	1. Refer to whistle blower program.	Same as above
BOD.017 – The audit committee members demonstrate a willingness to call unscheduled meetings when necessary to address significant financial reporting issues.	1. Review Audit Committee minutes, 2. Interview cross section of Committee, 3. Summarize findings from all interviews, evidence and reviews and file with Repository promptly.	Same as above
BOD.018 – The audit committee responds to issues raised by the external auditor on a timely basis.	1. Review External Auditor's issues, 2. Reconcile to Audit Committee minutes, 3. Review finding with Head of Audit Committee, if any discrepancies, 4. Summarize findings from all interviews, evidence and reviews and file with Repository promptly	Same as above

4. MANAGEMENT'S PHILOSOPHY AND OPERATING STYLE - usually this section is based on judgmental factors that are based on reviewing a prior period's date and management's reactions to the data. The focus is usually on:

COMPONENT: CONTROL ENVIRONMENT	POINT OF FOCUS: MANAGEMENT'S PHILOSOPHY AND OPERATING STYLE	
CONTROL	CONTROL ASSESSMENT STEPS	CUSTOMARY OWNER / REFERENCES
MPOS.001 – Turnover in management or supervisory personnel is monitored on a regular, periodic basis by CEO and CFO. Exit Interviews and reasons for significant turnover are evaluated. Focus is usually on critical operating areas e.g. Financial Accounting, IT, etc.	1. Review HR Senior Management and key Supervisory turnover report, 2. Determine Exit Interview program and reports on key individuals to Board and Committees, 3. Determine who is responsible for review and whether their findings are reported to Board, CEO and CFO, and 4. Summarize findings from all interviews, evidence and reviews and file with Repository promptly	Senior HR Officer
MPOS.002 – Management regards the accounting function as a means of monitoring and exercising control over the entity's various activities.	1. Part of CEO and CFO interview	CEO / CFO
MPOS.003 – The central accounting and financial departments (including any reporting functions) have appropriate and the necessary authority over decentralized accounting personnel in business units or regions,	1. Review Finance Division roles and responsibilities, 2. Review with CFO and Controller 3. Review with cross section of decentralized finance personnel, and 4. Summarize findings from all interviews, evidence and reviews and file with Repository promptly.	CEO / CFO
MPOS.004 – Senior company	1. Review Communications and correspondence of	Legal /

COMPONENT: CONTROL ENVIRONMENT	POINT OF FOCUS: MANAGEMENT'S PHILOSOPHY AND OPERATING STYLE	
CONTROL	CONTROL ASSESSMENT STEPS	CUSTOMARY OWNER / REFERENCES
management, on a regular and periodic basis, maintains bi directional communications with subsidiary or divisional operations. These communications are used to emphasize and reinforce the responsibility for appropriate conduct and compliance with all company and regulatory guidelines.	Senior Company Management, 2. Review Code of Ethics and related procedures for company, 3. Include as part of Employee Survey, and 4. Summarize findings from all interviews, evidence and reviews and file with Repository promptly.	Compliance Officer
MPOS.005 – Management demonstrates, on a consistent, ongoing basis, a commitment to a sound internal control environment and ethical values as expressed in the Code of Conduct (or Ethics) The management demonstration is not limited only to communications but is reflected by the action during the course of doing business.	1. This is usually determined from the anonymous employee survey, and 2. Summarize findings from all interviews, evidence and reviews and file with Repository promptly.	Legal / Compliance Officer
MPOS.006 – When improper practices are reported to management (e.g. non compliance with any company or regulatory guidelines), the necessary corrective action is taken and immediately communicated to all appropriate parties., and	1. Review HR files in order to identify instances, 2. From anonymous Employee surveys, determine whether communications are executed to appropriate parties, and 3. Summarize findings from all interviews, evidence and reviews and file with Repository promptly.	Legal / Compliance Officer
MPOS.007 – Management reviews, approves and implements the accounting policies and procedures that best reflect the economic realities of the business.	1. Review Management's policies and procedures for the adoption of financial and accounting policies and guidelines and the basis for adoption, 2. Review External Auditor's Management letter for any of these items, and 3. Summarize findings from all interviews, evidence and reviews and file with Repository promptly.	Legal / Compliance Officer

5. ORGANIZATIONAL STRUCTURE – This component is usually designed to ensure that the "*right people are in the right place*" to achieve the company's business and governance objectives. The focus is also on ensuring your company's organization structure and its defined roles and responsibilities are designed to facilitate the company's business objectives. This class usually includes the following individual points of focus:

COMPONENT: CONTROL ENVIRONMENT	POINT OF FOCUS: ORGANIZATIONAL STRUCTURE	
CONTROL	CONTROL ASSESSMENT steps	CUSTOMARY OWNER / REFERENCES
OS.001 - Your company has defined key managerial and organizational unit roles and responsibilities.	1. Review Organizational Chart and job descriptions, 2. Review Tables of Authorities and Responsibilities, 3. Summarize findings from all interviews, evidence and reviews and file with Repository promptly.	Senior HR Officer
OS.002 - Your company has defined appropriate lines of reporting, based on its size and the nature of its activities.	1. Same as above.	Senior HR Officer
OS.003 - The organizational structure facilitates the flow of	1. Same as above.	Senior HR Officer

COMPONENT: CONTROL ENVIRONMENT	POINT OF FOCUS: ORGANIZATIONAL STRUCTURE	
CONTROL	CONTROL ASSESSMENT STEPS	CUSTOMARY OWNER / REFERENCES
information across all business activities.		
OS.004 - Reporting relationships facilitate the flow of information to appropriate people in a timely manner.	1. Same as above, 2. Include in Employee and Officers' survey 3. Summarize findings from all interviews, evidence and reviews and file with Repository promptly.	Senior HR Officer
OS.005 - Management periodically evaluates the entity's organizational structure and makes changes as necessary based upon changes in the company's business or industry.	1. Determine Management's procedures for evaluating organization structures, 2. Determine results of these reviews, 3. Summarize findings from all interviews, evidence and reviews and file with Repository promptly.	CEO ; Senior HR Officer
OS.006 - The organizational structure is not overly complex and does not include numerous or unusual legal entities.	Usually this is performed by a Committee of the Board or an External Consultant engaged by the Board or its Committees.	
OS.007 - The business purpose of separate legal entities is evident and reasonable.	1. Determine Legal Entity to Business Unit relationships, 2. Request supporting information for Legal Entities, 3. Interview key financial divisional personnel, 3. Summarize findings from all interviews, evidence and reviews and file with Repository promptly.	Chief Administrative Officer
OS.008 - The entity has established procedures to identify related parties.	1. Review related policies and procedures, 2. Review list of company identified related parties, 3. Summarize findings from all interviews, evidence and reviews and file with Repository promptly.	Legal / Compliance Officer

6. ORGANIZATION OF AUTHORITIES AND RESPONSIBILITIES – The assignment of authority and responsibility is critical to the management of your company. It provides the basis on which key roles are defined and provides the basis by which you can assess the accountability and control delegation internally.

   This process should outline the company's delegation of authority beginning with the Board, through to the CEO, members of your company's Executive Committee, and ending with individual signing officers.

COMPONENT: CONTROL ENVIRONMENT	POINT OF FOCUS: TABLE OF AUTHORITIES AND RESPONSIBILITIES	
CONTROL	CONTROL ASSESSMENT STEPS	CUSTOMARY OWNER / REFERENCES
TOAR.001 - Authorities and responsibilities are assigned based on specific job functions.	1. Review Authorities and Responsibilities table of assignment in the company, 2. Ensure linkage to specific job functions, 3. Identify differences and review with senior HR and Finance Executives, and 4. Summarize findings from all interviews, evidence and reviews and file with Repository promptly.	Chief Administrative Officer / Chief HR Officer
TOAR.002 - Job descriptions contain specific references to control related responsibilities,	1. Review cross reference job descriptions for company – ensure that each role is represented in this review,	Chief Administrative Officer / Chief

COMPONENT: CONTROL ENVIRONMENT	POINT OF FOCUS: TABLE OF AUTHORITIES AND RESPONSIBILITIES	
CONTROL	CONTROL ASSESSMENT STEPS	CUSTOMARY OWNER / REFERENCES
	2. Ensure that Control Responsibility Officers, Business Unit SOX Managers, etc. are covered in these job descriptions, and 3. Ensure that the references are equal to better than those defined in Chapter 2.	HR Officer
TOAR.003 - Employees are empowered, when appropriate, to correct problems or implement improvements,	1. Include as question in Employee Survey, and 2. Summarize findings from all interviews, evidence and reviews and file with Repository promptly.	Chief Administrative Officer / Chief HR Officer
TOAR.004 - Management determines and clearly communicates the responsibilities, objectives and expectations for the critical control departments (e.g. Finance and Accounting, IT, etc.) departments, and	1. Review the Management approved Mandates for the SOX Department and other control related departments (including Finance, IT, etc.), 2. Determine whether authorities, responsibilities, and objectives are clearly defined and have been communicated to responsible officers, 3. Review HR files for communications on sample cross section, and 4. Summarize findings from all interviews, evidence and reviews and file with Repository promptly	Senior Administrative Officer / Senior HR Officer
TOAR.005 - Ensuring that there are appropriate numbers of people, with the necessary skills and qualifications, based on the organization structure and requirements of your company. Emphasis should be placed on critical areas such as Accounting, Data Processing and other key operational elements.	1. Interview Key Business Unit Managers for key areas on this subject, 2. Include as question in Employee Survey, 3. Interview Senior HR Officer, 4. Review External Auditor's Management letter for comments on this subject, 5. Determine if Internal Audit has conducted any reviews on behalf of Audit Committee, and 5. Summarize findings from all interviews, evidence and reviews and file with Repository promptly.	Senior Administrative Officer

7. HUMAN RESOURCES POLICIES AND PRACTICES – This component should focus on your company's personnel hiring and retention policies and procedures. It should be targeted at ensuring that the "*right people are hired and retained for the right jobs*". To ensure that your company achieves this, this component should focus on:

COMPONENT: CONTROL ENVIRONMENT	POINT OF FOCUS: HR POLICIES AND PRACTICES	
CONTROL	CONTROL ASSESSMENT STEPS	CUSTOMARY OWNER / REFERENCES
HR.001 - Ensuring that your company has current hiring, training, promotion and compensation policies and procedures that are clearly defined, communicated and implemented throughout your company,	1. Request current hiring, training promotion and compensation policies and procedures, 2. Review for completeness, accuracy and clarity, 3. Reconcile with Employee Survey and other interviews, and 4. Summarize findings from all interviews, evidence and reviews and file with Repository promptly	Chief Administrative Officer / Chief HR Officer
HR.002 - Your company's management focuses the necessary attention on these critical functions	1. Include as part of Senior Management interviews, and	Chief Administrative Officer / Chief

COMPONENT: CONTROL ENVIRONMENT	POINT OF FOCUS: HR POLICIES AND PRACTICES	
CONTROL	CONTROL ASSESSMENT STEPS	CUSTOMARY OWNER / REFERENCES
periodically to ensure that they are being performed effectively,	2. Review Executive Committee or Senior Management Committee minutes for discussions and reviews.	HR Officer
HR.003 - Problems or non compliance to policies or procedures are promptly identified and the necessary remedial action implemented promptly,	1. Include as part of Senior Management interviews, 2. Review HR records for non compliance and remedial actions, and 3. Determine if there are any gaps between con compliance and remedial action..	Chief Administrative Officer / Chief HR Officer
HR.004 - Ensuring that information gathering on this component (via performance appraisal meetings) is done on a regular, periodic basis and involves the full participation of both employees and management. These performance appraisals should be the foundation for implementing/enforcing promotion, and compensation policies and procedures. They should also provide a communications vehicle by which employees are apprised of these company policies and procedures,	1. Review performance appraisal procedures, 2. Sample a cross section of performance appraisals, 3. Review employee Survey for employee opinions of performance appraisal, 4. Review employee feedback process on performance appraisals, and 5. Summarize findings from all interviews, evidence and reviews and file with Repository promptly.	Chief Administrative Officer / Chief HR Officer
HR.005 - Ensuring that personnel background checks are performed in order to ensure no prior unacceptable activities on the part of the prospective employee, and	1. Review Background check procedure, 2. Random sample new hires in last fiscal year, and 3. Summarize findings from all interviews, evidence and reviews and file with Repository promptly.	Chief Administrative Officer / Chief HR Officer
HR.006 - Ensuring that the existing Training and Development programs demonstrate commitment to ensuring that your staff at all levels have the skills necessary to perform their jobs and to identify and develop high performing staff so that they can fulfill their potential	1. Review Employee Survey, 2. Review training and development programs with emphasis on internal control, finance, accounting and regulatory training programs, 3. Check for attendance records maintained in personnel files, 4. Reconcile differences between items 1 through 3, and 5. Summarize findings from all interviews, evidence and reviews and file with Repository promptly.	Chief Administrative Officer / Chief HR Officer

COSO – RISK ASSESSMENT

This component ensures that company management has developed and communicated entity wide objectives for its future performance. These objectives should be supported by strategic plans that have been developed and communicated to all pertinent management staff.

THE POINTS OF FOCUS IN THE RISK ASSESSMENT

As such, your assessment should cover the following areas:

1. **ENTITY WIDE OBJECTIVES** – Ensure that management has developed entity wide objectives as guidance to the company's employees. These objectives should be communicated to the Board of Directors and all employees.

2. **STRATEGIC PLANS** – Ensure that the Strategic Plans support the entity wide objectives and that management has allocated the necessary high level resources and established the priorities within these plans.

   This ensures the translation of your entity wide objectives into corporate strategic goals and major initiatives over an appropriate planning horizon. The key control elements assume that you have (or are developing) an overall planning system that addresses your planning objectives within an appropriate horizon.

3. **BUSINESS PLANS AND BUDGETS** – should be reconciled to your strategic plans and entity wide objectives to ensure consistency across all plans.

   You should ensure that these business plans reference and reflect the company's historical data and experiences and that they are prepared at an appropriate level of detail for their audience. Depending on the management level, the granularity of these plans should be appropriate.

   All plan levels should reconcile to the master plan if your Business Plan has multiple levels.

4. **ACTIVITY LEVEL OBJECTIVES** – Depending on your company's planning methods, major activities are usually planned at a detailed level e.g. marketing and sales. COSO provide a representative list of these activities in their reference manual.

   You should ensure that Activity Level Plans are reconciled to Business Plans and that they are communicated to all responsible parties. These plans should include tangible metrics in order to provide a level of specificity for proactive management of these activities. These management activities should include comparisons of results versus plans.

   Activities that are critical to entity wide objectives should be identified as *critical success factors* and should be closely monitored by management periodically.

   For all activities, the responsible management personnel, at the pertinent operating level, should participate in the development of these plans and must be actively required to support the objectives.

5. **RISKS** – The identification of risks is critical to the success of your company.

   You should assess whether your company has the necessary processes for the identification, assessment, management, monitoring and reporting of principal risks (both internal and external) that impact your business objectives.

   This component should also determine whether the Board and Audit Committee's review and assessment of appropriateness of risk processes is conducted to ensure that the executive team and their policies and procedures (within their functional areas/ regions) manage and mitigate risks appropriately.

   You should therefore ensure that your company has the necessary mechanisms to identify the following:

- EXTERNAL SOURCE RISKS – your company must have the necessary mechanisms to identify risks from external parties e.g. competitor's actions, political considerations, economic conditions, technology risks, non compliance with laws and regulations, etc.

- INTERNAL SOURCE RISKS – you should ensure that the necessary mechanisms exist to identify risks from internal sources - these usually relate to Human Resources (including Labor relations, Technology (e.g. Backup / Recovery) etc.

    The company's anti fraud program should occupy a pre eminent position in this segment of the Risk Assessment processes. The focus should be on the controls that are designed to identify and prevent any fraud that would result in a material misstatement of the financial statements, any fraud perpetrated by senior management or any other fraud that could result in a material loss for your company.

    Emphasis should be placed on:

    - Management identifies fraud risk factors including management override of controls.
    - Management identifies risks relating to non routine transactions.
    - Management identifies risks relating to the ability of an employee to initiate and process unauthorized transactions.

- ACTIVITY LEVEL RISKS – these should be identified within each activity level plan ensuring that risks are related to any plan objectives established. All identified risks are documented and communicated throughout the organization, as appropriate.

6. CHANGE MANAGEMENT – In an effort to heighten awareness of risks and changes affecting the entity, management communicates the results of their risk assessment and changes in their business environment to all appropriate employees.

    Your company's change management processes and controls should ensure that you can identify and react promptly to:

    - Events that can impact Entity Level and Activity level plans. If the risk is identified at the entity level, then all affected activity level plans must be reassessed.

    - Events that impact the environment and require active management participation e.g.
        i. Operating environment changes,
        ii. New technology that can impact the entity,
        iii. Supply source changes,
        iv. Product Changes,
        v. Acquisitions or divestures,
        vi. Foreign Operations, and
        vii. Corporate restructuring, etc.

COSO – INFORMATION AND COMMUNICATION

Accurate, timely and relevant information is the lifeblood for managing any company.

Information and communication is the component of internal control framework that ensures that pertinent information is identified, captured, and communicated in a form and timeframe that enables your company's personnel to carry out their responsibilities.

Information systems produce reports containing operational, financial, and compliance-related information that make it possible to operate and control your company's business. These systems use internally-generated data, as well as information from external sources with data elements pertaining to external events, activities, and conditions necessary to make informed business decisions and generate reliable external reports.

Effective communications must also occur in a broader sense, throughout the organization. *All personnel must receive a clear message from top management that control responsibilities must be taken seriously.* These individuals must understand their own role in the internal control system, as well as how individual activities relate to the work of others. They must also have a mechanism for communicating significant information upwards within the organization.

The objective of information and communication is to ensure that information relevant to the preparation of reliable financial statements and the maintenance of internal controls and records is identified, captured, and communicated to the appropriate personnel on a timely basis.

THE POINTS OF FOCUS FOR INFORMATION AND COMMUNICATION

The points of focus for this Component are usually:

1. RELIABLE REPORTING AND RELATED APPLICATION SYSTEMS - are necessary to achieve your company's objectives. To ensure the reliability of these systems, you should focus on the following elements:

COMPONENT: INFORMATION / COMMUNICATIONS	POINT OF FOCUS: RELIABLE REPORTING	
CONTROL	CONTROL ASSESSMENT STEPS	CUSTOMARY OWNER / REFERENCES
RR.001 - Company management has a strategic plan for IT that is linked to your company's overall strategies. The objectives of the IT plan include the preparation of accurate and timely financial reports.	1. Request IT Strategic Plan, 2. Determine whether there is linkage to Business Plans, 3. Focus on the Financial Reporting systems, and 4. Summarize findings from all interviews, evidence and reviews and file with Repository promptly..	Dependent on your company hierarchy.
RR.002 - Procedures are in place to provide assurance that relevant information is identified, captured, processed, and reported by information systems in an appropriate and timely fashion.	1. Review Senior Management interviews and Surveys, and 2. Review IT Logs.	Dependent on your company hierarchy.
RR.003 - Control activities are in place to ensure the accuracy and integrity of data used in the preparation of all financial analyses and reports.	1. Review IT internal control framework objectives and procedures, 2. Review IT Error Logs on Financial Reporting Systems, 3. Review with Finance Division and IT any outstanding accuracy or integrity problems or concerns, and 4. Summarize findings from all interviews, evidence and reviews and file with Repository promptly.	Dependent on your company hierarchy.
RR.004 – Management ensures that	1. Review the existing IT structure and key	Dependent on

COMPONENT: INFORMATION / COMMUNICATIONS	POINT OF FOCUS: RELIABLE REPORTING	
CONTROL	CONTROL ASSESSMENT STEPS	CUSTOMARY OWNER / REFERENCES
the IT Department or Division is: 1. Adequately staffed with qualified personnel, and 2. Has aligned its objectives and strategies with those of the business units that it supports.	vacancies in IT, 2. Review IT personnel turnover rate, 3. Conduct CIO interview focusing on design of IT Department, and 4. Summarize findings from all interviews, evidence and reviews and file with Repository promptly.	your company hierarchy.

2. APPROPRIATE INFORMATION IS OBTAINED AND PROVIDED TO MANAGEMENT IN A TIMELY MANNER – information is captured from all levels of management and reposted after validation and reconciliation processes. Your primary focus should be on ensuring that the report change points are clearly controlled:

COMPONENT: INFORMATION / COMMUNICATIONS	POINT OF FOCUS: INFORMATION TO MANAGEMENT IS TIMELY	
CONTROL	CONTROL ASSESSMENT STEPS	CUSTOMARY OWNER / REFERENCES
IM.001 - Internal information regarding financial results is generated by the financial information systems is reported regularly and on demand to the appropriate levels within the company.	1. Request Financial Information production schedule from Finance Division	CFO / Controller
IM.002 - Company operating results are reviewed and compared against budgets at regular periodic intervals at all management levels. Written explanation for variance in excess of management guidelines are provided for Senior Management review.	1. Review Senior Management and Board minutes for	CFO / Controller
IM.003 - There is a process for decentralized operations or departments to request changes to reports either generated by the accounting function or automatically generated by the system to meet their specific needs. However, these must adhere to strict central financial reporting controls and approval.	1. Review Finance Division and Business Unit outstanding IT requests reports, 2. As in next step, review change management process, and 3. Summarize findings from all interviews, evidence and reviews and file with Repository promptly.	CFO / Controller
IM.004 - If a number of requests are received to change reports, the reasons for such requests are examined, assigned a priority for IT processing and approved by Senior Management prior to any changes.	1. Review Change Management process in both the Business Units and IT Department, and 2. Determine selection criteria for approvals	CFO / Controller
IM.005 - Managers and personnel at various levels are interviewed or surveyed to determine the information that is needed or desired throughout the company is received at the summarization or detail level required.	1. Include in Business Unit Management interviews	CFO / Controller

3. **INFORMATION IS RECEIVED AND DISSEMINATED TO APPROPRIATE LEVELS ON A TIMELY BASIS** – the focus is on ensuring that the appropriate information raeches the appropriate levels on a timely basis.

COMPONENT: INFORMATION / COMMUNICATIONS	POINT OF FOCUS: INFORMATION DISSEMINATION	
CONTROL	CONTROL ASSESSMENT STEPS	CUSTOMARY OWNER / REFERENCES
ID.001 - Business Unit Managers receive financial analytical information so they can identify necessary actions to be taken within the next fiscal period (usually quarterly or monthly). This information may not only be budget vs. actual performance data but can also be forecast information generated internally or externally.	1. Review with random group of Business Unit Managers their opinion of this point of focus or include in Manager's surveys, 2. Sample key analytical reports for a representative group of Business Units with their managers, 3. Review frequency and minutes of Senior Management and Controllers meetings,	CFO Company Controller
ID.002 - Financial controllers meet periodically with line management to discuss operational results and to identify any errors, discrepancies, budget amendments, etc. The Financial Controllers are responsible for documenting the reasons for variances and forward these explanations to the Central Finance Department.	4. Review Error and Discrepancy Logs for IT and Finance Divisions, 5. Review with IT Management their design concepts and implementation procedures for the distribution of information based on management level, 6. Review remediation steps and actual resolutions, and 7. Summarize findings from all interviews, evidence and reviews and file with Repository promptly.	
ID.003 - Information is to all levels of management based on their responsibilities. The higher the management level in the hierarchy, information will be provided at both a summary and detail level for all subordinate units.		
ID.004 - Financial controllers receive from the Central Finance function all information for their related operating Business Units at both a summary and detail level.		
ID.005 - Information is distributed to all company levels on a timely basis in order to permit effective monitoring and responsive feedback to the Central Finance Department.		
ID.006 - There are established and agreed upon timelines and specific target dates for each step in the period-end reporting. The timelines must allow for Senior Management review, and.		
ID.007 – All information distributed throughout the company must meet the following criteria before dissemination: • It must be *accurate*, • It must be *validated* versus at least one other source, • It must be *relevant* based on the report or analysis in which it is included,		

Component: Information / Communications	Point of Focus: Information Dissemination	
Control	Control Assessment Steps	Customary Owner / References
• It must be *timely*, • It must be presented in an *appropriate and understandable format*, and • It must comply with the company security requirements.		

4. **CHANGE MANAGEMENT PROCESS FOR INFORMATION AND COMMUNICATIONS REQUIREMENTS** – the review and approval processes are the primary focus in this point of focus.

Component: Information / Communications	Point of Focus: Change Management	
Controls	Control Assessment Steps	Customary Owner / References
CM.001 - Your company has a process to address information needs arising from new accounting standards. This process should include the active participation of the IT and key regional finance departments and should not be limited only to the Central Finance Department. In some instances, it may also require External Vendor participation.	1. Determine who is responsible for disseminating new Accounting Standards, and 2. Determine company's training and implementation methods for new Accounting Standards.	CFO
CM.002 - Management understands the information systems requirements / needs for financial reporting.	1. Review with CEO, CFO and other Senior Management their key objectives for the IT function and other related information issues.	CIO
CM.003 - The corporate level resources devoted to information systems for financial reporting are appropriate and proportional in relation to those devoted to other areas of the entity, and	1. Review staffing (including vacancies for critical information systems)	CIO
CM.004 - Management establishes metrics and other indicators to assess the appropriateness and efficiency of the financial information systems.	1. Review with Senior management what these metrics and indicators are, 2. How often them perform these reviews? 3. The sources of this information.	CEO / CFO

5. **EMPLOYEE'S RESPONSIBILITY FOR INTERNAL CONTROL EFFECTIVELY COMMUNICATED** – Management must ensure that it communicates the necessity for employee participation in the internal control processes. Management must emphasize that this participation is mandatory at all levels within the organization.

Component: Information / Communications	Point of Focus: Internal Controls Communications	
Controls	Control Assessment Steps	Customary Owner / References
ICC.001 - Management communicates authorities and responsibilities across / throughout the organization (including external	1. Review Authorities and Responsibilities organization chart 2. Review communications assignments for all levels	Senior Administrative Officer / Senior HR Officer

Component: Information / Communications	Point of Focus: Internal Controls Communications	
Controls	Control Assessment Steps	Customary Owner / References
vendors, where applicable),	3. Include as part of employee survey, and 4. Include as part of management interviews.	
ICC.002 - Management uses formal and informal communications, training, meetings, or on-the-job supervision to communicate financial reporting and internal control requirements.	1. Acquire training material and schedules related to subject, and 2. Ensure that financial reporting and internal control training adequately covered depending on role.	Senior Administrative Officer / Senior HR Officer
ICC.003 - New employees in the corporate accounting department are required to attend training regarding their role in the internal control structure and how its effects on their functions and responsibilities.	1. Review training material and 2. Review HR records of random sample of new hired employees.	Senior Administrative Officer / Senior HR Officer
ICC.004 - Employees know the objectives of the company as related to financial reporting and how their activities affect those objectives.	1. Include as part of employee survey.	Senior Administrative Officer / Senior HR Officer
ICC.005 - The CFO meets with corporate controllers, at least annually, to discuss their role in meeting the company's objectives related to financial reporting.	1. Include as part of CFO interview, 2. Review Annual or Quarterly Financial Meeting minutes, and 3. Include as part of sub assertion form for Legal Entity signoffs	Senior Administrative Officer / Senior HR Officer

6. WHISTLE BLOWER PROGRAM – this program should establish within your company a confidential, secure program by which all personnel can submit information or complaints about non compliance with company or regulatory guidelines. The program should incorporate the policies and procedures for the receipt, retention, monitoring and processing of complaints.

    The Whistle Blower Program should focus on accounting, internal accounting controls or auditing affairs and the confidential, anonymous submission by your employees of concerns regarding questionable accounting or auditing issues.

Component: Information / Communications	Point of Focus: Whistle Blower Program	
Controls	Control Assessment Steps	Customary Owner / References
WBP.001 - There is a means for employees to communicate upstream, anonymously if so desired, other than through a direct supervisor.	1. Review mandate for Whistle Blower Program – determine whether complete, 2. Determine security features in order to ensure anonymity is guaranteed – ascertain whether program is run by third part firm or other method is used for security firewall,	Audit Committee Member
WBP.002 - There is a mechanism by which third parties can communicate financial reporting issues, anonymously if so desired. This can be included in an *overall* Whistle Blower Program.	3. Determine whether third parties can use whistle blower program, 4. Review usage of program by Region, Critical area, etc., and	
WBP.003 - The communication channels, established by management or the audit committee, have been used in the	5. Review logs of subjects covered e.g. fraud, internal control, ethics, etc.	

COMPONENT: INFORMATION / COMMUNICATIONS	POINT OF FOCUS: WHISTLE BLOWER PROGRAM	
CONTROLS	CONTROL ASSESSMENT STEPS	CUSTOMARY OWNER / REFERENCES
last fiscal year.	6. Review management's remedial actions based on highest severity complaints, and 7. Include as part of employee survey.	
WBP.004 – Any non-compliance Problems have been reported and resolved appropriately in the past fiscal year.		
WBP.005 - Reported problems are investigated promptly and disciplinary actions are taken after investigation or confirmation.		
WBP.006 - All financial reporting improprieties are reported to the audit committee promptly. Management does not impose or allow retribution on employees for reporting any improprieties.		

7. THE COMPANY'S COMMUNICATIONS REFLECT AN ATTITUDE ENDORSING SOUND INTERNAL CONTROL BOTH INTERNALLY AND EXTERNALLY – Company management must not only communicate the need for sound internal controls – but should also demonstrate this by their actions and ongoing communications with personnel. This should be done on a regular, periodic basis.

COMPONENT: INFORMATION / COMMUNICATIONS	POINT OF FOCUS: COMPANY COMMUNICATIONS – INTERNAL CONTROL	
CONTROLS	CONTROL ASSESSMENT STEPS	CUSTOMARY OWNER / REFERENCES
CCIC.001 - There is an established series of communication channels that operate within the company for dissemination of the company's entity-wide objectives regarding financial reporting.	1. Review with CEO and CFO in their interviews, 2. Review employee surveys, 3. Random senior Divisional Management for their opinions, and 4. Review written communications on subject	CEO
CCIC.002 - The CFO meets regularly with divisional management (both business and financial) to communicate expectations regarding financial reporting objectives for the company as a whole, In most companies, this is conducted at least semi annually.		
CCIC.003 – Management formally and informally communicates to personnel and other parties that a sound system of internal control is a priority of the company.		

COSO – MONITORING

Your company's monitoring processes should examine the quality of the internal control systems on a regular, periodic basis. Effective monitoring is accomplished through *ongoing* monitoring activities, separate evaluations, or a combination of these activities.

Ongoing monitoring occurs in the course of operations and requires regular management and supervisory activities, and other actions that your personnel should take in the performance of their duties.

The scope and frequency of separate evaluations will depend primarily on an assessment of risks and the effectiveness of existing ongoing monitoring procedures.

Internal control deficiencies should be reported throughout the organization with significant deficiencies and material weaknesses reported to top management and the board promptly.

THE POINTS OF FOCUS FOR MONITORING

For this component, the focus should on the following processes/activities:

1. THE ROLE, SCOPE, AND RESPONSIBILITIES OF THE INTERNAL AUDIT DEPARTMENT - are clearly defined and are appropriate for your company.

COMPONENT: MONITORING	POINT OF FOCUS: INTERNAL AUDIT DEPARTMENT	
CONTROLS	CONTROL ASSESSMENT STEPS	CUSTOMARY OWNER / REFERENCES
IA.001 - The scope of internal audit's activities are reviewed in advance with management, the audit committee, and the external auditors. This review focuses on the objectives and business units that will be audited to ensure that the proper focus is placed on high risk areas within the company.	1. Review Internal Audit Engagement files for reviews and approvals.	Chairman of Audit Committee
IA.002 - Internal audit has the necessary staffing levels to execute their plans and achieve their audit objectives and assignments.	1. Review with Chief Internal Auditor and Chairman of Audit Committee.	
IA.003 - Internal audit has the authority to review any element of the company's operations,	1. Confirm with Chairman of Board and Chairman of Audit Committee, and 2. Confirm with Chief Auditor.	
IA.004 - The audit plan is designed to be responsive and reactive to the company's risk assessments. In some instances, the audit team will also be expected to perform external vendor reviews based on the terms within the outsourcing contracts.		
IA.005 - The internal audit personnel are experienced, qualified, competent and trained to meet their roles and responsibilities.	1. Review Audit Staffing with Chief Auditor and Chairman of Audit Committee based on personnel files.	

2. THE INTERNAL AUDIT DEPARTMENT ADHERES TO PROFESSIONAL STANDARDS - The Internal Audit Department adheres to standards promulgated by professional organizations e.g. Institute of Internal Auditors.

COMPONENT: MONITORING	POINT OF FOCUS: INTERNAL AUDIT STANDARDS	
CONTROLS	CONTROL ASSESSMENT STEPS	CUSTOMARY OWNER / REFERENCES
IAS.001 - Internal audit is independent of the activities that they audit. Where conflicts of interest are	1. Review with Chief Auditor and Chairman of Audit Committee, 2. Confirm with External Auditor,	Chief Auditor

COMPONENT: MONITORING	POINT OF FOCUS: INTERNAL AUDIT STANDARDS	
CONTROLS	CONTROL ASSESSMENT STEPS	CUSTOMARY OWNER / REFERENCES
identified, IA takes the necessary action or requests a management exemption (e.g. family relationships between unit being married and audit team member)	3. Review any conflict of interest forms, and 4. Review External review files.	
IAS.002 - Internal audit has direct access to the audit committee and the board of directors. This should be demonstrated or evidenced by at least tow occurrences within a fiscal year.		
IAS.003 - Internal auditors are prohibited from having an operating role in the activities that they monitor. In addition, they should identify any social relationships with the operating unit prior to any engagement commencing.		
IAS.004 - Internal audit is evaluated by an external party at least once per fiscal year. This review must cover, at a minimum, all the above referenced points.		

3. THE COMPANY IS RESPONSIVE TO INTERNAL AND EXTERNAL RECOMMENDATIONS – usually evidenced by management's subsequent actions after receipt of recommendations.

COMPONENT: MONITORING	POINT OF FOCUS: INTERNAL / EXTERNAL RECOMMENDATIONS	
CONTROLS	CONTROL ASSESSMENT STEPS	CUSTOMARY OWNER / REFERENCES
IER.001 - Senior Managers, with appropriate level of authority, decide which of the internal and external auditors' recommendations will be implemented.	1. Review Internal Audit recommendations on random sample basis for last fiscal year, 2. In addition, select top ten of most material internal audit recommendations (ensure that action plans and their periodic reviews are also included),	CEO
IER.002 - Management takes appropriate action on non compliance to company policies and procedures,	3. Do the same for the External Auditor recommendations – with emphasis on Management letter, and 4. Review for all of the above, management's review and remedial actions taken.	
IER.003 - Action plans are implemented and there is follow-up to verify implementation by both financial and non financial means. The company standard operating procedures requires this to be performed at least once quarterly (modify frequency based on materiality or size of action plan).		
IER.004 - Management is required to respond, on a timely basis, to the internal audit department's findings and recommendations, or questions on financial results and variances from budget. Responses (including action plans) to internal or external audit findings		

COMPONENT: MONITORING	POINT OF FOCUS: INTERNAL / EXTERNAL RECOMMENDATIONS	
CONTROLS	CONTROL ASSESSMENT STEPS	CUSTOMARY OWNER / REFERENCES
are provided to the audit committee or board of directors for their review at least quarterly.		
IER.005 - Corporate accounting personnel investigate and respond accordingly to financial reporting issues identified at subsidiary levels.		
IER.006 - Management responds timely and appropriately to comments identified in the management letters.		
IER.007 - Management responds, in writing, to concerns raised in the management letter. The audit committee requires business unit management letters to be provided to them, with written responses from business unit management.		
IER.008 - Recommendations for improvements are adopted and deficiencies have been corrected.		

4. COMMUNICATIONS FROM EXTERNAL PARTIES - this section determines whether your company addresses problems or concerns from External parties appropriately.

COMPONENT: MONITORING	POINT OF FOCUS: EXTERNAL PARTIES COMMUNICATIONS	
CONTROLS	CONTROL ASSESSMENT STEPS	CUSTOMARY OWNER / REFERENCES
EPC.001 – Reports of financial improprieties by external parties (e.g. suppliers or regulators) are fully investigated and documented.	1. Determine process for external parties complaints, 2. Determine who is in charge of process at Senior Management level,	CFO
EPC.002 - Reported improprieties from individuals other than employees are investigated and resolved promptly.	3. Determine Internal process for investigations and validation,	
EPC.003 - Controls that should have prevented or detected problems are reassessed when problems occur – refer to Finance Error Log for additional details.	4. Determine process for review and remedial action, 5. Determine whether internal control system is re assessed based on confirmed cases – and timeliness of remedial action, 6. Review 10% of external complaints on a random sample basis, and 7. Review top five instances based on materiality.	

5. SELF ASSESSMENT/ EVALUATION OF THE INTERNAL CONTROLS – This section promotes control awareness and accountability. This should be conducted on a logical basis and is managed at the appropriate management level. The assessment/evaluation should be conducted using the appropriate tools that have been approved by the SOX Department e.g. checklists, questionnaires, etc.

The personnel assigned to perform the evaluation should have a clear understanding of your company's and the respective business unit's activities, an understanding of how the internal control system is supposed to work and the ability to provide management with an objective evaluation of whether the control objectives are being achieved.

COMPONENT: MONITORING	POINT OF FOCUS: CONTROL ASSESSMENTS	
CONTROLS	CONTROL ASSESSMENT STEPS	CUSTOMARY OWNER / REFERENCES
CA.001 - Personnel are required to acknowledge compliance with the code of conduct on a periodic basis.	1. Include as part of employee Survey, 2. Include as part of sub certification process, 3. Ensure that all critical control functions are required to be reviewed and approved on a periodic basis, and 4. Determine whether third parties are used for independent verification purposes.	Chief Auditor
CA.002 - Signatures are required to verify performance of significant control functions e.g. reconciliations.		
CA.003 - The results of self-assessments regarding the company's code of conduct and significant control activities are independently verified (refer to Internal Audit).		
CA.004 - The personnel that perform self-assessments for the control activities being performed by process owners complete the self-assessment based on "first-hand knowledge" of control activities that they have observed. Refer to Chapter 9 for assessment guidelines.		

SUMMARY

In this chapter, we have outlined the entity level program. You should commence developing your program and the related workbooks and assessment tools based on the information above.

The following should be completed for the entity level program

1. Map of the COSO Components to the points of focus to be used in your company's program,

2. Assign Senior Company Management to be owners of each point of focus and or control,

3. Determine the controls and the evidence required for each point of focus,

4. Develop workbook and interview forms that outline the evidence required to support the existence and operating effectiveness of the control,

5. Develop the time table and sample population that will be used in the assessment, and

6. Provide all above information to the communications unit so that they can apprise business units and management of timing of the events that will impact their schedules.

EXAMPLE OF ENTITY LEVEL CONTROL MAP

COMPONENT	Control Environment
POINT OF FOCUS:	Code of conduct and other policies regarding acceptable business practices, conflicts of interest, and expected standards of ethical behavior.
CONTROL	EVIDENCE / ASSESSMENT STEPS
Management maintains and communicates a code of conduct as defined in the point of focus and that is applied company wide.	1. Obtain and review Code of Conduct and Statement of Corporate Governance for completeness. 2. Validate that the Code of Conduct contains defined standards, stated communication policies, guidance, commitment, accountability and the appropriate tone at the top. Validate that it contains guidelines for conflict of interest situations. Validate that it prohibits certain loans to Directors and Executive Officers.

COMPONENT	Control Environment
POINT OF FOCUS:	Code of conduct and other policies regarding acceptable business practices, conflicts of interest, and expected standards of ethical behavior.
CONTROL	EVIDENCE / ASSESSMENT STEPS
In this instance the point of focus and control are the same	Typical review points for item 2: a. Is your company's Code of Conduct comprehensive, well communicated and effectively implemented? b. Has the Board been provided with timely, relevant accurate and complete reports that will enable it to assess whether you have a process for ensuring adherence to the Code of Conduct? c. Is there a process in place to assure the CEO that remedial action has been taken in response to departures from approved policies and procedures or violations of the Code of Conduct? d. Is there a mechanism in place to satisfy the CEO that Management adheres to the Code of Conduct and demonstrates commitment to integrity and ethical behavior? e. Is this commitment communicated effectively throughout your company, both in words and deeds?

TYPICAL ANONYMOUS EMPLOYEE SURVEY QUESTIONS

The following areas are usually covered in the Employee Survey. We have not covered fraud questions in this survey.

SAMPLE ANONYMOUS EMPLOYEE QUESTIONNAIRE	
SURVEY QUESTION	YOUR RESPONSE
1. STRATEGIC PLANS	
• Are your aware of company's Strategic Plans?	☐ Yes ☐ No
• Do you understand your Department or Business Unit's contribution to plan?	☐ Yes ☐ No
• Do you understand the Plan?	☐ Yes ☐ No
2. CODE OF ETHICS OR CODE OF CONDUCT	
• Have you reviewed the company's Code of Ethics or Conduct?	☐ Yes ☐ No
• Do you understand it?	☐ Yes ☐ No
• Are you aware of the company's whistle blower program?	☐ Yes ☐ No
• Do you believe that the program is affective?	☐ Yes ☐ No
• If you were aware of infractions of the Code of Conduct or fraudulent activities – would you use this program?	☐ Yes ☐ No
• Do you know of any infractions of the Code?	☐ Yes ☐ No
• Have you advised anyone of these infractions?	☐ Yes ☐ No
• Did you use the whistle blower program to advise management of these infractions?	☐ Yes ☐ No
• Did you advise your immediate management of these infractions?	☐ Yes ☐ No
• Do you believe that the Board and Senior Management adhere to this code?	☐ Yes ☐ No
• Do you know of any improvements or changes that need to be made to the code?	☐ Yes ☐ No
3. INTERNAL CONTROL	
• Do you understand our company's internal control objectives?	☐ Yes ☐ No
• In your job are you responsible for any internal control?	☐ Yes ☐ No
• In your opinion, are there any improvements that should be added to our framework? Please provide any specific references or examples.	☐ Yes ☐ No
• Are you aware of any changes that need to be made to the internal controls within your Department?	☐ Yes ☐ No
• Have you advertised your immediate management?	☐ Yes ☐ No
• If you have not advised your immediate management, who will you advise?	☐ Yes ☐ No
• Do you feel that your recommendations will be reviewed in a constructive, objective manner?	☐ Yes ☐ No
4. YOUR JOB	
• Do you have a complete, formal job description?	☐ Yes ☐ No
• Does if fairly represent your actual duties?	☐ Yes ☐ No
• If no, have you forwarded changes/recommendations to the HR Department or	☐ Yes ☐ No

SAMPLE ANONYMOUS EMPLOYEE QUESTIONNAIRE	
SURVEY QUESTION	YOUR RESPONSE
to your immediate supervisor?	
• When have you last received a performance evaluation?	Please provide date:
• In your performance evaluation with your immediate manager, are you provided the constructive feedback on your performance,	☐ Yes ☐ No
• Are you provided with the opportunity to provide constructive feedback on the company's policies and procedures?	☐ Yes ☐ No
• Do you feel empowered to make decisions necessary for the performance of your job?	☐ Yes ☐ No
• Have you had your authorities and responsibilities formally defined in your job description?	☐ Yes ☐ No
• Do you have the necessary tools to perform your job?	☐ Yes ☐ No
5. TRAINING AND EDUCATION	
• Are you provided adequate training to meet your job requirements?	☐ Yes ☐ No
• Are you apprised of the latest regulations, policies and procedures that impact the internal control functions?	☐ Yes ☐ No
• Do you require additional training?	☐ Yes ☐ No
• Have you advised your immediate supervisor?	☐ Yes ☐ No
• Have you received a response?	☐ Yes ☐ No
6. COMMUNICATIONS	
• In your opinion, does company management clearly communicate our internal control objectives?	☐ Yes ☐ No
• If no, what recommendations would you make to improve this process?	Please state:
• Do you believe that management clearly sends a message that violations of the Code of Ethics will not be condoned?	☐ Yes ☐ No
• Does management clearly communicate when disciplinary actions are taken to correct non compliance with company policies and guidelines?	☐ Yes ☐ No
• Do you believe that the communications can be improved?	☐ Yes ☐ No
• If yes, please explain how the communications can be improved:	
7. POLICIES, PROCEDURES AND GUIDELINES	
• Does your management provide you with the latest policies, procedures and guidelines to achieve your job objectives?	☐ Yes ☐ No
• Are you provided with the opportunity to review the policies, procedures and guidelines with your immediate management upon receipt or soon after receipt (two weeks)?	☐ Yes ☐ No
• Can you refer to authors or other sources for clarification for any ambiguous policies or procedures?	☐ Yes ☐ No
• Does the SOX department keep you apprised of regulatory or company guidelines that pertain to SOX?	☐ Yes ☐ No
• If the communications with the SOX Department clear, timely and comprehensive?	☐ Yes ☐ No
• Do you feel that you can request information from the SOX Department freely?	
• Do you have any recommendations for the SOX Department to improve their processes?	
8. RATINGS (ASSIGN A RATING OF 1 THROUGH 5 WITH 5 BEING THE BEST AND 1 BEING THE WORST)	
• Rate the of information regarding company news, priorities and objectives	RATING:
• Rate the credibility of information you receive from the company	RATING
• Rate the clarity of messages you receive from the company	RATING
• Rate the consistency of messages you receive from the company	RATING
• Rate the opportunities for employees to voice their opinions to leaders	RATING
9. SENIOR MANAGEMENT	
• Do you believe that the company's executive management demonstrates the ethical vales in their decision making and performance?	☐ Yes ☐ No
• Do you believe that your immediate management demonstrates the ethical	☐ Yes ☐ No

SAMPLE ANONYMOUS EMPLOYEE QUESTIONNAIRE	
SURVEY QUESTION	YOUR RESPONSE
vales in their decision making and performance?	

TYPICAL CEO INTERVIEW QUESTIONNAIRE

The table illustrates the type of interview questionnaire that should be developed for use in Entity Level Control assessments. In this instance, we have provided *some* of the interview points that should be addressed by the CEO.

The interview is usually conducted by qualified senior personnel.

The questionnaire is a compilation of questions that address several controls within the Entity Level Program. The Entity Level Control Manager has two options:

1. Distribute the results in their entirety to all Control owners, or

2. Provide the owners who supplied the questions with the specific responses.

The interview master list, in an earlier section of this calendar should be used as the basis for developing the rest of required interview sheets.

Some interviews are conducted based on samples of personnel at a specific level (e.g. IT personnel), the sample lists should be prepared in advance and filed within the repository for reply tracking purposes.

Your company should review in these "sample" interviews whether to identify the respondent to the control owners.

Where anonymous surveys are used, your company may consider the services of a qualified external third party to conduct these surveys and to provide the responses back to the Entity Level Control program

Entity Controls Questionnaire – CEO	CEO Response	Comments/ Description of Supporting Evidence or Documentation	Assessment Design / Operational Effectiveness
CONTROL ENVIRONMENT			
The organization has adopted adopt a written code of conduct and ethics applicable to directors, officers and employees. Management actively communicates the message that integrity and ethical values cannot be compromised to all employees. Management must continually demonstrate, through words and actions, a commitment to high ethical standards.			
1. Is our company's Code of Conduct comprehensive, well communicated and effectively implemented? What, in your opinion, supports your assessment?	☐ Yes ☐ No	The supporting evidence received from the CEO should be input into the Evidence column.	☐ Yes ☐ No Type:
2. Has the Board been provided with timely, relevant accurate and complete reports that will enable it to assess whether we have a process for ensuring adherence to the Code of Conduct?	☐ Yes ☐ No		☐ Yes ☐ No Type:
3. Is there a process in place to assure you that remedial action has been taken in response for non compliance or violations with/of the Code of Conduct? *Please provide supporting evidence.*	☐ Yes ☐ No		☐ Yes ☐ No Type:
4. Is there a mechanism in place to satisfy you that all company management adheres to the Code of Conduct and demonstrates commitment to integrity and ethical behavior? *Please describe the mechanism and the methods you have used to ensure that this mechanism operates effectively (e.g. Internal Audit reviews, HR reports, etc.)*	☐ Yes ☐ No		☐ Yes ☐ No Type:
5. Is this commitment communicated effectively throughout our company, both in words and deeds? *Please provide supporting evidence.* *Is there an assessment process to ascertain the level of understanding within the organization?*	☐ Yes ☐ No		☐ Yes ☐ No Type:
6. Does Management lead by example? *Please provide supporting evidence.*	☐ Yes ☐ No		☐ Yes ☐ No Type:
7. Is the management structure appropriate (i.e. not dominated by one or a few individuals) and is there effective oversight by the Board of Directors? *Please provide supporting evidence.* *Please provide table of delegated authorities and responsibilities.*	☐ Yes ☐ No		☐ Yes ☐ No Type:
Executives must fully understand their control responsibilities and possess the requisite experience and levels of knowledge commensurate with their positions. Management must specify the level of competence needed for particular jobs, and translate the desired levels of competence into the requisite knowledge and skills.			
8. Is there a process in place to assure that the Board and you that Senior Management has the competence and experience necessary for their assigned level of responsibility or the complexity of	☐ Yes ☐ No		☐ Yes ☐ No Type:

Entity Controls Questionnaire – CEO	CEO Response	Comments/ Description of Supporting Evidence or Documentation	Assessment Design / Operational Effectiveness
the business? *Please provide a description of the process and all related evidence.* *Please provide minutes or other evidence of Board review..*			
9. Is there a process in place to set targets for, and periodically evaluate the performance of, Senior Management on a regular basis? *Please provide a description of the process and all related evidence.* *Please provide sample performance evaluations for some of the Senior Executives.*	☐ Yes ☐ No		☐ Yes ☐ No **Type:**
10. Does Senior Management set realistic business objectives and financial targets? *Please provide all related evidence to support your conclusion.*	☐ Yes ☐ No		☐ Yes ☐ No **Type:**
The philosophy and operating style of management should have a positive pervasive effect on our company.			
11. Are you, in your opinion, visible and accessible across the Company? *What supports your opinion?*	☐ Yes ☐ No		☐ Yes ☐ No **Type:**
12. Do you meet regularly with the Senior Executives, other Company Management and regional management as well as the heads of any oversight functions? *Please provide format and minutes of meetings.*	☐ Yes ☐ No		☐ Yes ☐ No **Type:**
The organizational structure must be appropriate to fulfill the business objectives of the organization. The organizational structure shouldn't be so simple that it cannot adequately monitor the enterprise's activities nor so complex, or involving numerous or unusual legal entities that it inhibits the necessary flow of information. The correctly balanced structure will promote the required flow of information throughout the company			
13. Is there a process in place to periodically review the organizational structure to ensure that it is adequate for the size, complexity, business activities, and locations we operates in? *Please provide evidence of last review and date of next scheduled review.*	☐ Yes ☐ No		☐ Yes ☐ No **Type:**
14. Is the structure re-evaluated relative to significant internal or external events? *Are there any examples or evidentiary material to support your conclusion?*	☐ Yes ☐ No		☐ Yes ☐ No **Type:**
The assignment of responsibility, delegation of authority and establishment of related policies should be effective and provide a basis for accountability and control.			
15. Has the Board delegated to you the responsibility for developing and implementing policies and practices for the effective management of the	☐ Yes ☐ No		☐ Yes ☐ No **Type:**

Entity Controls Questionnaire – CEO	CEO Response	Comments/ Description of Supporting Evidence or Documentation	Assessment Design / Operational Effectiveness
company's operations? *Please provide evidence of this delegation of authority.*			
16. Is there a process in place to delegate responsibilities from you (the CEO) to Senior Management and to periodically review the level of delegation? *Please describe the process and provide evidence of periodic reviews.*	☐ Yes ☐ No		☐ Yes ☐ No Type:
17. Is there a process in place to define which matters need to be escalated to you for review or approval? *Please provide table of escalated events and their related processes.*	☐ Yes ☐ No		☐ Yes ☐ No Type:
Human resource policies are in place to recruit and retain competent people enabling our company to achieve its goals.			
18. Is there a process in place to ensure that executives appointed by the Board are individuals who are suitably qualified and capable of managing the operations effectively and prudently? *Please describe the process.*	☐ Yes ☐ No		☐ Yes ☐ No Type:
19. Is there a process in place to allow the Board to periodically assess the quality of Senior Management? *Please describe the process and provide evidence of board review.*	☐ Yes ☐ No		☐ Yes ☐ No Type:
20. Do you present, at least annually, an updated succession plan to the Board for review and approval? *Please provide copy of latest succession plan*	☐ Yes ☐ No		☐ Yes ☐ No Type:
RISK ASSESSMENT			
The company must have entity-wide objectives, supported by related strategic plans in order to have effective control.			
21. Do you have a process in place to ensure that our strategic plan is reviewed and updated (at least annually) and submitted to the Board for review and approval? *Please explain process and provide evidence of last review.*	☐ Yes ☐ No		☐ Yes ☐ No Type:
22. Our risk-assessment process must identify and consider the implications of relevant risks, at both the entity level and the business level. The risk-assessment process should consider external and internal factors that could impact achievement of the objectives, should analyze the risks, and provide a basis for managing them. *Please describe our risk assessment process that you and the Senior Management employ.*	☐ Yes ☐ No		☐ Yes ☐ No Type:

Entity Controls Questionnaire – CEO	CEO Response	Comments/ Description of Supporting Evidence or Documentation	Assessment Design / Operational Effectiveness
In addition, please provide supporting material for this process.			
23. Is there a process in place to ensure that the Risk Management policy is reviewed and updated on a periodic basis and submitted to the Board for approval? *Please describe the process and evidence of last review.*	☐ Yes ☐ No		☐ Yes ☐ No **Type:**
24. Mechanisms are in place to identify and react to changing economic, industry and regulatory conditions. *Please describe these mechanisms and provide any supporting documents.*	☐ Yes ☐ No		☐ Yes ☐ No **Type:**
25. Are the Board of Directors and/or the Audit Committee and you informed on a timely basis about changes that may have a significant effect on our company? *Please provide a description of the mechanism or process and example of latest advice.*	☐ Yes ☐ No		☐ Yes ☐ No **Type:**
INFORMATION AND COMMUNICATION			
Information is identified, captured, processed and reported by information systems. Relevant information includes industry, economic and regulatory information obtained from external sources, as well as internally generated information.			
26. Are there effective processes in place to provide you and Board of Directors with sufficient and timely information to allow them to fulfill your/their responsibilities? Are these processes periodically reviewed? *Please provide a description of these processes and examples of latest information packages received.*	☐ Yes ☐ No		☐ Yes ☐ No **Type:**
Effective communication within the company occurs downwards, across, upwards and with parties external to the organization.			
27. Is the Board of Directors advised of all material issues involving legal and reputation risk? *Please provide description of the process. Please provide examples of last updates.*	☐ Yes ☐ No		☐ Yes ☐ No **Type:**
28. Is there a process in place for you to effectively communicate our company's ethical standards to key constituents: shareholders, customers, external vendors, employees, regulators etc.? *Please describe process and supporting material.*	☐ Yes ☐ No		☐ Yes ☐ No **Type:**
29. Is there a process in place to promote the effectiveness of the Board of Directors by providing the Board with sound advice on the organizational structure, objectives, strategies, plans and major policies?	☐ Yes ☐ No		☐ Yes ☐ No **Type:**

Entity Controls Questionnaire – CEO	CEO Response	Comments/ Description of Supporting Evidence or Documentation	Assessment Design / Operational Effectiveness
Please describe process and supporting material.			
30. Does Senior Management facilitate the Board's oversight role by providing relevant, accurate and timely information to the Board, enabling it to oversee the management and operations of our company, assess policies and determine whether we are operating in an appropriate control environment? *Please describe process and supporting material.*	☐ Yes ☐ No		☐ Yes ☐ No Type:
31. Does Senior Management facilitate effective oversight through fostering candid and robust Board discussions? *Please describe process and supporting material.*	☐ Yes ☐ No		☐ Yes ☐ No Type:
Management reports on the operations and financial condition of the institution, the performance of risk management and other control systems during the period under review, and any significant non-compliance with controls, the institution's code of conduct, or with laws and regulations.			
32. Does our company have processes in place to ensure that the appropriate disclosures are made to the Board and the Audit Committee, our external auditors and all regulatory bodies? *Please describe process and supporting material.*	☐ Yes ☐ No		☐ Yes ☐ No Type:
33. Do you receive sufficient and timely information to allow you to fulfill your disclosure obligations to the Board and the Audit Committee, our external auditors and all regulatory bodies? *Please provide materials to support your opinion.*	☐ Yes ☐ No		☐ Yes ☐ No Type:

Chapter 4 – Communications requirements for Sarbanes Oxley

Intent of this chapter

This chapter focuses on the methods used to implement a SOX communications infrastructure. It focuses on organizing the

- SOURCES from which communications information originate – how they should be coordinated and organized,

- CHANNELS or paths that should be developed for delivering the information, and

- The INFORMATION REQUIREMENTS of the SOX Audience – *appropriate information to the appropriate level.*

Overview

The communications effort required to coordinate and manage the communications effort is extensive, complex and diverse. A comprehensive, communications management architecture is a necessity during both the initial and ongoing phases.

SOX COMMUNICATIONS OVERVIEW

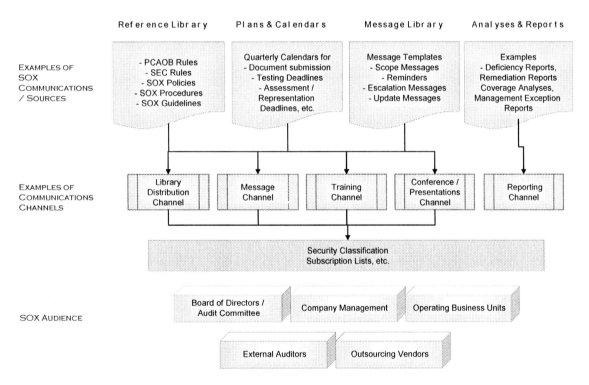

If not properly managed, the plethora of SOX communications may overwhelm both the senders and receivers.

The diagram above provides an overview of the communications infrastructure requirements. The diagram illustrates four layers as the minimum requirements for a communications management architecture that are:

1. The SOURCE MATERIAL that needs to be communicated – in this diagram, we illustrate four of the major classes of communications / sources. It is the responsibility of the SOX Department to assemble and disseminate this information after review and approval,

2. The recommended CHANNELS[13] for use in communications – these channels should be adopted / modified depending on the size and complexity of your company,

3. SECURITY CLASSIFICATIONS are optional based on your company's environment and security requirements. We would recommend that the highest security classifications and other measures be employed in all SOX communications because of the confidentiality of the information contained within these communications,

4. The SOX AUDIENCE – in the diagram, we illustrate only the key members of the SOX Audience because of space limitations.

Content lists and descriptions for each of the communication categories are provide in the latter sections of this chapter but are not illustrated in the diagram

COMMUNICATIONS OVERVIEW

The SOX department is normally required to maintain a minimum of four communications / publication processes. These processes, with their respective procedures, provide the SOX Department with the basis of a sound, robust and controlled communications environment.

COMMUNICATIONS MATERIAL / SOURCES

Communications usually originate based on the following materials and sources:

1. REFERENCE LIBRARY – This library maintains all current and previous versions of all SEC, PCAOB and other External Regulations, internal control policies, procedures, guidelines, training kits and other pertinent documentation. This information is maintained with version and date controls,

2. PLANS & CALENDARS – Fiscal Year plans, Quarterly plans, Final Fiscal Yearend plan, etc.,

3. MESSAGE LIBRARY – this library should maintain the standard message formats that will be used during the life cycle. This does not inhibit the normal email traffic flow that is a part of any company wide exercise but instead provides a formalized series of templates that should be used for SOX specific processes,

4. REPORTS & ANALYSES – the Analyses and Reports reviewed in Chapter 7.

CHANNELS

A channel is defined for the purposes of this chapter as "The *path* along which communications are transmitted."

In the diagram, we highlight the following channels:

---

[13] Channel - The path along which a communication is transmitted.

1. LIBRARY CHANNEL – this is usually a one-way path by which approved subscribers can access manuals, training material, regulations etc,

2. MESSAGE CHANNEL – a *bi-lateral* path used to move all dynamic electronic messages via a secure email facility. Wherever possible, email should originate and be received in a central SOX mailbox that is monitored and managed by specific individuals within the SOX Department,

3. REPORTING CHANNEL – path used to distribute all SOX analyses and reports in electronic format,

4. TRAINING CHANNEL – delivery path for all SOX training programs.

5. CONFERENCE / PRESENTATION CHANNEL – most companies use an annual (or more frequent) series of conferences to communicate with their SOX Audience any plans, procedure or policy changes, etc.

SECURITY CLASSIFICATIONS

All SOX Communications should be classified and restricted based on your company's internal security policies and procedures.

We would recommend that all communications emanating from the SOX Department have a minimum level of security control as these communications relate to financial statement preparations and other material that may have not been publicly disseminated.

SOX AUDIENCE

This subject is covered in depth in a later section of this chapter.

COMMUNICATION SOURCES AND MATERIALS

As outlined in the overview, communications emanate from a minimum of four sources viz. Reference Libraries, Plans & Calendars, Message Libraries, and Analyses & Reports.

REFERENCE LIBRARIES

The preparation and compilation of materials in the reference library may be assigned to other units within the SOX Department (usually the Policy and Procedures (Methodology) Manager) or to other Departments within your company.

For example, in larger organizations, ensuring that the legal and regulatory information contained in the Repository Reference Library sections is the direct responsibility of the Legal and Compliance Departments – the storage and delivery of the material is the responsibility of the Repository.

This library can be maintained in physical or digital format, depending on your company's requirements and capabilities. The use of a digital format usually provides a faster, more cost efficient distribution capability. However, you must ensure that your Audience is advised of future revision dates for their internal planning purposes via update communications.

A catalogue should be maintained of the contents of the reference library. This catalogue should be published as part of a SOX Quarterly Bulletin and be maintained as the introduction page for a digital library or on a Repository web page. The catalogue should contain:

1. The present contents in this Reference Library with the capability to download or view, if the contents are in digital format,

2. Additions made to the Reference Library within a specific period (e.g. monthly, quarterly, etc.) or in date sequence. There should be a brief synopsis outlining the impact of these changes appended to all additions,

3. Listing of references that have been changed within a specific period – *with links to previous versions*, and

4. Reference material that has been withdrawn (discontinued) from circulation and use. A brief note explaining the reason for the withdrawal and whether there is a substitute reference should be supplied. The reference libraries should not contain "*reference dead ends*".

Depending on your Audience and its requirements, some companies maintain subscription lists for this list of publications and the individuals who are to automatically receive update and other library notices.

SOX Department Management should periodically review the contents of the library and designate items as either mandatory or optional for Business Unit review purposes.

Items are designated as mandatory (e.g. PCAOB documents, SEC regulations, etc.) or optional. The determination of whether an item is mandatory is linked directly to the role the individual is responsible for within your organization.

For example, Business Unit Control Managers are *required* to receive all PCAOB documents, SEC Regulations, Internal Policies, Internal Procedures, etc. Optionally, Business Unit Managers may elect to not receive SOX Department Update Notices.

The list should also maintain alternate recipients in the event of planned or unplanned absences by the primary recipient. The subscription list should be confirmed quarterly.

REFERENCE LIBRARY CONTENTS

The Reference Library should contain, at a minimum, the following contents (please ensure that your company adheres to all copyright and subscription conditions of authors and publishers):

1. PUBLIC COMPANY ACCOUNTING OVERSIGHT BOARD (PCAOB) – All applicable regulations and interpretations,

2. SECURITIES AND EXCHANGE COMMISSION RULES (SEC RULES) – All applicable rules, regulations and interpretations,

3. YOUR COMPANY'S POLICIES for Financial Reporting, the Internal Control Framework and all other related materials,

4. COSO DOCUMENTATION including the Evaluation workbooks published by COSO,

5. YOUR COMPANY'S PROCEDURES AND ROLE DEFINITIONS for all pertinent Financial Procedures and the control framework over Financial Reporting,

6. INTERNAL CONTROL GUIDELINES AND STANDARDS for documentation of processes, controls, assessments (tests), deficiency reporting, assertions (or representations), etc.,

7. PLANS & CALENDARS detailing all planned activities and deadlines. These should include External Audit activities, wherever possible,

8. SOX DEPARTMENT MANAGEMENT UPDATES – most companies issue a quarterly (or more frequent) SOX Bulletin outlining the SOX activities, present status of the certification, items requiring special attention, etc. These should be maintained by publication date, and

9. LIBRARY NOTICES / CATALOGUES as outlined above.

PLANS & CALENDARS

Plans & Calendars are reviewed in more detail in Chapter 5. This section examines the communication requirements for Plans and Calendars *and not the actual construction of these plans and chapters.*

A fiscal year calendar projection of key activities should be published prior to the beginning of a new fiscal year. For example, if your company has a fiscal yearend of December 31, the preliminary calendar should be published on December 10 – with a one week *comment and feedback* period in which your audience can raise concerns or objections.. This one week period provides the operating Business Units with the opportunity to request change or exemptions based on regional business requirements or holidays.

The process steps required for the execution of the activities/ events in this calendar are usually documented in the procedures documentation section of the library. For one time only activities, these should also be provided in the calendar for ease of reference.

Quarterly updates should be published prior to the beginning of a new quarter with *confirmed* activity dates for events occurring within the quarter. Usually the preliminary fiscal year calendar can only provide approximate activity dates.

Specific activities (e.g. deficiency and/or remediation updates) may require more frequent communication notices within a quarter, *especially the final fiscal quarter*. These should be communicated via special update bulletins in the final quarter.

Communications of Plans & Calendars should be done via multiple channels, viz.

1. THE LIBRARY DISTRIBUTION CHANNEL through which the SOX audience can download or view of the latest copy of the Calendar if its is maintained in a digital format,

2. THE MESSAGE CHANNEL should be used to "*push*" the latest calendar to the SOX audience immediately on publication,

3. THE TRAINING CHANNEL should be used, wherever possible, to provide detailed information on the latest calendar to all trainees, and

4. CONFERENCES / PRESENTATION CHANNEL. Regardless of the method (whether web conference, video conference or physical attendee conference), conferences and presentations should be used to distribute and review the latest Plans & Calendars.

MESSAGES (EMAILS)

SOX certification processes require constant communications between the SOX Department and the SOX community. We would recommend that these messages be based on standard message templates that are developed by the SOX Department (with the assistance of your Legal and Compliance Departments, if necessary) for use throughout the fiscal year.

The use of a standard series of message templates ensures that your messages / emails are consistent in their format, meet company standards, meet any external regulatory requirements, require a limited amount of preparation time and are developed to assist the recipients to adhere to any instructions/ requirements promptly.

Training programs should include a section on standard messages and the required responses from the SOX community[14]. Message Logs should be maintained for all messages. Logs and should be used as follow-up lists where responses are required.

We would recommend the use of a central SOX mailbox from which all general SOX Department mail should originate and to which all general or company wide responses should be addressed. The use of this central mailbox provides a central portal through which all company wide SOX activities can be monitored, analyzed and controlled.

The management of this mailbox should be assigned to a specific individual within the Repository unit. The use of this mailbox does not obviously preclude the use of personal email facilities for "*one off*" messages.

ANALYSES & REPORTS

The formats, data and other details of these analyses and reports are covered in chapter 8. This chapter focuses on the communications methods to be used to communicate and distribute the analyses and reports.

A report distribution list that is confirmed / updated monthly with the SOX Community should be developed and maintained. This report list must contain at a minimum the following information:

1. The recipients for the analyses and reports – name, title or job function, business unit id, email address or mail drop,

2. The sources/originators that prepare these analyses and reports – name, title or job function, business unit id, email address or mail drop,

3. The production frequency of these reports e.g. on demand, daily, weekly, etc.,

4. The security level of the report and the recipient e.g. restricted to senior management, etc., and

5. The summary report for a specific analysis or report (some reports are produce by Business Unit or specific index – the corporate or other summaries should also be maintained in a cross reference in the report distribution list)

---

[14] We recommend that all messages contain a prefix in their subject line so that recipients can react appropriately. For example, a message prefaced with "ACTION REQUIRED with 48 HOURS" will provide the recipient with the necessary information to prioritize and respond to this message promptly.

Upon preparation / delivery of these reports, copies of all reports should be maintained with their distribution dates, recipients, delivery medium used and pertinent information that support the production and delivery of the analysis or report.

THE SOX COMMUNICATIONS AUDIENCE

As with any communications infrastructure, a fundamental understanding of the audience and their communications requirements must be included in the planning and implementation.

SOX AUDIENCE MEMBERS

The SOX Audience usually comprises of the following individuals or departments. At the end of this chapter, we provide a comprehensive communications table for each of these individuals.

- Board of Directors,
- Audit Committee,
- Disclosure Committee,
- Chief Executive Officer,
- Chief Financial Officer,
- External Auditors,
- Internal Auditors,
- Business Units,
- Legal Department,
- Compliance Department,
- HR Department,
- External Vendors, and
- IT Department.

COMMUNICATIONS & PUBLICATIONS CONTENT

One of the most effective methods for communicating with the internal control constituency is the development and publication of a SOX Quarterly bulletin that provides detailed information on all upcoming events and the responsibilities of the various units or individuals for their performance.

The department may be required to issue communication updates on any one of the categories on an interim or "*as needed*" basis. These stand alone communications should be referenced or summarized in the following quarter's bulletin for continuity purposes.

The SOX Quarterly Bulletin should provide the following items:

1. SOX DEPARTMENT QUARTERLY UPDATE –provides a summary of all pertinent SOX information for the next quarter and the results obtained from the prior quarter. This bulletin should provide the SOX Audience with updates on all Reference Library material, Plans and Calendars, Training Materials, etc.,

2. SOX INTERNAL DOCUMENTATION AND PUBLICATIONS FOR SOX PROCESSES (usually referred to as the SOX Methodology) – the policies and procedures required to implement an internal control framework the bulletin should advise of any changes to existing documents. In addition, new documents should be highlighted with a brief synopsis and how the complete document can be acquired,

3. CALENDARS & PLANS – these should be developed from an internal standard SOX life cycle template and amended during each quarter – the bulleting should outline the next quarter's activities in detail,

4. NEW NON PLAN TASKS – these are unplanned items that require immediate communication to the assigned/responsible SOX Audience member,

5. REGULATORY AND EXTERNAL PUBLICATIONS – these are the rules, regulations and interpretations usually maintained within a library. The actual documents may be maintained within the library system (recommended) or the links to the sites containing these documents, and

6. TRAINING – the schedule, kits and registration forms for training, etc. for the next quarter.

The following communications are not communicated as part of the Quarterly SOX Bulletin but are prepared and distributed separately because of the customization required.

1. FINANCIAL STATEMENT RISK ASSESSMENT COVERAGE REQUIREMENTS – these are the initial communications defining the requirements for the fiscal year. These should be customized to specific Business Units and must detail the Significant Accounts (and Notes or Disclosures) and Processes for which the Business Units is responsible.

   These lists are distributed separately because of the unique requirements for each Business Unit.

2. ISSUE LISTS – External Audit and other SOX communities may raise issues that need to be addressed during the certification process. Items on these lists may involve Business Units or departments other than the SOX Department.

   Because of the sensitive nature of these items, we would recommend that Business Units only receive the items pertaining to their specific and not the entire company's list.

   Management and the Board should receive the entire company wide list.

3. SUB CERTIFICATIONS – These are the quarterly sub certifications required of all SOX personnel. These sub certifications should be customized and sent to each certifier in a customized package with specific instructions and date by which the certification must be executed,

4. SOX REPORTS – these are the SOX reports that should be provided by the SOX Department based on the aforementioned Report Distribution List, and

5. AD HOC COMMUNICATIONS– these are the messages whose format is maintained in the Standard SOX message library and used as required. Typical examples are late notices, escalation notices, etc.

DESCRIPTION OF CONTENT TABLES

The communications/publications tables illustrated in the following sections contain recommendations that should be modified to your use..

In each table, we list the following columns:

1. COMMUNICATION / PUBLICATION DESCRIPTION: A description of the communication or publication requirement,

2. SOURCE: The section in the Repository in which the communication / publication should be filed. It is not the individual or department preparing the communication or publication,

3. UPDATES: Many of the communications and publications required regular periodic updates. We have indicated by a "yes" in the column whether we recommend these updates be performed,

4. LATE NOTICES: Several of the communications require an action to be performed by a Business Unit or other party by a prescribed date. As such, if the assigned individual is late, additional communications may be required,

5. ESCALATION NOTICES: In this communication strategy, we have assumed that your company will develop (or has developed) a standard escalation policy and procedures as part of its standard SOX Procedures. Items meeting the escalation criteria should automatically generate Escalation communications, and

6. EXCEPTION NOTICES: Exceptions Notices are generated when the required body of work that has been delivered (or submitted) does not meet the internal or external business rules and therefore requires the individual or department to correct the exception.

TOOLS REQUIRED TO SUPPORT COMMUNICATIONS STRATEGY

In addition to the standard tools and channels (e.g. email, presentations, web interfaces, etc.) required to support a SOX Communications strategy, there are several additional tools and/or manual processes that are needed.

1. TRACKING SYSTEMS: Many communications or publications have required target dates by which the recipient has to respond or perform an action. These target dates must be tracked and late and / or escalation notices automatically generated. Some organizations attempt to do this with a project management system.

2. VALIDATION SYSTEMS: *This only applies to organizations not using a real time validation input system (e.g. web interface with real time validation features, etc.).* If your organization uses spreadsheets or word processing documents that are collected and converted into a database, then the conversion process should include validation processes that ensure the integrity of the data imports into the database or documentation systems.

   Invalid data should be rejected and a validation exception report be produced for the originating department clearly outlining the cause of the problem. An acceptance report for valid records should also be produced.

SOX QUARTERLY BULLETINS

The items listed in the table below should be issued as one, comprehensive package to the entire SOX community.

The purpose of this communication is three fold:

1. To advise the community the *present state* of all SOX efforts,
2. To provide advance notice of *upcoming events*, and
3. To elicit *feedback* from the SOX community.

This bulletin should include the minimum following items:

Communication / Publication Description	Source	Updates	Late Notices	Escalation Notices	Exception Notices
SOX Department Manager's message/summary on present state of SOX efforts	NA	No	No	No	No
Table of significant upcoming events	NA	No	No	No	No
Highlights of changes to policies, processes and regulations	NA	No	No	No	No
List of current policy and or procedural infractions that need to be corrected within the Business Units	NA	No	No	No	No
Listing of frequently asked questions (and their answers)	NA	No	No	No	No
Regulatory and External Publications Listing of current documents within the library	NA	No	No	No	No
Significant personnel appointments in the SOX Department or internal control functions	NA	No	No	No	No

FINANCIAL STATEMENT RISK ASSESSMENT RESULTS

The communications in this section are the foundation upon which the transaction level SOX processes and controls are based. In order to provide these communications, your organization should have completed the Financial Statements Risk Assessment process in chapter 7.

Communication / Publication Description	Source	Updates	Late Notices	Escalation Notices	Exception Notices
Business Unit responsibilities (by Business Unit) for Significant Accounts and processes for this quarter	Repository	Yes	No	Yes	Yes
Financial Statements Note Requirements Matrix detailing the responsibilities for specific Business Units to provide information for specific Financial Statement Notes.	Repository	Yes	No	Yes	Yes

The Financial Statement Risk Assessment process should be executed on a quarterly basis. The communications to the Business Units of their responsibilities must be in two formats:

1. INCREMENTAL FORMAT: Identifying all changes from the previous period's responsibility chart and/or the previous fiscal yearend. For example, if Business Unit Alpha is now assigned Cash in Q2 but was not assigned this Significant Account in Q1, this incremental change should be identified as new ADD for Q2.

    We do not recommend that Business Units be required to remove processes and controls from their portions of the internal control framework based on a change in significant accounts - as these significant accounts may subsequently reassigned to the Business unit in later quarters,

2. CUMULATIVE FORMAT: Identifying the cumulative coverage required of that unit. Using the previous example, Business Unit Alpha is now assigned Cash,

3. All Business Units and the Finance Division should be required to confirm that they have met their coverage responsibilities for the Financial Statement Notes coverage on a quarterly basis via the SUB CERTIFICATION process,

4. The UPDATE column indicates "yes", because a Business Unit may advise of errors in preparation of the assignment of responsibilities. This is usually due to a post closing adjustment. The SOX Department should carefully review all requests before officially approving an update to the responsibilities.

The review and approval working papers must be stored in the Repository for a potential later review by the External Auditors or the Internal Audit Department.

SOX Internal Documentation and Publications for SOX processes

The list of items or required items is contained in the table below. When planning this segment of the communications infrastructure, the following should be taken into account:

1. A SUBSCRIPTION LIST - every Business should be required to have two individuals (minimum) responsible for receiving and disseminating all policies, procedures, etc. within their departments. In addition, this subscription list would be used to generate update notices for changes in the subject material.

2. EXCEPTION NOTICES should be generated if a department's subscription list falls below the minimum threshold level (no individual assigned to receive the notices or not the correct rank in the organization hierarchy to receive the communication),

3. TEST INSTRUCTIONS may generate late notices and escalation notices as these are usually "action" items that require Business Unit execution within a specified period. The SOX Department must generate Late Notices for all tardy items to the responsible Business Units. If further remedial action or senior company management intervention is required, an escalation notices may be generated.

Communication / Publication Description	Source	Updates	Late Notices	Escalation Notices	Exception Notices
Process and Control Documentation[15]	Publication Library	Yes	No	No	Yes
Test Guidelines	Publication Library	Yes	No	No	Yes
Deficiency Management Process	Publication Library	Yes	No	No	Yes
Entity Control Maps & Key Points of focus	Publication Library	Yes	No	No	Yes
Sub certification Process	Publication Library	Yes	No	No	Yes
Entity Control Evidence Process	Publication Library	Yes	No	No	Yes
IT Controls standard documentation	Publication Library	Yes	No	No	Yes
Outsource controls documentation	Publication Library	Yes	No	No	Yes
Standard Control Test Instructions	Publication Library	Yes	Yes	Yes	Yes
Annual Control Test Instructions	Publication Library	Yes	Yes	Yes	Yes
Fiscal Yearend Test Control Instructions	Publication Library	Yes	Yes	Yes	Yes

Calendar & Plans

1. PRELIMINARY CALENDARS – most companies produce preliminary fiscal calendars to assist the next year's planning and budget cycles. These are the same format as the Final calendars but may not contain detailed target dates,

2. FINAL CALENDARS - Final Calendars should be communicated for each quarter at the end of the preceding quarter in order to provide Business Units with the opportunity to include their required tasks in their internal plans and budgets.

---

[15] Process and Control documentation should include Segregation of Duty requirements, walkthrough requirements, risk identification, etc.

3. ISSUE LISTS - These may impact the SOX certification processes, since these items can be promoted to deficiencies if they are not resolved by a specific time frame (External Auditor issues are the usual example of these promotions). Issue lists are maintained and stored in the Repository. They are usually assigned to various Business Units or company management for resolution.

   The issue list (for general, company wide issues) should be published as one of the calendar events requiring them to provide updates by a specific date. If issues are of a confidential nature and should not be for general publication, these should be delivered using a more secure method other than the calendar.

4. NON PLAN TASKS - These are usually "one off" items arising from a meeting or are derivative tasks generated by an analysis of SOX data, External Audit or Regulatory request, etc.,

COMMUNICATION / PUBLICATION DESCRIPTION	SOURCE	UPDATES	LATE NOTICES	ESCALATION NOTICES	EXCEPTION NOTICES
Preliminary Fiscal Year Calendar	SOX Admin	Yes	No	No	No
Preliminary Quarterly Calendar (Q1) only	SOX Admin	Yes	No	No	No
Final Quarterly Calendar	SOX Admin	Yes	Yes	Yes	Yes
Final Fiscal Yearend Calendar	SOX Admin	Yes	Yes	Yes	Yes
Issues Lists	SOX Admin	Yes	Yes	Yes	Yes
Non Plan Task Lists	SOX Admin	Yes	Yes	Yes	Yes
Remediation Plans	SOX Admin	Yes	Yes	Yes	Yes

REGULATORY AND EXTERNAL PUBLICATIONS

Regulatory Publications are usually provided on the Regulator's web site. The Repository Unit should be assigned to monitor on a regular basis (at least weekly) these websites and to provide the web addresses for the latest information as part of the SOX Quarterly Bulletin.

LIBRARY LISTING

The SOX Department should maintain a library listing of all available Regulatory and External Publications on a web site or in a catalogue. This listing should be published as a part of the SOX Quarterly Bulletin. The following is a list of what the catalogue should contain:

COMMUNICATION / PUBLICATION DESCRIPTION	SOURCE	UPDATES	LATE NOTICES	ESCALATION NOTICES	EXCEPTION NOTICES
PCAOB Updates	Publication Library	Yes	No	No	No
PCAOB Rules	Publication Library	Yes	No	No	No
SEC Rules	Publication Library	Yes	No	No	No
Other Regulators' Rules	Publication Library	Yes	No	No	No
External Account Firms publications and Links	Publication Library	Yes	No	No	No
COSO Framework (including Evaluation tools)	Publication Library	Yes	No	No	No
All elements of COBIT Framework	Publication Library	Yes	No	No	No

SUB CERTIFICATIONS

The sub certification process is explained in detail in a later chapter. The SOX Department has the responsibility for:

1. Establishing the target dates by when sub certifications should be received,
2. Establishing the target dates by which corrections are required,
3. Sending to all certifying personnel their custom forms for certification (in most organizations, these forms are customized to the specific responsibilities of the certifier), and
4. Providing certification summaries to the CEO, CFO and Board after receipt of all sub certifications.

These are the basic communications sent for sub certifications. They should be generated from the Forms Library and data within the repository. Refer to Chapter 11 for the data usage.

Communication / Publication Description	Source	Updates	Late Notices	Escalation Notices	Exception Notices
Publication of sub certification customized forms by certification hierarchy level	Data	Yes	Yes	Yes	Yes
Target Dates for Quarterly sub certifications for SOX 302 / 906	Forms Library	Yes	Yes	Yes	Yes
Target Dates for SOX 404 certifications	Data / Forms Library	Yes	Yes	Yes	Yes
Reconciliation and correction dates by which certifiers are to return corrections	Data / Forms Library	Yes	Yes	Yes	Yes
Summary Report publication date	Data / Forms Library	No	No	No	No

SOX Department Reports

These are the standard Reports that are usually provided on a periodic basis to the SOX community. The delivery methods used to deliver these reports depend on your company's IT infrastructure. This list is provided to assist you in developing your initial Report Distribution List. For more details on each report, please refer to the chapter on Reporting and Metrics.

Communication / Publication Description	Source	Updates	Late Notices	Escalation Notices	Exception Notices
Monthly Calendar / Plan Progress Report	SOX Admin	Yes	No	No	No
Monthly SOX Issues List report	SOX Admin	Yes	No	No	No
Quarterly Documentation Status Report (including Validation statistics)	Repository	Yes	No	No	No
Quarterly Assessment (Test) Status Reports	Repository	Yes	No	No	No
Quarterly Transaction Deficiency Reports	Repository	Yes	Yes	Yes	Yes
Quarterly Entity Controls Deficiency Report	Repository	Yes	Yes	Yes	Yes
Quarterly Deficiency Combination Report	Repository	Yes	Yes	Yes	Yes
Quarterly Deficiency Aggregation Report	Repository	Yes	Yes	Yes	Yes
Quarterly Remediation Plan Report	Repository	Yes	Yes	Yes	Yes
Quarterly Significant Changes Report	Repository	Yes	No	No	No
Quarterly Documentation Validation Results (can be amalgamated into Documentation Report if done by Business Unit)	Repository	Yes	Yes	Yes	Yes
Quarterly Assessment (Test) Exception Results (can be amalgamated into Assessment (Test) Report if done by Business Unit)	Repository	Yes	Yes	Yes	Yes
Quarterly End to End Process summary	Repository	Yes	Yes	Yes	Yes
Quarterly End to End Process Broken links summary	Repository	Yes	Yes	Yes	Yes
Final Documentation Status Report (including Validation statistics)	Repository	Yes	No	No	No
Final Assessment (Test) Status Reports	Repository	Yes	No	No	No
Final Transaction Deficiency Reports	Repository	Yes	Yes	Yes	Yes
Final Entity Controls Deficiency Report	Repository	Yes	Yes	Yes	Yes
Final Deficiency Combination Report	Repository	Yes	Yes	Yes	Yes

Communication / Publication Description	Source	Updates	Late Notices	Escalation Notices	Exception Notices
Final Deficiency Aggregation Report	Repository	Yes	Yes	Yes	Yes
Final Remediation Plan Report	Repository	Yes	Yes	Yes	Yes
Final Significant Changes Report	Repository	Yes	No	No	No
Final Documentation Validation Results (can be amalgamated into Documentation Report if done by Business Unit)	Repository	Yes	Yes	Yes	Yes
Final Assessment (Test) Exception Results (can be amalgamated into Assessment (Test) Report if done by Business Unit)	Repository	Yes	Yes	Yes	Yes
Final End to End Process summary	Repository	Yes	Yes	Yes	Yes
Final End to End Process Broken links summary	Repository	Yes	Yes	Yes	Yes

You should maintain an archive of all reports issued based on period and date issued keys.

Ad Hoc Requests / Communications

Because of the dynamic nature of the certification process, the SOX Department should be prepared to address and communicate unscheduled items as they arise. We have provided a sample of the types of *ad hoc* requests that may be required within your company.

We recommend the preparation of the following standard request / communication formats prior to fully implementing your communications infrastructure.

1. Financial Statement Significant Account Coverage Ad hoc requirements – As previously covered each Business Unit is responsible for documenting the internal control framework within its own unit for specific, assigned Significant Accounts, Notes, Processes, etc. The SOX Department usually analyses the documentation received from all Business Units and identifies any Business Units that have not complied with their assigned list.

The SOX Department is required to send an Exception Notice advising the Business Unit of the problem and requiring correction by a specific date.

Communication / Publication Description	Source	Updates	Late Notices	Escalation Notices	Exception Notices
Notification of Financial Statements Coverage Exception (advising business Unit that they have not covered all Significant Accounts, Processes or Notes requirements) requesting correction by a specific date	Message Library	Yes	Yes	Yes	No
Exception Notice sent to company management requesting management intervention for missed correction date	Message Library	Yes	Yes	Yes	No

2. Calendars & Plans ad hoc requirements – Calendars and Plan will inevitably change during the course of a quarter. The SOX Department must be prepared to broadcast changes on an ad hoc, but controlled, basis to the SOX community in a structured manner.

In addition, the SOX Department will require standard formats for update requests, rejection notices, late notices, exception notices, etc. Therefore, we recommend that standard message formats be prepared and store in the message library for the following:

Communication / Publication Description	Source	Updates	Late Notices	Escalation Notices	Exception Notices
Request for Task Update	Message Library	Yes	Yes	Yes	Yes
Request for Issue Update and / or resolution	Message Library	Yes	Yes	Yes	Yes
Request for Remediation Plan Update	Message	Yes	Yes	Yes	Yes

Communication / Publication Description	Source	Updates	Late Notices	Escalation Notices	Exception Notices
	Library				
Late Notice for Task	Message Library	Yes	No	Yes	Yes
Late Notice for Issue Update	Message Library	Yes	No	Yes	Yes
Late Notice for Remediation Plan	Message Library	Yes	No	Yes	Yes
Escalation Notice for Task	Message Library	Yes	No	No	Yes
Escalation Notice for Issue Update	Message Library	Yes	No	No	Yes
Escalation Notice for Remediation Plan	Message Library	Yes	No	No	Yes
Exception Notice for Remediation Plan	Message Library	Yes	No	No	Yes
Request for Test Update Status	Message Library	Yes	Yes	Yes	No
Rejected Test Results	Message Library	Yes	Yes	Yes	No
Invalid (bad threshold or guideline) Test Results	Message Library	Yes	Yes	Yes	No
Late notification for Test	Message Library	Yes	Yes	Yes	No
Advice of External Audit Issue (advising of new item added to Issue List)	Message Library	Yes	Yes	Yes	No
Advise of assignment of a non plan task with details of assignment, target date etc.	Message Library	Yes	Yes	Yes	No

3. SUB CERTIFICATIONS AD HOC REQUIREMENTS – late notices for sub certifications, etc.

Communication / Publication Description	Source	Updates	Late Notices	Escalation Notices	Exception Notices
Late sub certification	Message Library	Yes	Yes	Yes	No
Invalid sub certification (assuming that an automated real time validation system is not used)	Message Library	Yes	Yes	Yes	No

4. SUBSCRIPTION AND REPORT DISTRIBUTION LIST AD HOC REQUIREMENTS – the SOX Department should periodically request the Business Units and other members of the SOX Audience to confirm their requirements for the Report Distribution list and the SOX Subscription lists.

Communication / Publication Description	Source	Updates	Late Notices	Escalation Notices	Exception Notices
Confirmation of Report Distribution Lists	Message Library	Yes	Yes	Yes	No
Confirmation of Subscription Lists	Message Library	Yes	Yes	Yes	No

TRAINING

The communications required for advising your community of upcoming training sessions.

Communication / Publication Description	Source	Updates	Late Notices	Escalation Notices	Exception Notices
Training Calendars / Schedules	Train Library	Yes	No	No	No
Training Registrations	Training Library	Yes	No	No	No
Training Material	Training Library	Yes	No	No	No

SOX AUDIENCE COMMUNICATIONS REQUIREMENTS

This table does not include ad hoc messages since these can be sent to anyone in the SOX Audience.

Communication Requirement Y= Yes N = No O = Optional	Board of Directors	Audit Committee	CEO	CFO	External Auditors	Internal Auditors	Business Units	Legal and Departments	External Vendors
SOX Department Manager's message/summary on present state of SOX efforts	O	O	Y	Y	Y	Y	Y	Y	Y
Table of significant upcoming events	Y	Y	Y	Y	Y	Y	Y	Y	Y
Highlights of changes to policies, processes and regulations	Y	Y	Y	Y	Y	Y	Y	Y	Y
List of current policy and or procedural infractions that need to be corrected within the Business Units	Y	Y	Y	Y	Y	Y	Y	Y	Y
Listing of frequently asked questions (and their answers)	O	O	Y	Y	Y	Y	Y	Y	Y
Regulatory and External Publications Listing of current documents within the library	Y	Y	Y	Y	Y	Y	Y	Y	Y
Significant personnel appointments in the SOX Department or internal control functions	Y	Y	Y	Y	Y	Y	Y	Y	Y
Financial Statement Risk Assessment									
Business Unit responsibilities (by Business Unit) for Significant Accounts and processes for this quarter – *Units only receive their assignments – not a global assignment sheet*	O	O	Y	Y	Y	Y	Y	Y	N
Financial Statements Note Requirements Matrix detailing the responsibilities for specific Business Units to provide information for specific Financial Statement Notes - *Units only receive their assignments – not a global assignment sheet*	O	O	Y	Y	Y	Y	Y	Y	N
Internal Control Framework Documentation									
Process and Control Documentation[16]	O	O	Y	Y	Y	Y	Y	Y	Y
Test Guidelines	O	O	Y	Y	Y	Y	Y	Y	Y
Deficiency Management Process	O	Y	Y	Y	Y	Y	Y	Y	N
Entity Control Maps & Key Points of focus *(Board and Audit Committee receive only summaries)*	Y	Y	Y	Y	Y	Y	Y	Y	N
Sub certification Process	Y	Y	Y	Y	Y	Y	Y	Y	Y
Entity Control Evidence Process	Y	Y	Y	Y	Y	Y	Y	Y	Y
IT Controls standard documentation	O	O	Y	Y	Y	Y	Y	Y	N
Outsource controls documentation	O	O	Y	Y	Y	Y	Y	Y	Y
Standard Control Test Instructions	O	O	Y	Y	Y	Y	Y	Y	Y
Annual Control Test Instructions	O	O	Y	Y	Y	Y	Y	Y	Y
Fiscal Yearend Test Control Instructions	O	O	Y	Y	Y	Y	Y	Y	Y
Calendars & Plans									
Preliminary Fiscal Year Calendar - *(Board and Audit Committee receive summary)*	Y	Y	Y	Y	Y	Y	Y	Y	Y
Preliminary Quarterly Calendar (Q1) only	O	O	Y	Y	Y	Y	Y	Y	Y
Final Quarterly Calendar - *(Board and Audit Committee receive summary)*	Y	Y	Y	Y	Y	Y	Y	Y	Y
Final Fiscal Yearend Calendar - *(Board and Audit Committee receive summary)*	Y	Y	Y	Y	Y	Y	Y	Y	Y
Issues Lists	O	Y	Y	Y	Y	Y	Y	Y	N
Non Plan Task Lists	O	O	Y	Y	Y	Y	Y	Y	O
Remediation Plans - *(Audit Committee receive summary)*	O	Y	Y	Y	Y	Y	Y	Y	O
Library									
PCAOB Updates	O	O	Y	Y	Y	Y	Y	Y	Y
PCAOB Rules	O	O	Y	Y	Y	Y	Y	Y	Y
SEC Rules	O	O	Y	Y	Y	Y	Y	Y	Y
Other Regulators' Rules	O	O	Y	Y	Y	Y	Y	Y	Y
External Account Firms publications and Links (E.G. Audit Firm)	O	O	Y	Y	Y	Y	Y	Y	Y
COSO Framework (including Evaluation tools)	O	O	Y	Y	Y	Y	Y	Y	Y
All elements of COBIT Framework	O	O	O	O	O	O	O	O	O
Sub Certifications									
Publication of sub certification customized forms by certification hierarchy level (Board and Committee members receive	O	O	Y	Y	Y	Y	Y	Y	Y

---

[16] Process and Control documentation should include Segregation of Duty requirements, walkthrough requirements, risk identification, etc.

COMMUNICATION REQUIREMENT Y= YES N = No O = OPTIONAL	BOARD OF DIRECTORS	AUDIT COMMITTEE	CEO	CFO	EXTERNAL AUDITORS	INTERNAL AUDITORS	BUSINESS UNITS	LEGAL AND DEPARTMENTS	EXTERNAL VENDORS
templates)									
Target Dates for Quarterly sub certifications for SOX 302 / 906	O	Y	Y	Y	Y	Y	Y	Y	Y
Target Dates for SOX 404 certifications	O	Y	Y	Y	Y	Y	Y	Y	Y
Reconciliation and correction dates by which certifiers are to return corrections	O	Y	Y	Y	Y	Y	Y	Y	Y
Summary Report publication date	Y	Y	Y	Y	N	N	N	N	N
STANDARD SOX REPORTS									
Monthly Calendar / Plan Progress Report - *(Board and Audit Committee receive summary)*	Y	Y	Y	Y	Y	Y	Y	Y	N
Monthly SOX Issues List report - *(Board and Audit Committee receive summary)*	Y	Y	Y	Y	Y	Y	Y	Y	N
Quarterly Documentation Status Report (including Validation statistics) - *(Board and Audit Committee receive summary)*	Y	Y	Y	Y	Y	Y	Y	Y	N
Quarterly Assessment (Test) Status Reports - *(Board and Audit Committee receive summary)*	Y	Y	Y	Y	Y	Y	Y	Y	N
Quarterly Transaction Deficiency Reports- *(Board and Audit Committee receive summary)*	Y	Y	Y	Y	Y	Y	Y	Y	N
Quarterly Entity Controls Deficiency Report- *(Board and Audit Committee receive summary)*	Y	Y	Y	Y	Y	Y	Y	Y	N
Quarterly Deficiency Combination Report - *(Board and Audit Committee receive summary)*	Y	Y	Y	Y	Y	Y	Y	Y	N
Quarterly Deficiency Aggregation Report - *(Board and Audit Committee receive summary)*	Y	Y	Y	Y	Y	Y	Y	Y	N
Quarterly Remediation Plan Report - *(Board and Audit Committee receive summary)*	Y	Y	Y	Y	Y	Y	Y	Y	N
Quarterly Significant Changes Report - *(Board and Audit Committee receive summary)*	Y	Y	Y	Y	Y	Y	Y	Y	N
Quarterly Documentation Validation Results (can be amalgamated into Documentation Report if done by Business Unit)	O	O	Y	Y	Y	Y	Y	Y	N
Quarterly Assessment (Test) Exception Results (can be amalgamated into Assessment (Test) Report if done by Business Unit)	O	O	Y	Y	Y	Y	Y	Y	N
Quarterly End to End Process summary - *(Board and Audit Committee receive summary)*	O	O	Y	Y	Y	Y	Y	Y	N
Quarterly End to End Process Broken links summary - *(Board and Audit Committee receive summary)*	O	O	Y	Y	Y	Y	Y	Y	N
Final Documentation Status Report (including Validation statistics) - *(Board and Audit Committee receive summary)*	O	O	Y	Y	Y	Y	Y	Y	N
Final Assessment (Test) Status Reports - *(Board and Audit Committee receive summary)*	O	O	Y	Y	Y	Y	Y	Y	N
Final Transaction Deficiency Reports - *(Board and Audit Committee receive summary)*	O	O	Y	Y	Y	Y	Y	Y	N
Final Entity Controls Deficiency Report - *(Board and Audit Committee receive summary)*	O	O	Y	Y	Y	Y	Y	Y	N
Final Deficiency Combination Report - *(Board and Audit Committee receive summary)*	O	O	Y	Y	Y	Y	Y	Y	N
Final Deficiency Aggregation Report - *(Board and Audit Committee receive summary)*	O	O	Y	Y	Y	Y	Y	Y	N
Final Remediation Plan Report - *(Board and Audit Committee receive summary)*	O	O	Y	Y	Y	Y	Y	Y	N
Final Significant Changes Report - *(Board and Audit Committee receive summary)*	O	O	Y	Y	Y	Y	Y	Y	N
Final Documentation Validation Results (can be amalgamated into Documentation Report if done by Business Unit)	O	O	Y	Y	Y	Y	Y	Y	N
Final Assessment (Test) Exception Results (can be amalgamated into Assessment (Test) Report if done by Business Unit)	O	O	Y	Y	Y	Y	Y	Y	N
Final End to End Process summary	O	O	Y	Y	Y	Y	Y	Y	N
Final End to End Process Broken links summary	O	O	Y	Y	Y	Y	Y	Y	N
TRAINING									
Training Calendars / Schedules – *External Vendors receive only*	O	O	Y	Y	Y	Y	Y	Y	Y

Communication Requirement Y= Yes N = No O = Optional	Board of Directors	Audit Committee	CEO	CFO	External Auditors	Internal Auditors	Business Units	Legal and Departments	External Vendors
their sections.									
Training Registrations	O	O	Y	Y	Y	Y	Y	Y	Y
Training Material – *External Vendors receive only their sections.*	O	O	Y	Y	Y	Y	Y	Y	Y

Message Formats

We recommend that you adopt a standard format for its messages in order to permit its recipients to more efficiently process the messages they receive. The recipient needs to be apprised of the message priority from simply reading the subject line. This table illustrates the subject lines and their priorities.

Priority	Subject Line Construction	Security Restriction	Comments
Highest	URGENT : *Subject*	All messages should have one of the following security Restrictions classification codes viz. 1. For your eyes only 2. Confidential – Senior Management only 3. Restricted to Management only 4. Internal to Company only 5. No security restrictions	This is an urgent message that requires a response upon receipt
High	ACTION REQUIRED by (date): *Subject*		This message requires the recipient to perform an action and to report on the results to the SOX Department by a specified date
High	REPLY REQUIRED by (date): *Subject*		This message requires the recipient to reply to the SOX Department by a specific date
Normal	SOX: *Subject*		Standard message that can be processed at the recipient's convenience
Process when time available	UPDATE: *Subject*		This is a message that contains a policy, procedural, guideline update than can be processed at the recipient's convenience.

Summary

Next Steps

We would suggest that you complete the following steps based on the information contained in this chapter:

First, identify the information sources and formalize (document and implement) the processes and timelines by which these sources will provide the SOX Department the necessary information for delivery to the SOX community.

In the table below, we provide an example using the recommended library listing. The affirmation column designates whether the department should advise that there are no updates on a regular, periodic basis e.g. monthly. You should coordinate the activities represented in this table with the Originators/Sources and prepare the procedures for joint approval. Complete a similar table for all sources provided in this chapter.

Communication / Publication Description	SOX Department Destination	Originator / Source	Required Dates	Affirmation Notice
PCAOB Updates	Publication Library	Legal or Compliance Department	Receipt + 48 hours	Yes
PCAOB Rules	Publication Library	Legal or Compliance Department	Receipt + 48 hours	Yes
SEC Rules	Publication Library	Legal or Compliance Department	Receipt + 48 hours	Yes
Other Regulators' Rules	Publication Library	Legal or Compliance Department	Receipt + 48 hours	Yes
External Account Firms publications and Links	Publication Library	SOX Department	Receipt + 48 hours	Yes

COMMUNICATION / PUBLICATION DESCRIPTION	SOX DEPARTMENT DESTINATION	ORIGINATOR / SOURCE	REQUIRED DATES	AFFIRMATION NOTICE
COSO Framework (including Evaluation tools)	Publication Library	SOX Department	Receipt + 48 hours	Yes
All elements of COBIT Framework	Publication Library	IT Department	Receipt + 48 hours	Yes

1. Next, develop the preliminary list of all publications and their intended recipients. Distribute this list for comment to key representatives within the community.

2. Develop the procedures for the central SOX mailbox and the standard message library.

CHAPTER 5 - SARBANES OXLEY PLANS & CALENDARS

INTENT OF CHAPTER

This chapter focuses on the development of the plans and calendars for both *initial and ongoing* phases. It starts with a complete fiscal year cycle and decomposes this annual calendar into quarterly or monthly calendars.

For each component, this chapter provides with standard planning templates for each of the main sections of the calendar. This chapter discusses the activities and events that should be included in the plans and calendars – it does not discuss the steps or processes that should be executed for each of these activities – *these are reviewed in subsequent chapters*.

- Financial Statements Risk Assessment,
- Process and Control documentation submission timelines,
- Assessment (Testing timelines),
- Deficiency Management Processes,
- Sub Certification process, and
- External Auditor Coordination

OVERVIEW

Certification activities require sound organizational planning in order to ensure the optimization of your company's resources, time and costs. The purpose of this chapter is to provide you with the information necessary to construct the plans (*both initial and ongoing*) and a Calendar that are customized to meet your company's requirements.

The publication of the calendar detailing all anticipated activities for the fiscal year provides two *tangible* benefits to the entire SOX community:

1. It ensures that the internal controls community has the opportunity to incorporate the Plans & Calendars into their unit's Business Plan development for the upcoming fiscal year. Therefore, these Business Units can plan their cost, personnel and other resource requirements, inclusive of all SOX activities, for the entire fiscal year, and

2. It coordinates the activities *on a company wide basis* for the entire internal control community which includes both internal and external parties. This coordination effort is critical to the ultimate success of the SOX certification effort.

In later steps, the Calendar will be used as a *benchmark* against which performance is measured for Board and Management Reporting. Any variations based on a *plan versus actual* comparison will highlight for the Board and Management tasks that may require their intervention or further attention.

The prompt identification of these variances normally ensures prompt remediation efforts within the SOX community.

The SOX Department should develop two views of the Sarbanes Oxley Calendar

1. INITIAL PHASE CALENDAR - a series of one-time activities required to achieve the initial SOX certification and to establish the ongoing processes for subsequent quarterly and yearend certifications,

2. ONGOING PHASE CALENDAR - a series of ongoing, sustainable activities required to achieve Quarterly and Annual SOX objectives

The two calendar views usually differ on the following:

- Only the INITIAL PHASE calendar contains

    o The selection of an internal control framework model (companies do not usually change the framework model year over year – it is usually a very unusual step)
    o The development of a SOX Department, and
    o The initial development work required for designing policies, procedures, etc.

- The ONGOING PHASE calendar focuses on the ongoing nature of its activities and not on the initialization efforts. Therefore, its usually does *not* include the following:

    o Selection of an internal control framework,
    o Setting up the SOX Department – instead your company should focus on ensuring the department focuses on developing a sustainable process and reducing the time and cost factors from year one,
    o Streamlining the processes and procedures for efficiency purposes.

INITIAL PHASE PLANS & CALENDARS

The INITIAL PHASE Plans & Calendar for the initial SOX certification effort generally comprises of eleven(11) macro steps in which your company should:

1. Select and customize an Internal Control Framework for Financial Reporting,

2. Define the job descriptions[17] and employ the personnel required to support a Sarbanes Oxley Certification Process (we refer to this generically as the *SOX Department* and the *Business Units* throughout this volume),

3. Design, document, quality assure, approve and implement a Sarbanes Oxley Methodology that includes the Polices, Procedures, Guidelines, Management Thresholds, Formats, etc.. This must also include all IT requirements – including General Computer Controls, Business Units Computing Controls and End User Computing Controls, etc.,

4. Design and implement a SOX communications infrastructure (as outlined in Chapter 4 of this volume),

5. Design and implement a Repository Unit (within the SOX Department) with the necessary tools to support secure storage of all documents, working papers and other evidence. This repository must maintain all SOX records on a version and periodic archival basis. The Repository will be the primary source for all SOX data and information for analysis and reporting to the entire SOX Audience,

6. Design and perform a Risk Assessment on the Financial Statements in order to identify the Significant Accounts and Processes and disclosure requirements. This assessment

---

[17] Job descriptions (as highlighted in the Entity Controls chapter must not only define the job itself but also the qualifications and experience required from any potential candidate. It should also include the training regimen that the successful applicant will be required to embark on upon employment.

must extend to the identification of the responsible business units (based on your Company's Organizational Hierarchy) that should be held accountable for the implementation, documentation and assessment of processes and controls for these significant accounts and processes (refer to chapter on Financial Statements Risk Assessment),

7. Design and perform a Risk Assessment on your Company's Entity Control Program (refer to chapter 3),

8. Design an Assessment (Test) Regimen for ensuring that controls are designed and operating effectively,

9. Design and implement a Deficiency Management process for identifying, recording, analyzing, combining and aggregating all entity and process (transaction level) control deficiencies,

10. Design and implement a Sub Certification process that provides Company Management and the Board assurances that all accountable Business Unit Managers have performed their duties as outlined in your Company's Policies and Procedures, and

11. Design and implement a comprehensive Management Reporting System (as reviewed in detail in Chapter 8).

ONGOING PHASE PLANS & CALENDARS

The ONGOING PHASE CALENDAR requires that your Company has previously designed and implemented the standard processes (chapter 2) as a *prerequisite* to maintaining an ongoing, sustainable process.

The preparation of the ONGOING PHASE calendar takes into account the "*lessons learned*" in the initial SOX certification phase and modifications are made to items 2 through 11 of the INITIAL PHASE CALENDAR, where required.

The selection of the internal control framework is usually not changed during the subsequent, ongoing certifications and, therefore, is usually not a part of the Ongoing Phase Calendar.

NORMAL CALENDAR PREPARATION ASSUMPTIONS

When developing the SOX Calendar, we would recommend that the following assumptions be used in its preparation:

1. HIGH RISK ITEMS should receive the highest priority for implementation, evaluation and assessment activities. These should be conducted at *the earliest available opportunity*. In the event of a deficiency identified in these high risk areas, your company should have ample time to remediate the deficiency before the fiscal yearend,

2. EXTERNAL AUDITOR ACTIVITIES are closely coordinated and incorporated into your Company's SOX Calendar. These activities must be requested from your Auditors early in the fiscal year in order to ensure that there is adequate preparation and discussion time. The External Auditor may not be in a position to provide specific dates at the beginning of the fiscal year for some activities and will instead provide general dates (week or monthly targets).

Prior to commencing a new quarter, you should request your External Auditor to provide a more defined timetable, with specific dates and Business Unit identifications, for incorporation into the final Quarterly calendar.

3. Despite the fact that some activities are usually performed only at yearend, we recommend that these activities be performed for at least two quarters in Year 1 and 2 of SOX activities.

   A typical example of this is the process by which you ensure that your internal control framework covers the required Significant Accounts, Processes and Notes (sometime referred to as the "*scope coverage*")..

   We would recommend that you perform these activities, even though your Business Units may not have completed their documentation and assessment activities for the entire framework, on a regular, periodic basis.

   The results of these periodic activities provide *interim* benchmarks for both your company management and the Business Units involved. For example, you can use the coverage reconciliation to confirm which Significant Accounts or Processes have *not* been covered by Business Units with the Unit Managers – this will eliminate any inadvertent omissions that are only identified at yearend – *when it may be too late to correct.*

4. PRELIMINARY CALENDARS should be issued at the beginning of the fiscal year. As plans and events change or are confirmed (e.g. External Audit Activities, General Computer Control tests, etc.), calendars should be modified and issued as FINAL calendars before the *beginning* of the quarter or month to which they apply.

   The majority of changes usually occur in the third and fourth quarters of the fiscal year.

CALENDAR INPUT SOURCES

The calendar should be prepared from four sources as illustrated in the diagram below::

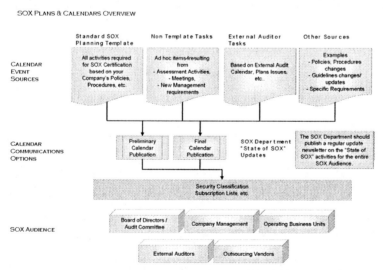

1. SOX STANDARD PLANNING TEMPLATE – You should develop and maintain a standard calendar planning template from which each fiscal year's calendar should be generated.

   The template should list the proposed activities in date sequence.

   It should not provide the detailed procedures for any of the calendar activities as this should be a part of your Company's methodology (Policies, Procedures, Guidelines, etc.) and SOX Departmental procedures. Instead, the template should focus on *what* activities are to be performed by *when* (target date),

2. SOX ISSUES AND NON PLAN TASK LISTS – Issues and other unforeseen activities will arise during the certification process. Therefore, a process for identification and management

should be developed to ensure their inclusion into the plans & calendars upon identification,

3. EXTERNAL AUDITOR GUIDELINES AND CALENDAR EVENTS – The Calendars should be prepared including External Auditor events and tasks in order to provide Business Units with *one definitive perspective* of all SOX activities – *both internal and external*. This assists the Business Units to plan their key activities,

4. OTHER SOURCES – these are usually changes required in the plans or calendars based on Regulatory or Management changes.

In this diagram, we have illustrated two options for publication of the SOX Calendar.

- OPTION 1 - publish the calendar as a stand alone document focusing only on the tasks and events for the period covered,

- OPTION 2 – publish together with any plan, methodology and guideline changes that impact the next quarter as a "State of SOX" Monthly or Quarterly Bulletin. This has been discussed in Chapter 3 as part of the overall communications strategy.

STANDARD CALENDAR PRACTICES OF SOX DEPARTMENT

MEETINGS AND CONFERENCES

The SOX Department should organize regular periodic meetings or conferences for the following:

1. SOX DEPARTMENTAL MEETINGS that review results and upcoming events. These should be designed as action meetings with the results published as a list of tasks[18], issues[19], decisions[20] and assumptions[21] that have to be resolved for the operational aspects of the SOX Calendar – *and not in the traditional minutes format in use in most companies*,

2. ANNUAL SOX BUSINESS UNIT CONFERENCE where the upcoming year of SOX activities, new policies and procedures and all other SOX related items can be reviewed. This can be a section of a general corporate annual conference or a separate SOX conference.

COMMUNICATIONS AND PUBLICATIONS

We would recommend the publication of quarterly (or monthly) SOX Newsletter should be issued to communicate all upcoming events, policy and procedural changes and all other matters that impact the SOX certification process,

STANDARD SOX PLANNING TEMPLATE

This template should have two key cycles. The first is a standard quarterly cycle which details the activities that should be completed within any fiscal quarter. The second should

---

[18] TASK – a body of work assigned to a specific individual to be performed by a specific date and time whilst meeting a specific standard for that type of work.
[19] ISSUE – an item requiring resolution or approval by Senior Company Management. An issue champion is appointed to achieve the objective by a specific date and time.
[20] DECISION – a selection from one of more SOX operational options that will be implemented by the Department by a specific date. This decision must be communicated and approved on a timely basis.
[21] ASSUMPTION – an item requiring confirmation. This item has an appointed champion who has to confirm by a specific date and time.

comprise of all fiscal yearend or annual activities that are not included in the standard quarterly cycle.

MAINTENANCE OF TASK AND ISSUE LISTS

It is assumed that your Department will maintain a comprehensive list of issues and tasks that need to be resolved. These will usually originate from the aforementioned SOX meetings, data analyses, External Auditors, Regulators, etc. These are identified throughout this document as NON PLAN items for ease of reference and should be included in all FINAL calendars.

CALENDAR PUBLICATION DATES

The proposed calendar publications listed below assume a fiscal yearend of December 31 (the calendar used in the examples below is the fiscal year 2006). Quarterly and Fiscal

FISCAL YEAR 2006	PRELIMINARY CALENDAR	LAST COMMENT DATE	FINAL CALENDAR
Quarter 1	December 1, 2005	December 29, 2005	January 3, 2006
Quarter 2	March 1, 2006	March 29, 2006	April 3, 2006
Quarter 3	June 1, 2006	June 29, 2006	July 5, 2006
Quarter 4	September 1, 2006	September 28, 2006	October 2, 2006
Fiscal Yearend	November 15, 2006	December 11, 2006	December 31, 2006

STANDARD TEMPLATE

The Calendar template is usually subdivided into the following sections for ease of reference. We have provided the timing components in generic format e.g. Q1 = Quarter 1, M1 = Month 1. The frequency for each major subsection is identified in the table below by quarter.

SUB SECTION (NOT IN PRIORITY / TIMING SEQUENCE)	FREQUENCY OF SUB SECTION	TIMING				
		Q1	Q1	Q1	Q1	YE
METHODOLOGY FINALIZATION AND UPDATE – This is usually a prerequisite to the fiscal year and is not performed during the fiscal year, therefore we have not designated any timing within the current year	As required / on demand	No	No	No	No	No
RISK ASSESSMENT OF FINANCIAL STATEMENTS (Scoping) – Publication of responsibility for all Business Units – both Incremental and Cumulative[22] reports	Quarterly and at Fiscal Yearend	√	√	√	√	√
ENTITY LEVEL CONTROL PROGRAM activities including the business unit / regional assessments	Quarterly and at Fiscal Yearend	√	√	√	√	√
Preparation and Quality Assurance of PROCESS AND CONTROL DOCUMENTATION by all responsible departments within the company	Quarterly and at Fiscal Yearend	√	√	√	√	√
Timetable for all ASSESSMENT (TESTING) ACTIVITIES and results and Evidence submission to the Repository	Quarterly and at Fiscal Yearend	√	√	√	√	√
Timetable for DEFICIENCY MANAGEMENT PROCESSES including Deficiency Identification, confirmation, remediation plans, combination and aggregation activities.	Quarterly and at Fiscal Yearend	√	√	√	√	√
Timetables for SENIOR MANAGEMENT, BOARD AND BOARD COMMITTEE REPORTING based on Board Scheduled meetings	Quarterly and at Fiscal Yearend	√	√	√	√	√
Timetable for all SUB CERTIFICATION PROCESSES	Quarterly and at Fiscal Yearend	√	√	√	√	√

---

[22] INCREMENTAL and CUMULATIVE – The SOX Department should communicate two lists of Significant Accounts / Processes required to be covered by the Internal Control Framework. The INCREMENTAL list should identify all changes from the prior period's list. The CUMULATIVE list should include all significant Accounts / Processes required to be covered in this period.

Sub Section (not in Priority / Timing sequence)	Frequency of Sub Section	Timing				
		Q1	Q1	Q1	Q1	YE
External Audit coordination – including Issue resolution	Quarterly and at Fiscal Yearend	√	√	√	√	√
Training timetables	Quarterly or as required	√	√	√	√	No

Methodology Finalization and Update Calendar Activities

Advising your Community of future methodology changes is a professional courtesy that should be always extended. In addition to fostering their goodwill (and very few operating departments look at governance activities with much goodwill), it allows your entire company to incorporate into their business plans and budgets operational procedural changes that may emanate from these methodology changes.

We normally recommend that all methodology changes should be packaged together with the release of the Final Quarterly Calendar. Therefore, this section of the calendar should provide the Business Units with detailed information on any additions, changes or deletions to any policy, procedural or guideline changes.

Annual Review of Methodology

You should schedule and perform, in November and December of the preceding fiscal year, a review of the entire SOX Methodology. All manuals or other material should be changed as required. The Methodology must include, at a minimum the following elements. The elements are covered in more detail in subsequent chapters.

1. Process and Control Documentation[23] - This must include all Significant Process and Control documentation policies, procedures, guidelines, formats, etc. They must provide specific, detailed instructions to the Business Units on how execute the tasks necessary for the upcoming fiscal year.

   - Process outlining how Business Units should organize the documentation process for the Significant Accounts and Processes for which they are responsible based on the SOX Department's risk assessment,

   - How to document Significant Processes (methods and tools to be used should be clearly defined),

   - How to identify key controls or control steps within the process (define methods and tools). Controls are NOT always process steps and may be documented separately in some companies,

   - Methods to be used to establish process links for end-to-end processes – in many instances, a business unit may be responsible for a process that is "handed off" or transferred to another process performed by a different business unit. The two processes, when combined are referred to as an "end to end" process,

   - Methods to be used to identify process jumps between business units and processes – in some processes, based on a decision point in the process (e.g. an error has occurred), the process may have to "jump" to a different Business Unit's Process. This "process jump" must be documented in a manner that assessment activities can be easily performed,

---

[23] Process and Control documentation should include Segregation of Duty requirements, walkthrough requirements, risk identification, etc.

- Segregation of duties documentation requirements and what methods and tools should be used by the Business Unit,

- Documentation of Systems used within processes – this should be documented based on your Company's End User Computing and IT localized requirements and must clearly define the methods and tools to be used.,

2. TEST GUIDELINES – Test Guidelines formally document your minimum assessment requirements.

   We normally recommend that the guidelines be formally mandated (by the Board and/or company management) for the entire year. In preparing this list, we have assumed that you allow examination, re-performance and synchronized test types and do NOT allow inquiry and observation test types. However, this is an option that you can modify.

   The following should be the ANNUAL minimum guidelines established:

   - Depending on the *control type* (e.g. routine, non-routine, estimation, etc.), your Company should mandate the minimum type of test required for the control type e.g. Provisioning / Estimation controls can only be tested by re-performance,

   - *Sample sizes* for tests by control type and control frequency,

   - Number of *test cycles* required within the fiscal year for each control type, and

   - Guidelines for *relationship* of Control Assessor (Tester) versus Control Performer – this is an integral part of the Segregation of duties, etc.

   The following should be the QUARTERLY guidelines published in each quarter's final calendar:

   - QUARTER 1 – all annual controls with performance dates within Q1, all estimation and other high risk controls, and one third of the routine controls within the business units,

   - QUARTER 2 – all annual controls with performance dates within Q2, all estimation and other high risk controls for the second cycle and all failed controls, one third of the routine controls within the business units and first cycle of synchronized tests,

   - QUARTER 3 – all annual controls with performance dates within Q3, all failed estimation and other failed high risk controls, one third of the routine controls within the business units and second cycle of synchronized tests,

   - QUARTER 4 – all annual controls with performance dates within Q4, final tests for all failed controls, and

   - FISCAL YEAREND – *this must be carefully coordinated with your external auditors.* These tests are usually for all year end closing controls and all controls that directly impact the preparation of Financial Statement Notes.

3. DEFICIENCY MANAGEMENT PROCESS – The Deficiency Management Process (detailed in later chapters) must provide the Business Units with clear instructions for identifying deficiencies, preparing remediation plans, etc.,

4. ENTITY LEVEL CONTROL COMPONENTS & KEY POINTS OF FOCUS – This section must clearly outline your Company's Entity Control program and the assessment processes that will

be used in Business Units in order to prepare these Units for these activities,

5. SUB CERTIFICATION PROCESS – All additions, changes or deletions to the methods, processes and formats for sub certifications should be included in this section.

6. ENTITY CONTROL EVIDENCE PROCESS – Same as previous section.

7. IT CONTROLS STANDARD DOCUMENTATION – The processes required to document and assess both the General Computer Controls, Business Unit Computing Controls and End User Computing Controls

8. OUTSOURCED CONTROLS DOCUMENTATION – The processes required to document and assess the Outsourced Processes and Controls. This should provide The Business Units with detailed instructions on how to review and assess the SAS70 received from External Vendors,

9. STANDARD CONTROL ASSESSMENT (TEST) INSTRUCTIONS – Any changes to the methods, guidelines and management thresholds for control assessment activities that the Business Units have to perform for that specific quarter,

10. ANNUAL CONTROL TEST INSTRUCTIONS – these are special controls that usually can only be tested once per year and on a specific date. Any changes to annual test requirements must be included in the Q1 preliminary calendar, and

11. FISCAL YEAREND TEST CONTROLS – Similar to annual controls, these are special high risk controls. Any methodology, guideline or threshold changes must be included with the fiscal yearend calendar to alert business units.

RISK ASSESSMENT OF FINANCIAL STATEMENTS (SCOPING) CALENDAR

This section of the calendar should detail the activities that are performed for the Risk Assessment of the Financial Statements and the assignment of responsibility to the various Business Units to ensure that specific Significant Accounts and Processes are covered by their section of the internal control framework

ASSUMPTIONS USED IN THE PREPARATION OF THIS SECTION

1. You have a predetermined set of financial assertions for each financial statement line and that these assertions are inherited by the subordinate significant account. These financial assertion sets have been reviewed with your External Auditors and have been mutually agreed between the two parties. For additional information, please refer to the Chapter on Risk Assessment of Financial Statements,

2. You will ensure coverage not only for a specific significant account but *also for the financial assertions required for the account*,

3. All individuals preparing the Significant Account analysis have executed special confidentiality agreements since they will be in possession of financial statements prior to public disclosure.

CALENDAR SCOPING ACTIVITIES

The Calendar must advise the Business Units of all *target dates* for Scoping activities and their Financial Statement coverage responsibilities. The calendar must provide the Business

Units with specific dates by which they should expect their assigned responsibilities from the risk assessment process.

Depending on your policies, the risk assessment of the Financial Statements is usually measured on a pragmatic, tangible basis on a quarterly or semi annual basis. The rationale behind this approach is simple – if there is a gap in the financial statement coverage – it should be discovered and remedied as early as possible in the fiscal year so that it can be tested within Q2 or Q3 of the fiscal year and *not in the final quarter*.

In our experience, External Auditors usually reserve Q4 for their testing activities.

All Financial Statement Risk Assessment Activities should be coordinated / confirmed with the Finance Division of your company.

RECOMMENDED CALENDAR TEMPLATE

Specific dates should be assigned to each line item. This table is in the step sequence of the process. This table may or may not be a part of the general population calendar. In some companies, only the last three lines (gray Shaded) are included in the general SOX Calendar.

FINANCIAL STATEMENTS RISK ASSESSMENTS			
PERIOD	DESCRIPTION	SOURCE	DESTINATION
Start of any quarter	Finance Division provides Yearend or Quarter End Financial Reporting files for assessment purposes	• Finance Division	• SOX Dept.
Start of any quarter	Finance Department approves or provides the Financial Statement to Significant Account Map or cross reference files (These files are normally maintained within the Finance Division for Financial Statements Consolidation purposes)	• Finance Division	• SOX Dept.
Start of any quarter	Finance Division provides detailed trial balances by significant account by region or business unit that will be held accountable for SOX documentation.	• Finance Division	• SOX Dept.
Start of any quarter	Based on the management thresholds established for the risk assessment, the risk assessment is executed to provide the listing of significant accounts required to be covered by each business unit. These files should contain the balances designated to each Business Unit	• Finance Division	• SOX Dept.
Start of any Quarter	Finance Division provides SOX Department with Listing of Financial Statement Notes that requires input from Business Units.	• Finance Division	• SOX Department
Start of any quarter	List of significant accounts should be provided to auditors with all default assertions by Business Unit for review.	• SOX Dept.	• External Auditors
Start of any quarter	Publication to each logical Business Unit of the Significant Accounts they are required to cover in two formats: 1. INCREMENTAL format i.e. changes since the last assessment, 2. CUMULATIVE format i.e. all accounts and/or processes required to be covered.	• SOX Dept.	• Business Units
Start of any Quarter	Your Company should provide guidance for Qualitative Accounts and a minimum list of Qualitative accounts that are required to be covered by the internal control framework	• SOX Dept.	• Business Units
Start of any Quarter	Business Units should receive a listing of Financial Statement Notes to which their input is required by the Finance Division	• SOX Dept.	• Business Units

Business Units should be allowed one week to review the required Significant Account and Process coverage requirements provided by the SOX Department. These units should have the right to file objections of changes for any mandated significant accounts.

Changes or objections should be received by the end of the first calendar month of the quarter:

CHANGES / OBJECTIONS FOR FINANCIAL STATEMENTS ASSIGNMENTS			
PERIOD	DESCRIPTION	SOURCE	DESTINATION
Month One of any Quarter	Last date for Significant Account objections to be filed	• Business Units	• SOX Dept.
Month One of any Quarter	Business Units file listing of Qualitative Accounts defining which they will cover and which they will NOT cover for the period.	• Business Units	• SOX Dept.

PROCESS AND CONTROL DOCUMENTATION CALENDAR

This governs the *timing* of the submission, validation and analysis of the documentation (and not the content or other documentation processes) that is to be submitted as evidence of their implementation and self assessments activities by the Business Units to the SOX Department's Repository on a quarterly (or other periodic) basis.

We have assumed that documentation is not submitted unless the process and control has been assessed (tested). Therefore, upon submission, the Business Unit will submit to the Repository the following

- Process documentation (e.g. Process Map, Narrative, process to process connectors, etc),
- Control documentation,
- Test Results,
- Deficiency Forms (if necessary)
- Remediation Plans (if necessary), etc.

TIMING FOR SUBMISSION OF DOCUMENTATION

Documentation should be submitted on a regular, periodic basis to the Repository.

The SOX Department should develop the guidelines for these submission cycles in order to ensure that Business Units are aware of *which* documentation is required by *what* dates.

The calendar should be heavily weighed to high risk controls and their assessments being submitted *earlier* in the fiscal year. The same sequence of events should be assigned to Entity Level controls documentation and assessment.

As previously stated, the rationale for this weighting is to ensure that any failures in the high risk and entity level controls are identified as early as possible so that remediation action can be taken before the fiscal yearend. In addition, the following factors should be taken into consideration in the development of this section of the calendar.

1. A more frequent, earlier cycle of submissions provides the Repository and the Business Units an opportunity to identify problems and to correct these before Q3/Q4,

2. Personnel Resource Load requirements for documentation and testing will be more evenly distributed throughout the fiscal year instead of being concentrated at yearend with its other competing activities,

3. The Assessment activities can be more closely coordinated with the External Auditors, and

4. Remediation activities should start earlier in the fiscal year so that you can achieve at least two cycles of testing for the remediated controls within the fiscal year.

Repository

It is assumed that your Company has established a Repository as outlined in *Chapter 3 – Prerequisites for Sarbanes Oxley (and Chapter 6 – the SOX Repository)*.

The repository will be responsible for acceptance of submissions, validation of documentation versus your Company's standards, rejection (if necessary), storage of documentation, etc. The timing of these tasks is outlined in the calendar template below.

You should have also established a series of validation rules prior to commencing any of these activities e.g. documentation formats, unique identifiers for processes and controls, Assessment reporting formats, Deficiency Management formats, etc.

Q1 / Q2 / Q3 Recommended Calendar Template

This recommended template provides the minimum activities that should be required within any of the first three quarters of the fiscal year.

STANDARD QUARTERLY CALENDAR TEMPLATE			
PERIOD	DESCRIPTION	SOURCE	DESTINATION
Q1/2/3	All **Annual** controls (including their tests) with anniversary dates within Q1/2/3 must be documented and submitted to the Repository	• Business Unit	• SOX Dept. Repository
Q1/2/3	**High Risk** controls (as many as can be documented or modified by the Business Unit in the each quarter) with the emphasis on performing these activities at the earliest point in the fiscal year	• Business Unit	• SOX Dept. Repository
Q1/2/3	A minimum of one third of all Routine controls must be documented and **assessed** within each quarter	• Business Unit	• SOX Dept. Repository
Q1/2/3	SOX Department Repository Unit executes validation routines versus your business rules for documentation submitted for Q1 / Q2 and Q3	• SOX Dept. Repository	• Business Units
Q1/2/3	Validation acceptances / exceptions provided to Business Units with requests for corrections by a **specific date in the following quarter**	• SOX Dept. Repository	• Business Unit
Q1/2/3	Deficiency Management Process commences for all identified deficiencies from the previous quarter – Listing sent and remediation tracking commences	• SOX Deficiency Unit	• and Business Units
Q3 only	Weekly External Audit Coordination commences	• SOX Dept. Managers	• External Auditors
Q3 only	Archive made of documentation to be used by External Auditors for their testing – in larger companies this may start in Q2.	• SOX Dept. Deficiency Unit	• External Auditors
Q3 only	External Issues List procedures commence	• External Auditors	• SOX Dept
Q3 only	Issue List published to Business Units, where applicable with	• SOX Dept.	• Business Units

STANDARD QUARTERLY CALENDAR TEMPLATE				
PERIOD	DESCRIPTION		SOURCE	DESTINATION
	• requests for responses by specific dates or • requests for remediation plans			
Q3 only	Management Report on External Auditors Issues jointly published monthly		• SOX Dept. and External Auditors	• Senior Company Management

Q4 RECOMMENDED CALENDAR TEMPLATE

Q4 is usually considered the "*remediation*" and "*clean up*" quarter. It is also the quarter with the most intense External Auditor activity that requires the SOX Department to ensure that the Business Units are aware of their responsibilities for assisting these Audit activities.

Q4 CALENDAR TEMPLATE			
PERIOD	DESCRIPTION	SOURCE	DESTINATION
Q4	All **Annual** controls (including their tests) with anniversary dates within Q4 must be documented and submitted to the Repository in time for the External Auditors to review.	• Business Unit	• SOX Dept. Repository
Q4	All **remediated** controls are submitted / validated with their new test results. These will be confirmed by Internal Or External Audit reviews in this quarter	• Business Unit	• SOX Dept. Repository
Q4	SOX Department Repository Unit executes validation routines versus your business rules for documentation submitted for Q4	• SOX Dept. Repository	• Business Units
Q4	Validation exceptions provided to Business Units with requests for corrections by a **specific date (less than fiscal yearend wherever possible).**	• SOX Dept. Repository	• Business Units
Q4	Deficiency Management Process commences for all Q4 identified deficiencies. Cumulative List of Q1/Q2/Q3/Q4 deficiencies sent and remediation tracking commences / continues.	• SOX Deficiency Unit	• Business Units
Q4	Weekly External Audit Coordination continues	• SOX Dept. Managers	• External Auditors
Q4	Archive made of documentation to be used by External Auditors for their testing. This archive should also be accompanied by a change list and audit trail identifying any changes between the Q3 and Q4 archives.	• SOX Dept. Deficiency Unit	• External Auditors
Q4	External Issues List procedures continue	• External Auditors	• SOX Dept
Q4	Issue List published to Business Units, where applicable with: • requests for responses by specific dates (before **fiscal yearend**) or • requests for remediation plans	• SOX Dept.	• Business Units
Q4	Senior Company Management Report on External Auditors Issues jointly issued monthly or more frequently as required	• SOX Dept. and External Auditors	• Senior Company Management
Q4	Advance notices provided of all Fiscal Yearend controls that will be required to be submitted at the fiscal yearend or shortly thereafter.	• SOX Dept.	• Business Units
Q4	Advance notices provided of all Financial Statements Notes controls that will be required to be submitted at the fiscal yearend or shortly thereafter.	• SOX Dept.	• Business Units
Q4	Cutoff date established for changes to Financial Statements Notes Coverage matrix	• Business Units	• SOX Dept.
Q4	Conversion date for External Audit Issues to be promoted to deficiencies established	• SOX Dept. • External Auditors	• Business Units
Q4	External Issue List issues to each pertinent Business Unit with conversion dates from previous	• SOX Dept. • External	• Business Units

| Q4 CALENDAR TEMPLATE ||||
PERIOD	DESCRIPTION	SOURCE	DESTINATION
	step	Auditors	

ASSESSMENT (TESTING) CALENDAR

These are the recommended activity dates that should be included in the Quarterly Calendars published to the Business Units.

RECOMMENDED CALENDAR TEMPLATE

The same assumptions as outlined in the documentation section above are used within this section.

We normally recommend the following assessment cycle should be used throughout the fiscal year. As previously mentioned, you should ensure that the assessments are front end loaded based on the control or processes risk weight. In other words, please test the high risk controls and processes in Q1 and the lower risk items in Q3.

| ASSESSMENT CALENDAR TEMPLATE ||||
PERIOD	DESCRIPTION	SOURCE	DESTINATION
All Quarters	All Tests for **Annual** controls (including their tests) with anniversary dates within Q1 must be documented and submitted to the Repository. *Documentation must be in your standard format and in compliance with your guidelines.*	• Business Unit	• SOX Dept. Repository
All Quarters	All Tests for other controls **based on process or control risk factor.**	• Business Unit	• SOX Dept. Repository
All Quarters	SOX Department Repository Unit executes validation routines versus your business rules for test documentation submitted.	• SOX Dept. Repository	• Business Units
All Quarters	Test Validation exceptions provided to the Business Units with requests for correction by a **specific date with the quarter.**	• SOX Dept. Repository	• Business Units
All Quarters	If available, issue list of untested End to End Process activities for SOX Department Management follow up.	• SOX Dept. Repository	• SOX Dept. Management

DEFICIENCY MANAGEMENT (INCLUDING REMEDIATION PLANS) CALENDAR

The following Deficiency Management steps should be included in the Quarterly calendars issued to the Business Units.

QUARTERLY DEFICIENCY CALENDAR TEMPLATE

PERIOD	DESCRIPTION	SOURCE	DESTINATION
Q1	Carryover of deficiencies from previous year rolled over into new fiscal year in Repository	• SOX Department	• SOX Department
Q1	Confirmation of all open deficiencies with Business Unit from SOX Departments	• SOX Department	• Business Units
Q1	Confirmation Notices filed with SOX Department by Business Units	• Business Units	• SOX Department
Q1 to Q4	Collection and Identification of all individual **transaction** deficiencies from Business Units	• Business Units	• SOX Dept. Deficiency Management Team
Q1 to Q4	Collection and Identification of all individual **entity** deficiencies from Business Units or from Corporate Entity Control Unit	• Business Units • Corporate Entity Control Unit	• SOX Dept. Deficiency Management Team
Q1 to Q4	Collection and Identification of all individual **"other"** deficiencies from Business Units	• Internal Audit, Legal and Compliance	• SOX Dept. Deficiency

Period	Description	Source	Destination
		Depts.	Management Team
Q1 to Q4	Input and validation of all deficiencies and remediation plans to the Deficiency Management System.	• Business Units	• SOX Dept. Deficiency Management Unit
Q1 to Q4	Exception lists of deficiency and remediation plans prepared for • Senior Company Management • Business Units (should contain only the applicable Business Unit's deficiencies and not the entire organizations)	• SOX Dept. Deficiency Management Unit	• Senior Company Management and Business Units
Q1 to Q4	Combination of deficiencies and elimination of duplicates (with x ref keys) these should be based on carry forward deficiencies from the previous yearend	• SOX Dept. Deficiency Management Unit	• SOX Dept. Management
Q1 to Q4	Aggregation of Deficiencies based on your Company's Methodology (based on internal Aggregation keys)	• SOX Dept. Deficiency Management Unit	• SOX Dept. Management
Q1 to Q4	List of aggregated deficiencies provided to CFO and Audit Committee	• SOX Dept.	• Senior Company Management
Q1 to Q4	All other Deficiency Management Reports provided to Senior Company Management in summary and detail format	• SOX Dept.	• Senior Company Management
Q1 to Q4	Warning List of Significant deficiencies about to be promoted to Material Weaknesses (3 months in advance of promotion)	• SOX Dept. Deficiency Management Unit	• SOX Dept. Management
Q1 to Q4	Late or changed remediation plans escalated to Senior Management for corrective actions on a **fortnightly** basis (note for Q1 and Q2, this list should be produced monthly, for Q3 and Q4 this list should be produced fortnightly.)	• SOX Dept.	• Senior Company Management
Q3 / Q4	Reconciliation to External Auditor Deficiencies commences in Q3 and extends through Q4. Listing provided to Senior Company Management and External Auditors	• SOX Dept.	• Senior Company Management • External Auditors
Q1 to Q4	All Entity Control Gaps identified and stored in Deficiency Management files	• SOX Dept. Deficiency Management Unit	• SOX Dept. Deficiency Management Unit
Q1 to Q4	All remediation plans for entity controls files with Repository and Deficiency Management Unit	• SOX Dept. Deficiency Management Unit	• SOX Dept. Deficiency Management Unit
Q1 to Q4	Entity Remediation Plans monitored and exceptions provided to Senior Company Management.	• SOX Dept. Deficiency Management Unit	• Senior Company Management
Q1 to Q4	Entity control remediation exceptions (late or invalid) reports prepared for Senior Company Management	• SOX Dept. Deficiency Management Unit	• Senior Company Management
Q1 to Q4	List of Orphaned End to End Process controls due to a deficiency reviewed and issued to Senior Company Management	• SOX Dept. Deficiency Management Unit	• SOX Dept. Management

SENIOR MANAGEMENT AND COMMITTEE REPORTING CALENDAR

This section outlines the basic calendar for Senior Management Reporting. Additional details are provided in Chapter 8.

The Calendar for these reports usually commences from the Corporate Governance Calendar. Usually the calendar is worked "*backwards*" from the various Board and Committee Meetings that occur at the end of each quarter.

EXAMPLE OF NORMAL CORPORATE CALENDAR

Dates provided in this example are for illustrative purposes only. The following are examples of a Corporate Calendar:

- Yearend Board meeting (for fiscal year 2005) is held on February 15, 2006
- Disclosure Committee Meeting (for fiscal year 2005) is held on February 1, 2006
- Audit Committee Meeting (for fiscal year 2005) is held on February 7, 2006

The SOX Department should have all necessary information ready and delivered to all Audit and Disclosure Committee Members *one week in advance of any of these meetings.*

The CEO and CFO information should be ready and delivered at least *48 hours* prior to the Committee packages being prepared in order to provide CEO and CFO opportunity to make any necessary changes.

PERIOD	DESCRIPTION	SOURCE	DESTINATION
All periods	**Monthly** CEO and CFO Management Reports prepared and delivered.	• SOX Dept.	• CEO and CFO
All periods	**Monthly** Audit Committee Reports delivered one week in advance of Committee meeting (after review by CEO and CFO)	• SOX Dept.	• Audit Committee Members
All periods	Input of all tasks and issues emanating from Committee meetings into Secure Repository.	• Audit Committee Members	• SOX Dept.
All periods	Warning of all Significant Deficiencies about to be promoted	• SOX Dept.	• Committee Members
All periods	Aggregation Reports	• SOX Dept.	• Committee Members

The following section is optional and assumes you would like to adopt a "*best practices*" approach for managing their SOX activities.

PERIOD	DESCRIPTION	SOURCE	DESTINATION
All periods	CEO and CFO (based on input of SOX Department provides regular schedule updates on all items from Committee meetings. It assumes that the SOX Dept. will maintain a confidential Audit Committee Task and Issue List. These will include: • Individual responsible for resolving the issue • Date by which issue will be resolved • Late or escalated items	• CEO / CFO / SOX Dept.	• SOX Dept. Deficiency Management Unit

SUB CERTIFICATION PROCESSES CALENDAR

Because of the diversity of geographical and hierarchical organization levels within some companies, we would recommend that you perform a Quarterly 302 and 404 sub certification on a quarterly basis.

Whilst the regulations do not require a quarterly 404 assertion directly, we believe that this practice reduces the number of unanticipated events or surprises at the fiscal yearend.

We would recommend that you perform a quarterly assertion process for all of the following:

1. LEGAL ENTITIES – these should be required in most companies with international or other complex operations,

2. LOGICAL BUSINESS UNITS e.g. some companies organize on continental or geographical lines e.g. Europe or France – These would provide sub certifications to the Corporate Heads of all summary business units,

3. SUMMARY BUSINESS UNITS e.g. Corporate Level Finance Department – These would be based on the assurances provided by the Logical Business Units.

SUB CERTIFICATION TIMETABLE

Similar to the management reporting section, these should be timed to provide the CEO and CFO with the necessary assurances at least one week prior to Board and Committee meetings.

PERIOD	DESCRIPTION	SOURCE	DESTINATION
Q1 to Q4	Issue all assertions 2 weeks in advance of Board or Committee meetings	• SOX Dept.	• Business Units • Legal Entities
Q1 to Q4	Significant Changes received from Business Units and entered into Repository for specific period.	• Business Units • Legal Entities	• SOX Dept.
Q1 to Q4	Deficiency Confirmation Listing received from Business Units and entered into Repository for specific period.	• Business Units • Legal Entities	• SOX Dept.
Q1 to Q4	Exceptions Listings Received from Business Units and entered into Repository for specific period.	• Business Units • Legal Entities	• SOX Dept.
Q1 to Q4	Summaries of all Significant Changes and Exceptions prepared for CEO and CFO review (deficiencies are prepared as part of Deficiency Management Process).	• SOX Dept.	• CEO • CFO
Q1 to Q4	Late or inaccurate sub certifications list prepared for CEO and CFO action	• SOX Dept.	• CEO • CFO
Q1 to Q4	Assertion Summary prepared for Audit Committee and Board of Directors	• SOX Dept.	• Board of Directors • Audit Committee

EXTERNAL AUDIT COORDINATION CALENDAR

The Calendar should provide all External Auditor activities to the Business Units, Board and Audit Committees.

Each Business Unit should have an opportunity to review the proposed engagement dates for the Auditors (within their units) and to provide feedback to the SOX Department at least one quarter in advance of the proposed dates in the event of scheduling conflicts within the Business Unit.

TRAINING CALENDARS

A listing of recommended courses is provided at the end of Chapter 2 – *Prerequisites for Sarbanes Oxley*. All Training Seminars should be published one quarter in advance of the proposed date.

Registrations should be finalized one month in advance of the Training date by the SOX Department.

SUMMARY

This chapter has provided you with the framework for developing the plans and calendars required for both the initial and ongoing efforts. Within each section of the framework, we have also provided the detailed requirements for each section.

NEXT STEPS

1. Develop a framework for your future plans and calendars – using the initial section of this chapter,

2. Develop a preliminary Standard SOX template that will be used quarterly. Modify the template provided in this chapter to meet your requirements. Review this calendar with your entire SOX Community and make further modifications as required,

3. Develop a preliminary fiscal yearend calendar and review with your External Auditors, and

4. Develop the procedures for all Non Plan items.

CHAPTER 6 – THE SOX REPOSITORY

The SOX Repository is the information nucleus of the SOX Department because it is the unit in which all SOX data is securely stored and analyzed. All company wide SOX analyses and reporting should only be based data that is resident in this Repository.

This chapter focuses on establishing and sustaining all the necessary Repository processes that are required. It also provides a brief introduction into the type of reports and metrics that should be provided to the SOX Community.

BACKGROUND

The Public Company Accounting Oversight Board's (PCAOB) Standard 2 is the standard used by most Auditors to perform Sarbanes Oxley Audits. Section 20 of the Standard (December 2004 edition) states that:

"Management's Responsibilities in an Audit of Internal Control over Financial Reporting:

20. For the auditor to satisfactorily complete an audit of internal control over financial reporting, management must do the following:[24]

a. Accept responsibility for the effectiveness of the company's internal control over financial reporting;
b. Evaluate the effectiveness of the company's internal control over financial reporting using suitable control criteria;
*c. **Support its evaluation with sufficient evidence, including documentation**; and*
*d. Present a **written assessment** of the effectiveness of the company's internal control over financial reporting as of the end of the company's most recent fiscal year."*

The responsibility for management to maintain evidence of its internal control framework activities, including assessment activities, exists in several sections of this standard and also indirectly in the Sarbanes Oxley Act itself (reference – *Inspection of Registered Public Accounting Firms*).

This chapter reviews the process for documenting and analyzing the assessment of the internal control framework and the maintenance of the required evidence.

IMPLEMENTATION STEPS

The steps required for the implementation of a Repository into four main classes for organizational purposes.

INITIAL SETUP

1. DEFINITION OF THE REPOSITORY FUNCTIONS. These have been previous discussed in Chapters 1 and 2 of this volume.

2. PREREQUISITES FOR THE REPOSITORY. These have been previous discussed in Chapters 1 and 2 of this volume.

---

24 24 Management is required to fulfill these responsibilities. See Items 308(a)and (c) of Regulation S-B and S-K, 17 C.F.R. 228.308 (a) and (c) and 229.308 (a) and (c), respectively.

3. INITIAL SET UP. The initial steps required to set up the Repository.

ONGOING REPOSITORY OPERATIONS

4. REPOSITORY DOCUMENTS – the documents that should be securely stored and maintained within the Repository. Some of these have been introduced to you in previous chapters.

5. REPOSITORY ACCEPTANCE / VALIDATION OF SOX DOCUMENTATION. The processes to be used when receiving documents into the Repository. This should include validation, rejection and inventory verification processes.

REPORTING AND ANALYSIS FUNCTIONS

6. IMPORT AND ANALYSIS FUNCTIONS. The processes to be used to import data elements into a relational data base management system (or similar tool) for analysis and reporting.

7. REPORTING FUNCTIONS. The reporting processes for preparing reports for the Business Units, SOX Department Managers, Senior Company Managers, Board and Committee members, External Auditors, etc.

SPECIAL FUNCTIONS

8. PREPARATION FOR AUDITS. The Repository should take special steps to be prepared for both Internal and External Audits. These steps should be part of the ongoing operations but must be closely managed.

DEFINITION OF THE SOX REPOSITORY

A Repository is the *secure* storage facility in which all documentation and analyses supporting management's assessment of the internal control environment are maintained..

The Repository is the primary source of data / information used in all internal and external reporting. The routines or code modules used for analysis and reporting should also be maintained within a special restricted *data library section* of the Repository.

Optionally, it is also the storage facility for all External Auditor SOX work papers that have been delivered to your company during the course of the audit. We strongly recommend you adopt this option as it provides a single source for all documentation.

THE SOX REPOSITORY

FUNCTIONS PERFORMED BY THE REPOSITORY DEPARTMENT

The Repository is the critical unit within the SOX Organization because of its mandate to provide accurate, validated information upon which management's SOX assessments are based.

This function is responsible the primary for the following tasks:

1. RECEIVING / ACCEPTING all documentation into the repository for process and control documentation, Assessment (Test) Testing, Deficiency updates, Remediation Plans. Entity Surveys, etc. based on your company's internal business rules,

2. VALIDATING all documentation received to ensure that they meet your business rules for SOX documentation designed by the Methodology Unit within the SOX Department. Items rejected must be identified, managed, followed up and escalated when required,

3. ANALYZING the documents received into the repository and, more importantly, identifying all *missing* documentation. The Repository staff must be responsible for ensuring that the data received is accurate (random sampling or other method), validated (based on your validation rules) and is complete (meeting financial statement scope requirements[25], etc.),

   In addition, the Repository function must also be responsible for the preparation of all analyses used by management in their assessment of the internal control framework.

4. REPORTING to management, external auditors, business units and other interested parties based on the data and analyses that are stored / prepared within the repository.

   The repository should also prepare the reports and presentations for Management, the Board and other Committees or this can be assigned to a separate group within the SOX Department. *It is however imperative that the information used in these presentations be accurate and validated and ONLY repository data should be employed in any management reporting.*

5. ESCALATING, as required, to company management all items requiring their attention including non compliance with Corporate and External regulations

Please note that whilst the repository is the source for all Policies, etc. It is not the preparer of this material in the SOX Department's organization chart – this is the role of the Methodology Unit.

PREREQUISITES FOR THE REPOSITORY

This section details the prerequisites that should be completed prior to the implementation of a Repository. The development of these items normally requires the dedication of two individuals with *practical SOX experience* for approximately 15-30 calendar days, depending on the size of your company. We have provided estimated time lines and decisions points throughout this section.

PROCESSES, METHODS AND TOOLS

Most of the data received by the Repository will be in an electronic format. The data that is received in physical format should be stored based on your company's existing standards for storage of confidential, regulatory, physical documents.

The processes, methods and tools listed in this section provide you with a step by step approach to implementing your Repository.

---

[25] FINANCIAL STATEMENT SCOPE REQUIREMENTS – the results of the Financial Statements Risk Assessment process which assigns the responsibility by Business Unit for Significant Accounts and Significant Processes. Refer to Chapter on Financial Statements Risk Assessment Process.

STEP 1 – ESTABLISH THE REPOSITORY STORAGE MEDIUM

Many companies maintain their documentation in an electronic format. Several of these companies use spreadsheets, word processing documents, graphics tools, etc. In rare instances, some documentation is also maintained in a non-digital format.

Many companies have compiled their SOX data into relational database management systems or documentation systems for analysis and reporting purposes. Your company needs to evaluate the best tools, formats and processes to be used to store, analyses and report on SOX information.

The various automation alternatives are reviewed in the last section of this chapter.

SOX REPOSITORY PROCESSES, METHODS AND TOOLS

Step 1 - Establish the storage medium to be used for Repository	Step 2 - Establish inventory of all SOX documents to be stored in Repository	Step 3 - Define content / elements for each document defined in Step 2	Step 4 - Define the validation rules for each document and its elements	Step 5 - Define the preliminary list of Reports and Analyses

Step 3a - Define supporting documentation of evidence

STEP 2 – DEVELOP / ESTABLISH INVENTORY OF REQUIRED SOX DOCUMENTS

The SOX Department should develop an inventory of all documentation that will be stored within the Repository. This inventory must establish the following:

1. THE NAME OF THE DOCUMENT required to be provided to the Repository – for example, all process documentation is to delivered to the Repository by March 31

2. THE ORIGINATOR/ SOURCE OF THE DOCUMENT – the Business Units (and the individual - title only) that should be submitting the document to the Repository,

3. THE FREQUENCY OR DATE by/for which the document is to be submitted to the Repository,

4. THE DOCUMENT FORMAT – the format in which the Repository requires the document to be filed in. Many companies use Spreadsheets, Word Processing documents.

The following is the minimum series of inventories that should be developed by the Repository team prior to the Initial Set Up phase for the Repository.

1. SOX METHODOLOGY DOCUMENTS that should be maintained within the Repository. These should be included:

    - SOX Policies,
    - SOX Process Documentation Procedures,
    - SOX Risk Assessment Procedures,
    - SOX Assessment Procedures and Guidelines,
    - SOX Sub Certification Procedures,
    - SOX Entity Level Program Processes,
    - SOX Analysis and Reporting Procedures, and
    - SOX Department Procedures.

2. PROCESS, CONTROL, DEFICIENCY AND REMEDIATION DOCUMENTATION required to be submitted by Business Units. This inventory will vary based on the results from Financial Statements Risk assessment which produces lists of significant processes and accounts that are required to be documented by specific business units or locations.

   Typically, this inventory usually comprises of the following information which is in turn used to ensure that all documentation is received at the end of the fiscal quarter::

   - Fiscal Period e.g. 200601
   - Business Unit ID – Finance _ Europe,
   - Significant Account – Account ABCD1234,
   - Significant Process – Process SVREG19

   The inventory can be decomposed into a more granular format depending on your company's use of standardized processes and controls as outlined in earlier chapters.

   For example, if a business unit has been assigned a significant Account of "Fixed Assets". There may be a standard process for "Depreciation Computations" which comprises of 26 process steps and 8 controls. Therefore the inventory would now contain the details of this standard process and the due date.

3. FINANCIAL STATEMENT DOCUMENTS and work papers that must be provided by the Finance Division for the Risk Assessment process and subsequent assignment of Significant Account coverage responsibilities to the operating Business Units,

4. ENTITY LEVEL CONTROL Plans – This should comprise of a list detailing the following (assuming a COSO framework):

   - COSO Component e.g. Control Environment,
   - Point of Focus e.g. Anti Fraud Program,
   - Control (if different from Point of focus),
   - Evidentiary Material e.g. Policy, Interview(s),
   - Assessment Results,
   - Remediation Plans, etc.

5. ASSESSMENT (TEST) RESULTS (Assessment Results forms), and

6. SUB CERTIFICATIONS required from the operating Business Units on a periodic basis which provides Senior Company Management with the current information on the state of the internal control framework within these units.

   - Period e.g. 200602
   - Business Unit ID or Legal Entity e.g. Finance Europe
   - Business Unit Role, and
   - Sub certification document/form required

STEP 3 – DEVELOP / ESTABLISH DOCUMENT FORMATS - CONTENT / ELEMENTS

For each document defined in the inventory in Step 2, the SOX Department must also define the required *format* for each document. This format must clearly define required elements (the ID and Dates are provided as examples and Optional Elements (Process Connectors are provided as an example)

1. The REQUIRED ID that must be included for that specific document. For example, control documents must contain a unique control ID that comprises of the Significant Process ID, the Business Unit ID and the Control Sequence number.

2. The REQUIRED DATES that must be included in each document. Typical examples of these are:

    - Anniversary dates for annual controls,
    - Date control was first implemented,
    - Date control was last reviewed by Business Unit Management,
    - Date control was last changed,
    - Date control was last tested (all previous test dates should be saved in separate file for audit archival purposes)

3. PROCESS TO PROCESS CONNECTORS – You must establish connectors for end to end process transitions. You should also ensure that that you clearly define the validation rules for process to process connections.

In the illustration below, we provide a detailed example of one document – The financial statements worksheet that should be used in the Risk Assessment process.

DELIVERABLE REQUIRED: Document content layouts for each document to be stored in the Repository. If the Repository tool is an automated system this should be acquired from your Vendor or your Database Administrator.

Example (illustrative purposes only): Financial Statements for Risk Assessment table:

- Period (must include period as some accounts will be added or retired depending on period) – REQUIRED.
- Financial Statement Line Number (or other unique ID) or Note ID – REQUIRED.,
- Financial Statement Description (as appears on public Financial Statements – REQUIRED.,
- Financial Assertions – REQUIRED.
    - Existence
    - Occurrence
    - Completeness
    - Rights & Obligations
    - Valuation
- Balance in U$ – REQUIRED.
- Balance Sheet Indicator – REQUIRED.
- Income Statement Indicator – REQUIRED.
- Notes Indicator – REQUIRED.
- Originator – REQUIRED.
- Date of record – REQUIRED.
- Comments - OPTIONAL

Key for content is Period, Financial Statement Line Number and Significant Account ID

STEP 3A – DEFINE SUPPORTING DOCUMENTATION REQUIREMENTS

In our experience, it is a prudent practice to ensure that the Repository maintains all supporting information that relates to SOX processes. These documents are usually prepared by other departments within the company for non SOX related purposes but are used within SOX processes.

The SOX Department should also develop an inventory of supporting documents required similar to that in Step 1. The format and contents of this supporting documentation may need to be negotiated with the primary suppliers and users of the evidence. Alternately, the SOX Department, depending on its mandate, may request from originating departments a specific SOX format for its use.

Typical examples of supporting documentation are:

1. CROSS REFERENCE OF FINANCIAL STATEMENT LINES TO SIGNIFICANT ACCOUNTS – whilst not a part of the actual SOX documentation; this information is critical to supporting the SOX Financial Statement Risk Assessment process and resulting analysis data for audit trail purposes,

2. INTERNAL AUDIT REPORTS identifying deficiencies that impact Financial Reporting. Usually these are operating unit audits that are conducted in the course of normal business for the Internal Audit Department. However, if any of the deficiencies identified have an impact on the company's financial reporting, these must be added to the SOX deficiency list,

3. FINANCE DIVISION ERROR LOGS - since these may become the source of identifying deficiencies. Normally, a Finance Error Log is maintained for audit and process improvement purposes but it can also double as a deficiency identification source by establishing where detective, preventative or monitoring types of controls have failed,

4. EVIDENCE LISTS – Some elements of the evidence list is critical in the Entity Level Control assessment. The list should maintain, at a minimum, the following:

    - The location of key documents (physical or electronic locations) e.g. HR Policies on the company web site, etc., and
    - Key company contacts for evidence preparation and maintenance e.g. Company Organization Chart and Assignment of Responsibilities in Manual ABD or on a company webpage.

DELIVERABLE REQUIRED: Document content layouts for each document to be stored in the Repository. If the Repository tool is an automated system this should be acquired from your Vendor or your Database Administrator.

Example (illustrative purposes only): Financial Statement to Significant Account Cross Reference:

- Period (must include period as some accounts will be added or retired depending on period)
- Financial Statement Line Number (or other unique ID) or Note ID,
- Financial Statement Description (as appears on public Financial Statements,
- Significant Account ID
- Significant Account Description
- Financial Assertions
    - Existence
    - Occurrence
    - Completeness
    - Rights & Obligations
    - Valuation
- Originator
- Date of record
- Comments

Key for content is Period, Financial Statement Line Number and Significant Account ID

STEP 4 – DEFINE DATA MANAGEMENT AND VALIDATION RULES

Ensuring that the Repository data is of the highest integrity and accuracy is the primary objective. Since the entire company's assessment will be based on the analyses and reports produce from this data, the integrity and accuracy of this data is paramount to the company's management assess of the internal control framework.

In order to ensure that the data meets these high standards, the SOX Department must establish the validation rules that all Repository data will be subjected to upon submission by the operating Business Units.

These validation rules are executed at the point of entry into the Repository and may vary based on the level of your company's automation. For example, if your company uses a web page for submission of SOX data, these validation rules should be executed at the time of submission and the user immediately advised of any validation errors. If your organization submits its data via spreadsheets or other digital format, these validation rules should execute at the time of import into the repository database.

The data management (e.g. backup, recovery, access security, etc.) for the Repository should be based on your company's *existing* IT standards.

In developing the validation and data management rules, the following should be considered:

1. Data should be stored in its *original* form when received from the Business Units.

   It is critical that no changes be made to the originals of these documents by anyone other than the originator as it may invalidate related documents.

   For example, if you change a Internal Control Document you may invalidate its related Assessment (Test) results, which was based on information that you changed in the original control document,

2. Data within each individual record should be validated versus an established set of business rules for record formats and content that clearly outline:

   - REQUIRED FIELDS or elements,
   - FORMAT OF DATA within fields (alpha / numeric),
   - PERMITTED LIST of values (as maintained and updated in master files),
   - RELATIONSHIPS BETWEEN DIFFERENT ELEMENTS within the same record (remediation plan date provided but type of deficiency not provided – then the logical question is why is there a remediation plan), and
   - ORIGINATOR / TIME STAMP - All data / documents should have an originator and time stamp based on the document's acceptance. This should be required for all formats of data including records within a relational database management system.

3. The dataset of records should be validated versus an established set of business rules for *datasets* (e.g. process sets, control sets by Business Unit).

   For example, if all significant process documentation has been submitted, the validation rules should compare the documents received versus the inventory list of anticipated documents to determine whether there are any *missing* documents.

   Another typical example is the process to process connection validation. This validation can only be performed when all process documentation for the entire company is received. The validation process checks all process to process connectors to ensure that there is a valid process on both sides of each connector. If there is a missing process, the originating department should be immediately advised.

   We have seen instances where an Accounts Payable process was linked to a completely unrelated type of process (an interest estimation process) and therefore invalidated the end to end connection. This is usually automated by the use of process / sub process codes.

4. Your company should optionally construct a conversion process / routine for gathering all documentation into a Relational Database Management System (or similar tool) for analysis and reporting purposes.

STEP 5 – DEFINE INITIAL ANALYSIS AND REPORTING REQUIREMENTS

The SOX Department, using this Repository's data, must produce the analyses and reports that assist the SOX community to assess the effectiveness of the internal control framework. Prior to producing these analyses, the Repository must be examined to ensure that its data is complete, accurate and valid.

Upon final closing, prior to publishing its analyses and reports, the Repository should examine the contents for the reporting period and produce the following reports:

1. DOCUMENTATION NOT RECEIVED – Based on the Inventories developed in Step 2, the Repository must compare the documents received to the Inventory and report on any missing documentation to company management for escalation purposes and to advise that reporting is incomplete,.

2. INVALID DOCUMENTATION RECEIVED – invalid documentation received from the Business Units are identified in the validation process. The Repository is responsible for advising SOX Department Management of all invalid documentation. The corrected documentation must be received prior to producing any analyses and reports.

In the chapter 8 - Reporting and Metrics, we provide you with a list of recommended analyses and reports that should be produced on a periodic basis. You should review this list and customize where necessary.

ESTABLISHING THE REPOSITORY

We have provided no specific references to any specific technical tools and have kept all statements in this section as generic as possible.

Depending on the tools that you will be using for your Repository, you should modify these steps to meet your tool's capabilities and requirements.

1. Establish Logical IT SECURITY ACCESSES to the Repository based on your company's information security policies and procedures,

2. Implement a DIRECTORY OR OTHER DATA STRUCTURE to accommodate document types, periods, versions of periods and sources e.g. if you are using spreadsheets or word processing documents, establish a directory for document type, within this directory establish a directory by fiscal period, file documents by business unit using the Business ID as part of the naming convention of the document,

3. Implement the DATA FORMATS for the relational database or other tool that you will use to analyze and to report on SOX data,

4. Install all VALIDATION processes/modules (that have been developed within the PREREQUISITES chapter) and test in the new Repository environment,

5. Install all ANALYSIS processes/modules (that have been developed within the PREREQUISITES chapter) and test in the new Repository environment,

6. Install all REPORTING modules (that have been developed within the PREREQUISITES chapter) and test in the Repository Environment

REPOSITORY DOCUMENTS

This is the minimum list of documents that should be maintained with your repository.

REFERENCE LIBRARY - SOX POLICIES, PROCESSES, GUIDELINES AND INSTRUCTIONS

These should be maintained by Version Number and Publication Date within the Reference Library section of the Repository.

Each document should be prefaced with a standard cover sheet listing the Subject, Author, Effective date, Approval Date, Version No., Previous Version, future Revision Date, etc.

- Internal Control Framework Policies,
- Entity Level Control Program – Policies and Procedures,
- Entity Level Control Program Test Guidelines,
- Transaction (Process) Level Process / Control Documentation Manual – this must include all validation, exception reporting and escalation processes,
- Transaction (Process) Level Process / Control Testing Guidelines – This will be updated and published on a periodic basis in order to provide the Business Units with the requirements to be achieved each quarter,
- IT Processes and Controls Policies and Procedures – this manual should clearly define the responsibilities of the IT Department and those of the Business Units,
- End User Computing Processes and Controls Policies and Procedures,
- IT General Computing Controls Procedures,
- Deficiency Management Procedures,
- Deficiency Aggregation Procedures,
- External Vendors Policies and Procedures Manual for all documentation and assessment processes,
- Sub certification Procedural manual – explaining the entire organization's roll up of certifications to the CEO/CFO Level, and
- Senior Management Reports and Preparation Procedures.

FINANCE STATEMENT RISK ASSESSMENT WORK SHEETS AND SUPPORTING DOCUMENTS

The repository should maintain all Financial Statement Risk Assessment worksheets by quarter and fiscal year. For additional details on this process, please refer to the chapter on Financial Statements Risk Assessment. This includes the following:

1. All files received from the Finance Division including financial statements and cross reference tables (for significant accounts and subordinate general ledger systems),

2. The Financial Statement Exception listings – listing by Significant Account of the Business Units that have failed to meet their coverage requirements,

3. All changes requested by Business Units for significant account coverage (this is the form used by a Business Unit to advise of their objection to the assignment of a significant account or process), and

4. Evidence of coverage by Significant Account and Business Unit – the data maintained must be reviewed / approved by the External Auditor.

TRANSACTION PROCESS/ CONTROL DOCUMENTATION

All process and control documentation should be stored within the Repository by quarter, fiscal year and by submission date.

This checklist should be developed jointly with the Business Coordination Unit of the SOX Department and be used as the basis for management reporting and escalation processes.

We would recommend that the Repository should include, at a minimum, the following items by quarter, fiscal year and Business Unit:

1. PROCESS FLOW CHARTS (Maps) – outlining the Process Flows within each business unit in prescribed format (must include all process to process connectors),

2. PROCESS DOCUMENTATION (NARRATIVE) – the description of each process step in prescribed format,

3. KEY CONTROL DOCUMENTATION – the description of each control in prescribed format. This should include any standard controls.

4. SEGREGATION OF DUTIES TEMPLATES – for the Business Unit and its processes,

5. ASSESSMENT documentation – evidence of walkthroughs and tests (see section below), etc.

ENTITY LEVEL PROGRAM DOCUMENTATION

All pertinent worksheets outlining the components, points of focus, controls, evidence, surveys, and interviews should be stored and maintained within the Repository.

ASSESSMENT (TEST) RESULTS

All test results should be stored by Control ID and Fiscal Period. Test results should be summarized by an automated process into the Repository database for analysis and reporting purposes.

Normally, because of volume and formats, the Repository should not be responsible for storing test evidence or working papers attributed to the test. These should be maintained within the local Business Unit's facilities. However, the results must provide the location of this evidence (e.g. a directory, a physical filing location, etc.)

We would recommend that the Repository should maintain the following documents (at a minimum) by Quarter, by Business Unit, by Fiscal Year with valid cross reference IDs to the specific control or process being tested.

1. TEST RESULTS by Quarter by Fiscal Year by Business Unit in Control ID sequence,

2. DEFICIENCY REPORTS (the form on which the Business Unit reports the deficiency – may be a part of the test template) by Quarter, by Fiscal Year, by Business Unit in Control ID Sequence, and

3. REMEDIATION ACTION PLANS by Quarter, by Fiscal Year, by Business Unit in Control ID Sequence.

These should all be converted into the relational database for analysis and reporting on a quarterly basis,

DEFICIENCY LISTINGS

Assuming that the information in the previous sections is converted into the Repository's relational database (or similar tool), the following must be produced and stored within the repository. Remediation Plan updates should be requested monthly from the Business Units.

These should be prepared on a monthly basis except at fiscal yearend when they should be prepared weekly.

1. DEFICIENCY LISTS BY BUSINESS UNITS – combined with the Deficiency update file displaying last three months of updates,

2. DEFICIENCY LISTS BY CONTROL RISK– combined with the Deficiency update file displaying last three months of updates,

3. DEFICIENCY LISTS BY FINANCIAL STATEMENT LINE - th,

4. REMEDIATION PLAN LISTS BY BUSINESS UNIT – combined with the Deficiency update file displaying last three months of updates,

5. REMEDIATION PLAN LISTS BY CONTROL RISK – combined with the Deficiency update file displaying last three months of updates,

6. REMEDIATION PLAN LISTS BY QUARTER, and

7. PERIOD OVER PERIOD RECONCILIATIONS FOR DEFICIENCIES – these are critical for determine data integrity within the Repository files, and

8. CLOSED DEFICIENCIES – maintained on a monthly or update basis.

SUB CERTIFICATIONS

This Repository should be responsible for the collection and validation of all mini certifications and assertions for Legal Entities, Business Units.

The Repository should store and catalogue all Assertion Exception forms by Business Unit/Legal Entity, Quarter and Fiscal Year.

SIGNIFICANT CHANGES

All significant changes received from Business Units or Legal Entities should be converted into the Repository Database by Source, Quarter and Fiscal Year.

Null reports should also be filed in order to execute completeness checks.

FINANCE DIVISION ERROR LOGS

In the course of the Finance Division's review of the Financial Statements or other error check mechanisms, there are occasions when errors are identified (and corrected)

It is customary for the Finance Division to maintain an Error log of these items (and the corrective action taken). It is also important that the Finance Division be instructed to document WHO identified the error – Internal personnel or External Auditors.

These logs must be stored in the Repository. They must then be processed by the SOX Department, Finance Division and Business Coordination Unit in order to determine:

1. The Business Unit responsible for the error – the error should be reviewed with the Business Unit to determine whether it was the Business Unit's control that failed or a control within the Central Finance Division,

2. Whether a control exists to prevent this error – and if "*yes*", the Control ID should be appended to the error record – this information depends on the answer to the previous question,

3. Whether a control exists to detect the error – and if "*yes*", the Control ID should be appended to the error record - this information depends on the answer to the first question,

4. The entity identifying the error – External or Internal. If an internal entity identified the error then the control identified in Step 2 must be marked operationally defective. If it was an External Party then both controls (Steps 2 & 3) must be marked as operationally deficient

5. The remedial action taken – Whether any remedial steps have been taken and whether the control has been retested,

6. The dollar amount of the error,

7. The currency of the dollar amount,

8. The Significant Account(s) to which this error is attributed, and

9. The Financial Statement Line to which this error is attributed

REPOSITORY ACCEPTANCE OF SOX DOCUMENTS

Upon completing the initial setup, the Repository should begin accepting documentation into the repository based on the procedures outlined in this section.

INITIAL RECEIPT

The following are the steps that should be employed upon receipt of documentation. This applies to all documentation.

1. Check the documentation versus the documentation Inventory list – *do not mark as received until the documentation successfully passes the validation step,*

2. Validate the documentation versus the business rules (preferably with the use of the validation modules developed in the PREREQUISITES section)

3. If the documentation fails the validation, it is to be returned to the Business Unit with a listing of all exceptions and the date by which the exceptions are to be corrected. If you are using an online system to capture this information, this step should be encompassed

in your online validation sequence – the user should receive an immediate invalid entry message with detailed correction message, and

4. The documentation log (listing of all documents submitted) is to be updated with the all pertinent details.

DOCUMENTATION INVENTORY PROCESS

The documentation inventory is the primary method of determining whether all required documentation is received on time.

Items that have not been received by their required date must be immediately escalated to the SOX Department Management for follow up action. This includes any items that have failed validation. *The repository should not accept invalid information.*

REJECTION ANALYSIS

The Repository should provide SOX Department Management with an analysis of the rejections on a periodic, document type, and business unit basis.

As the history files grow, emerging patterns can be easily identified so that remedial action can be taken with the Businesses Unit involved.

ANALYSIS FUNCTIONS

The Repository should perform, at a minimum, the following analyses for SOX Management Review. Collectively, these analyses should be combined into a QUARTERLY REPOSITORY ANALYSIS REPORT.

In addition, the Repository should be prepared to deliver certain specific "on demand" analyses when requested by Business Units or company management

TEST ANALYSES

Depending on the Guidelines that you develop, SOX Management should receive on a quarterly basis, a test analysis report outlining the progress of testing.

We have detailed these reports in our Reporting and Metrics Reports (Chapter 8) because of the density of calculations and other derived information that is required to perform this analysis/reporting function.

TRANSACTION DEFICIENCY DISTRIBUTION REPORT

This report should comprise of two sections – Summary and Detail Sections. The sum of the Detail sections must reconcile to the summary section totals.

SUMMARY (CORPORATE LEVEL) Section that details at the corporate level the following information:

- Vertical Axis – The Risk level of the control e.g. High Risk, Routine, Non Routine, etc.
- Horizontal Axis – Design Deficiencies, Operating Deficiencies, Other deficiencies, Total deficiencies

The DETAIL section should provide the same information by Business Unit on individual pages. These should be distributed to the Business Units and the Business Coordination Unit within the SOX Department.

EXTERNAL AUDITOR ISSUE REPORT

It should be recognized that Audit issues may occur at the Corporate Level, Business Unit Level, Process Level or individual control level. It is the responsibility of the SOX Department, upon receipt of an External Audit issue, to assign the responsibility to the correct level within your company. This assignment should be to the lowest level possible and not kept at a Corporate level, wherever possible.

These issues should be reported in both Summary and by organizational level. With the issues detailed by organizational level, it will provide management with the necessary information for remedial action.. All detail reports should reconcile to the totals on the Summary report. Issues should be ranked in a priority sequence *by the External Auditor* for reporting and remediation purposes.

OTHER DEFICIENCY DISTRIBUTION REPORT

This is similar to the External Auditor Issue Report with the following exceptions:

- the source of the deficiencies must be identified (e.g. NYSE, SEC, etc.),
- the deficiency must be cross referenced to a transactional control deficiency if a duplication exists.

TESTS (ASSESSMENT) EXCEPTIONS

This analysis should be provided in two sections – Summary and Business Unit Levels.

This report should outline all Tests that have not met Management guidelines with the summary section detailing the data at a corporate level. We would recommend that the risk level of the controls be used as the vertical axis.

SUB CERTIFICATION EXCEPTIONS

This should detail all sub certifications that have not been received by the required date for all organizational levels..

REMEDIATION PLANS DISTRIBUTION

This Analysis has to be executed in three sequences – Frequency, Quarter that the activity is targeted and Control Risk rating.

The analysis should provide summaries as follows:

1. RISK / QUARTER SUMMARY – detailing the Control risks on the Vertical axis and the distribution of remediation plans by quarter on the Horizontal axis,

2. RISK / QUARTER / BUSINESS UNIT – same as Risk Quarter Summary except each page should display the detail for specific Business Units,

3. FREQUENCY / QUARTER SUMMARY – detailing the Control Frequency on the Vertical axis and the distribution of remediation plans by quarter on the Horizontal axis. Special attention should be paid to the Annual and Fiscal Yearend Frequencies, and

4. RISK / QUARTER / BUSINESS UNIT – same as Frequency / Quarter Summary except each page should display the detail for specific Business Units,

REMEDIATION PLAN EXCEPTIONS

This analysis should identify all remediation plans that are not within Management Guidelines and would formatted as the reports in the previous section.

REPORTING FUNCTIONS

In this section, we focus on three classes of Reports

1. BOARD COMMITTEE REPORTING requirements,
2. SENIOR MANAGEMENT REPORTING requirements, and
3. EXTERNAL AUDIT REPORTING Requirements.

BOARD COMMITTEE REPORTING

These Board and its committees should receive the following minimum reports and/or presentations. The Repository will be required to provide the information required for these reports. The actual preparation of the reports/ presentations may be the responsibility of Units other than the Repository within the SOX Department.

1. FINANCIAL STATEMENT COVERAGE REPORT - This should be based on documentation received and validated in the repository for the fiscal year. The information should display Financial Statement Line on the Vertical Axis. The Horizontal Axis should display the Control Risk Level, The Number of Controls, the coverage percentage based on the Significant Account Analysis.

    This is a Summary report that must be supported by the Detail report in the Senior Management Section below.

2. ENTITY CONTROL COVERAGE REPORT - This is a progress report on the documentation and testing progress throughout the fiscal year. The report should display all COSO Components, points of focus and related controls and the assessment results.

    Exceptions should be highlighted for Board and Committee review.

3. ASSESSMENT (TEST) COVERAGE BY FINANCIAL STATEMENT LINE REPORT - The Report provides progress on assessment coverage and results on a cumulative basis for the fiscal year. The information should display Financial Statement Line on the Vertical Axis.

    The Horizontal Axis should display the Control Risk level, The Number of Controls, The number of controls tested to date, the percentage of controls tested to date, the number of deficiencies identified to date, the percentage of deficiencies versus the number of controls tested.

4. DEFICIENCY STATUS REPORT - The report should be subdivided by risk level, region and function.

    Usually the Board and its committees focus on the significant deficiencies and material weaknesses. Therefore the Committee should receive a status report by control risk factor and deficiency type. The Vertical axis should be the control risk type and the horizontal axis should be the deficiency type e.g. deficiency, significant deficiency, material weakness.

This Summary Report must be supported by a Business Unit detail report that displays the above information by Business Unit.

5. REMEDIATION STATUS - The report provides the status of all deficiencies (gaps) and remediation action plans with specific emphasis on material weaknesses and significant deficiencies.

    The report should display on the Vertical Axis the Control risk type and on the Horizontal Axis the Remediation quarters by Deficiency Type.

6. ISSUES AND CONCERNS REPORT - The information contained in this report is accumulated from all sources including External Auditors, Regulators, etc. This should be based on the External Auditor's priority code on the Horizontal Axis and by Business Unit on the Vertical Axis.

SENIOR MANAGEMENT REPORTS

The following are the recommended reports that should be issued to your company's Senior Management.

1. INTERNAL CONTROL FRAMEWORK SUMMARY - This report should have a vertical axis of Financial Statement lines. The Horizontal Axis should provide a subdivision by Control Type with related test and deficiency results,

2. SUMMARY AND SUPPORTING DETAILS OF TEST RESULTS - This report should be based on the same format provided to the various Board Committees. The Senior Management's report should contain an additional section providing the information at the Business Unit Level that summarized up to the Corporate Summary provided to the various committees.

3. COMPREHENSIVE DEFICIENCY REPORTS - The Senior Management's Deficiency Reports should summarize into the reports provided to the various Board Committees. The report must be organized by Business Unit so that Senior Management can take any necessary remedial action.

    These deficiency reports should also provide aggregated deficiencies and the action plans for remediation of these aggregated items at the same time.

4. REMEDIATION REPORTS - This report should provide the detail supporting the Board Committee reports in the previous section,

PREPARATION FOR AUDITS

The SOX Department can anticipate being audited by two entities – External Auditors and Regulators and/or your Internal Audit Department.

The preparation for an Audit should be based on the following list and the engagement letter issued by the Auditor or Regulator. We would recommend that the Repository perform these functions on a quarterly basis in the event of a surprise audit. However, we would recommend that the Repository execute the following steps in advance of an Audit or Quarterly, whichever is sooner.

SECURITY ACCESSES

Validate and confirm all Security Accesses to the Repository on a monthly basis. We assume that the IT Department and HR Department have a coordinated process whereby security accesses are updated throughout your company.

COMPLETENESS CHECKS

The Repository will execute and evidence completeness check to ensure that the Repository has received a full suite of documentation from all Business Units, Legal Entities and other pertinent parties.

The evidence for this is the Documentation Inventory listings referenced earlier in this chapter. The Department must demonstrate all escalation efforts, etc. necessary to complete the Repository requirements

AUDIT TRAILS

The repository is a storage unit that is not permitted to change or alter documentation received from their originators. The Repository is only permitted to change information it has derived from the source data provided by the Business Units or other sources.

The Audit trails within the Repository database must display all change records and the User IDs for all records. None of these should be Repository or SOX Department staff as that may invalidate the sub certifications.

EVIDENCE OF REPORTS TO AUDIT COMMITTEE

Copies of all Audit Committee and Board reports and presentations must be maintained within the Repository by preparation date and fiscal period.

AUTOMATION ALTERNATIVES FOR THE REPOSITORY

The Repository may be developed using different levels of automation. To determine which tools meet your needs best, you need to perform a functional review for the Repository as outlined in the table below.

POTENTIAL TOOLS

The tools examined in the comparison table below are:

1. SPREADSHEET OR WORD PROCESSING PROGRAMS – these are the simplest tools to use that already exist within most companies. Their usage is usually pervasive throughout an organization.

2. DOCUMENTATION SYSTEMS – these are systems that are used mainly to organize and store documents in a corporate environment. Some of these systems have comprehensive library capabilities

3. RELATIONAL DATABASE MANAGEMENT SYSTEMS – are usually operated by the IT division and require the construction of a user interface and validation routines, if developed from scratch. Usually requires extensive IT Resources, and

4. SOX MANAGEMENT SYSTEM – very few of these exist, despite the marketing hype that abounds these systems. Simply stated a SOX Management system must include all the functions listed in this chapter and subsequent chapters as outlined below

- Must be capable of processing both Entity and Transaction Level controls,
- Receipt and Storage Functions,
- Record Validation versus business rules (i.e., individual records),
- Dataset Validation versus Business Rules,
- Built in Financial Statement Risk Assessment process – including reconciliations,
- Built In Deficiency Management System (including combination and aggregation features),
- Built in Sub Certification system,
- Built in External Auditor interfaces,
- All Analysis functions,
- All Reporting functions, and
- All Special functions including fiscal yearend.

USER PERSPECTIVE ON SOX TOOLS

In conducting a survey of users in different clients, we have been provided a unique perspective on the tools used by a Repository.

BUSINESS UNITS – usually vote overwhelmingly for the Spreadsheet / Word Processing approach because of the following reasons:

1. It does not require special training and business units usually have personnel with expertise in both systems,

2. It's simple to use - if the SOX Department provides standard templates for required documentation,

3. Management functions are simpler and do not require specialized resources,

4. There are no additional costs (*direct or allocated*) to the Business Unit for use of the System, and

5. Business Unit Users can the entire framework on screen and can make changes in spreadsheet or word process table mode – a feature that is not possible in most systems,

SOX Departments usually prefer any of the other three solutions (and rarely prefer the spreadsheet or word processing option) with the Relational Database Management System usually slightly leading. The rationale for this is usually the following:

1. Submission and validation processes can be automated and force an integrity standard if the modules are properly developed,

2. The analytical functions are considered more extensive and this feature is viewed as a positive factor by the SOX Department. There is however a counter balance if the SOX Department requires IT support or personnel to assist this feature,

3. SOX Departments also like the capability to prepare customized analyses and reports if they have the necessary technical support,

4. For Documentation Systems and SOX Management Systems that do not have the capability to meet the various requirements, SOX Departments seek an "export" function

that permits them to export the data into a format from which they can perform the additional functions required. This need for additional subsidiary systems should be viewed as a negative.

	REPOSITORY TOOLS COMPARISON		
BASIC REPOSITORY FUNCTION	POTENTIAL TOOL	ADVANTAGE TO POTENTIAL TOOL	DISADVANTAGE TO POTENTIAL TOOL
STORAGE OF DOCUMENTATION AND EVIDENCE	Spreadsheet or Word Processing Document	1. Does not require training – most of user population can operate effectively,	1. Requires manual storage techniques to be used for Repository Management, 2. Period archives have to be manually controlled
	Document Management System	1. Most Documentation tools provide extensive storage capabilities 2. Usually provide automated archival functions.	1. Usually requires specialized training and special routines 2. Will not perform specialized SOX functions (e.g. Financial Statement Risk Assessment), 3. Will require supplementary systems at additional costs to meet SOX requirements.
	Relational Database Management System	1. Extensive storage and relational capabilities	1. Requires technical expertise 2. Requires User Interface and custom built programming 3. Will require analytical and reporting modules to be constructed
	SOX Management System	1. Should have all storage capabilities built in for all documentation types - not all systems provide full function capabilities	1. **Caveat emptor** – not all systems perform as advertised and not all systems perform the required functions.
SUBMISSION OF DOCUMENTATION OF DOCUMENTATION	Spreadsheet or Word Processing Document	1. Business Units with large volume of documentation prefer to submit by spreadsheet or word processing document versus entry of records by a User interface	1. Requires the SOX Department to perform extensive QA features unless there is an automated conversion program to upload to one of the following systems.
	Document Management System Relational Database Management System SOX Management System	1. If the system permits a bulk update of records, this should be viewed as an advantage for the system.	1. If the system does not have a bulk update feature, this should be viewed as a disadvantage.
VALIDATION PROCESSES	Spreadsheet or Word Processing Document	No known advantage.	1. Validation routines are not easily incorporated into either spreadsheets or word processing documents and cannot be easily modified or maintained.
	Document Management System	1. May have validation capabilities depending on the system	
	Relational Database Management System	1. Record validation can be incorporated in to the design of the data tables simply – assuming that the SOX Department has the necessary expertise or IT assistance	1. Usually requires IT expertise not available in SOX Department. 2. Maintenance requires IT or external assistance.
	SOX Management System	1. Depending on the system purchased, record and dataset validation may be available.	
ANALYSIS FUNCTIONS	Spreadsheet or Word Processing Document		1. Requires extensive technical and manual intervention in order to build a single document set from which analyses can be performed.

REPOSITORY TOOLS COMPARISON			
BASIC REPOSITORY FUNCTION	POTENTIAL TOOL	ADVANTAGE TO POTENTIAL TOOL	DISADVANTAGE TO POTENTIAL TOOL
			Usually requires all the spreadsheets and word processing documents to be converted into a single table.
	Document Management System	1. May be available in some systems	1. Specialized SOX analysis routines usually not available in these systems or require custom coding. For example these analyses are usually not available: • Financial Statement Risk Assessment • Deficiency Management Analyses • Financial Statement Coverage, etc.
	Relational Database Management System		
	SOX Management System	1. May be available in some systems	
REPORTING FUNCTIONS	Spreadsheet or Word Processing Document		1. Requires combination into a single source for company wide reporting – usually special conversion programs or extensive manual effort.
	Document Management System	1. May be available in some systems	1. Specialized SOX reports usually not available in these systems or require custom coding. For example these analyses are usually not available: • Financial Statement Risk Assessment • Deficiency Management Analyses • Financial Statement Coverage, etc.
	Relational Database Management System		
	SOX Management System	1. May be available in some systems	

In summary, the SOX Department needs to carefully evaluate the tools used within the Repository. All tools should be evaluated to ensure that they perform the functions outlined in this chapter.

In the evaluation ensure that you fully evaluate the following at a minimum:

1. The record formats that will be used - ensure that these format contain all the information you will need in the analyses and reports you have to produce,

2. Ensure that the system has a sound referential integrity capability (or ensure that the system uses an relational database management system for data management,

3. Ensure that the system is table driven with extensive master files that provide basic validation capabilities – do not permit hard coding of these validation rule – or you will become a maintenance addict (translation: you will be spending a lot of money on custom programming over an extended period of time)

4. Ensure that the system has bulk import capabilities with automated validation capabilities,

5. Ensure that all the analysis routines (deficiency, financial statements risk assessment, etc.) are built into the system,

6. Ensure that all reporting capabilities are built into the system on a real time basis, if possible,

7. Ensure that the system has an export capability for ad hoc analyses, and

8. Most importantly, ensure that your Vendor understand your SOX processes BETTER than you do!

Summary

With the contents of this chapter, you now have the detailed steps for developing or modifying your Repository. You should also review Chapter 8 on Reporting and Metrics for additional on the information that will be required from the Repository.

Chapter 7 – The Financial Statements Risk Assessment Process

Intent of this chapter

To provide you with the objectives, methods and tasks that need to be performed to achieve a comprehensive Financial Statement risk assessment analysis. In this chapter, the tools and steps used are provided in a generic format to assist you through this exercise.

Financial Statement Coverage Overview

To ensure comprehensive coverage of the Financial Statements and other Financial Reporting elements, Your Company should engage in a multi-step process to produce the necessary working documents. These working documents are required for assigning responsibility for the coverage to the Business Units of their documentation and assessment obligations.

Financial Statements analysis and Risk Assessment

Significant Account Analysis / Risk Assessment		Significant Account Reconciliation	
Beginning of Period		*End of Period*	
Inputs	1. Risk Assessment Worksheets 2. Deficiency Working Papers 3. Finance Error Logs 4. Previous Significant Changes 5. Financial Statements to Significant Account Cross References	Inputs	1. Business Unit Significant Account Requirements 2. Financial Statement Management Guidelines 3. Significant Account Extract from Repository
Processes	1. Risk Assessment Process 2. Financial Assertion assignment 3. Significant Account Decomposition 4. Business Unit / Location identification 5. Business Unit required coverage list 6. Significant Process linkage	Processes	1. Reconciliation of Significant Account documentation versus requirements 2. Identification of Threshold exceptions 3. Identification of Business Unit exceptions
Outputs	1. Corporate Quantitative Risk Assessment 2. Business Unit Significant Account Requirements 3. Business Unit Significant Process, etc	Outputs	1. Business Unit Exception List 2. Significant Account Exception List 3. Financial Statement Exception List

This chapter comprises of two main sections as illustrated in the diagram above.

1. The *left* section documents the risk assessment and the assignment of significant account responsibilities to the Business Units and Locations.

2. The *right* section illustrates the processes used to ensure that the Business Units have documented their obligations for Significant Accounts.

These two sections will collectively ensure that your company can demonstrate and support its:

1. Financial Statements risk assessment processes,

2. Assignment policies and processes for its significant account and process responsibilities,

3. Documentation and Assessment processes for the internal control framework with emphasis on Financial Statements coverage,

4. Management assessment of the completeness of coverage provided by its internal control framework over its financial reporting.

SECTION I - FINANCIAL STATEMENT RISK ASSESSMENT (THE INITIAL PROCESS)

This is the first step of two macro steps in the risk assessment of your Financial Statements. We have used a fictitious set of Financial Statements, throughout this chapter, for illustrative purposes.

PREREQUISITES

We have assumed that Management has established its Materiality Guidelines[26] for the Financial Statement coverage it deems necessary for the internal control framework.

For illustrative purposes throughout this chapter, we have assumed that management has established a threshold of 95% of total revenue for all significant accounts required to be covered. Some companies use different materiality measures that vary on other factors.

PCAOB REQUIREMENTS

When reviewing the Financial Statements, External Auditors are required under PCAOB Standard 2 – Section 65 to evaluate the following factors in order to determine whether an account is significant or not:

- Size and composition of the account;
- Susceptibility of loss due to errors or fraud;
- Volume of activity, complexity, and homogeneity of the individual transactions processed through the account;
- Nature of the account (for example, suspense accounts generally warrant greater attention);
- Accounting and reporting complexities associated with the account;
- Exposure to losses represented by the account (for example, loss accruals related to a consolidated construction contracting subsidiary);
- Likelihood (or possibility) of significant contingent liabilities arising from the activities represented by the account;
- Existence of related party transactions in the account; and
- Changes from the prior period in account characteristics (for example, new complexities or subjectivity or new types of transactions).

INPUT REQUIRED FOR THIS PROCESS

For this initial step, the following input (working) materials identified in the following sections should be assembled prior to commencing the Risk Assessment.

1. RISK ASSESSMENT WORKSHEET - For illustrative purposes, we will use only the Balance Sheet section of the Financial Statements in this chapter. The same methods and principles apply to the Income and Expense Statements. In the working paper examples

---

[26] MATERIALITY - PCAOB Auditing Standard No. 2 advises that the concept of materiality should be applied at both the financial statement level and at the individual account balance level. Materiality at both the financial statement level and the individual account balance level is relevant to planning and designing procedures. Materiality at the account balance level should be lower than materiality at the financial statement level.

provided, we have displayed the prior two fiscal years' balances (in the vertical axis) and the criteria from PCAOB Auditing Standard - Section 65 in the horizontal axis.

It also illustrates additional columns usually used in this initial risk assessment step.

2. ERROR LOGS - The last four quarters of Error Logs from Finance Division should be acquired for this analysis. These Error Logs will provide supporting material for determining which lines are susceptible to errors or misstatements based on last 4 quarters of fiscal statement preparation history.

3. SIGNIFICANT CHANGES - Significant Changes from last four Quarterly Business Unit representations (sub certifications) should be available for review and analysis by the Analysis team.

4. DEFICIENCIES - The working papers detailing all Deficiencies sorted by Financial Statement Line or Significant Account as outlined in Chapter 9 - *Deficiency Management*.

These deficiency work sheets will assist the team in analyzing the risk associated with the Financial Statement line from the individual and aggregated deficiencies.

5. FINANCIAL STATEMENTS TO SIGNIFICANT ACCOUNT CROSS REFERENCES - This *reverse* cross reference table is actually the financial statement consolidation cross reference table *in reverse* that permits provides the input to the logical process for decomposing the financial statement lines into their respective contributing significant accounts. In other words, the significant accounts are usually consolidated into the final financial statement lines based on a cross reference table. This table is prepared (or used) in reverse for this process.

Where the consolidation was based on a formula or judgmental factor, the Analysis team should also receive the supporting work sheets from the Finance Division.

PROCESS STEPS

There are six basic steps required for the financial statement analysis and risk assessment process:

1. Financial Statements Risk Assessment

2. Assignment of default Financial Assertions for each Financial Statement line,

3. Decomposition of Financial Statement lines into Significant Accounts and Processes

4. Identification of Business Units responsible (that will be assigned to cover with their internal controls) for Significant Accounts and Processes,

5. Development and Publication of Business Unit Coverage Responsibility Lists, and

6. Financial Statement Lines linked to Significant Processes.

OUTPUT

These events provide three basic outputs that comprise the majority of the entire Financial Statement coverage process.

Business Units should also receive from the SOX Department:

1. The SIGNIFICANT ACCOUNTS (Quantitative and Qualitative) that they are required to document within their controls,

2. The *projected* BUSINESS PROCESSES that are required to be documented by the Business Units, and

3. All NOTES AND DISCLOSURE requirements.

RISK ASSESSMENT TEAM COMPOSITION

The team assigned to perform this task should comprise of the following personnel:

1. SOX Department personnel responsible for assembling Significant Account and Process assignment lists for Business Units,

2. Finance Department personnel familiar with the assembly of the Financial Statements and the contents of the Finance Error Log[27], and

3. Representatives of Regional or Business Unit Finance units who will assist in identifying significant Business Units.

WORKSHEETS

The work sheet illustrated below represents a fictitious company's Balance Sheets for fiscal years 2004 and 2005. We are using the prior two years to prepare the assessment ofr 2006.

The work sheets are completed by using the recommended process outlined following the illustration.

	SIGNIFICANT ACCOUNT ANALYSIS (Balance Sheet) FOR Q1 2005														
	YEAR		RISK ASSESSMENT												
	2005	2004	Size and Composition	Loss Susceptibility	Account Volume	Nature of Account	Account and Reporting	Exposure to Losses	Cont Liabilities	3rd Party	Changes from Prior periods	Deficiencies?	Errors?	Significant Changes?	Significant Account?
Assets															
CURRENT ASSETS															
Cash and cash equivalents	$1,290	$1,399													
Restricted cash and cash equivalents	$28	$22													
Accounts receivable - net	$893	$877													
Inventories - net	$495	$338													
Deferred income	$89	$129													

---

[27] Most Finance Divisions maintain an error log of all errors identified during and after the closing cycle. This log is usually used to ensure a non recurrence of these errors by modifying and adopting new controls and procedures in the next closing cycle. For purposes of this chapter, we have assumed that your company's Finance Division maintains such a log.

	YEAR		RISK ASSESSMENT									Deficiencies?	Errors?	Significant Changes?	Significant Account?
	2005	2004	Size and Composition	Loss Susceptibility	Account Volume	Nature of Account	Account and Reporting	Exposure to Losses	Cont Liabilities	3rd Party	Changes from Prior periods				
taxes - net															
Other current assets	$125	$142													
TOTAL CURRENT ASSETS	$2,920	$2,907	DO NOT ASSIGN												
Investments	$56	$85													
Plant and equipment - net	$578	$580													
Goodwill	$806	$807													
Intangible assets - net	$27	$30													
Deferred income taxes - net	$1,308	$1,189													
Other assets	$250	$209													
TOTAL ASSETS	$5,944	$5,807	DO NOT ASSIGN												
LIABILITIES															
CURRENT LIABILITIES	$349	$307													
Trade and other accounts payable	$180	$267													
Payroll and benefit-related liabilities	$199	$186													
Contractual liabilities	$89	$72													
Restructuring liabilities	$988	$877													
Other accrued liabilities	$5	$42													
Long-term debt due within one year	$1,810	$1,751													
TOTAL CURRENT LIABILITIES	$1,352	$1,362	DO NOT ASSIGN												
Long-term debt	$50	$67													
Deferred income taxes - net	$116	$31													
OTHER LIABILITIES	$4,328	$4,210	DO NOT ASSIGN												
TOTAL LIABILITIES	$221	$216	DO NOT ASSIGN												
Minority interests in subsidiary companies															
Guarantees, commitments and contingencies															
SHAREHOLDERS' EQUITY	$1,440	$1,400													
Issued and outstanding shares:	$1,149	$1,169													
Additional paid-in capital	$0	$0													

SIGNIFICANT ACCOUNT ANALYSIS (Balance Sheet) FOR Q1 2005

	YEAR		RISK ASSESSMENT												
	2005	2004	Size and Composition	Loss Susceptibility	Account Volume	Nature of Account	Account and Reporting	Exposure to Losses	Cont Liabilities	3rd Party	Changes from Prior periods	Deficiencies?	Errors?	Significant Changes?	Significant Account?
Accumulated deficit	($193)	($188)													
Accumulated other comprehensive loss	$2,396	$2,381													
TOTAL SHAREHOLDERS' EQUITY	$5,944	$5,807	DO NOT ASSIGN												
TOTAL LIABILITIES AND SHAREHOLDERS' EQUITY	$1,290	$1,399	DO NOT ASSIGN												

SIGNIFICANT ACCOUNT ANALYSIS (Balance Sheet) FOR Q1 2005

Worksheets similar to that highlighted in this section should be developed for the Income Statement and Disclosures (Notes).

STEP 1 - INITIAL ASSESSMENT PROCESS

The Balance Sheet worksheet should then be reviewed in detail for each account and column. We recommend that you assign a risk factor to each intersection (row and column e.g. Cash and Cash Equivalents, Size and Composition) based on the following table (or a similar ranking METHOD of your preference).

- 5 = High Risk
- 3 = Medium Risk
- 1 = Low Risk

SIZE AND COMPOSITION

The SIZE AND COMPOSITION should be reviewed by the Analysis team and a Risk Factor code for each Financial Statement Line should be inserted into the worksheet. In order to review the composition of some accounts, the Analysis may require the consolidation cross reference tables used within the Finance Division for assembling the balances in the various financial statement lines.

As defined in the prerequisites, we have assumed that your management has established the materiality factor to be used for identifying the financial statement lines that should be assigned to the Business Units for their internal control framework coverage.

LOSS SUSCEPTIBILITY

Each statement line should be reviewed by the team for the susceptibility of incurring a loss due to errors and fraud. Some organization should make extensive use of internal and external audit reports together with internal fraud assessments.

Business Unit anti fraud assessments (from the Entity level Control program) should also be used by the Analysis Team in this assessment.

ACCOUNT VOLUME

The volume of activity in an account when reviewed with the complexity and type of transactions being processed within the account will provide the analysis team with and insight into the significance of the account.

We normally recommend an automated volume analysis of the quarter's journals in order to provide a volume ranking. In addition, depending on the General Ledger used within your organization a transaction analysis can also be provided (weighted by balances and transaction counts) to assist in determining the homogeneity of an account,

NATURE OF ACCOUNT

Depending on the General Ledger capability, an automated analysis should be executed to identify and rank accounts that are suspense, clearing, reconciliation and other transitory accounts by volume of transactions, balances, etc. This is usually done by reviewing the Chart of Accounts master tables and the ancillary classification files in order to identify these specific accounts.

ACCOUNTING AND REPORTING COMPLEXITY

Accounting and reporting complexities associated with the account. This is usually based on the judgment of the Financial Reporting team within your company he dependent factors should be established by this team and should include estimation and provisioning risk factors.

EXPOSURE TO LOSSES

Exposure to losses represented by the account (for example, loss accruals related to a consolidated construction contracting subsidiary),

CONTINGENT LIABILITIES

PCAOB DEFINITION: Likelihood (or possibility) of significant contingent liabilities arising from the activities represented by the account.

3RD PARTY TRANSACTIONS

PCAOB DEFINITION: Existence of related party transactions in the account should be reviewed by the Regional and Central Finance personnel to identify on both a centralized and Regional basis the risks with this category.

This analysis is usually performed by Regional Financial and Acquisition Department Managers they are individuals within the organization that would be most familiar with this category. You should determine which individuals within the organization are most qualified before commencing this section of the assessment.

In addition, these individuals should be assigned the role of External Vendor Liaisons for review the internal control frameworks and SAS70s received from the external vendors.

CHANGES FROM PRIOR PERIODS

PCAOB DEFINITION: Changes from the prior period in account characteristics (for example, new complexities or subjectivity or new types of transactions).

We recommend that a period over period analysis be done on both a balance and transaction analysis basis. The transaction analysis should include an analysis of amounts, transaction types and sources singularly and in combination.

DEFICIENCIES

If there are known deficiencies that have been identified for any Financial Statement lines or their related Significant Accounts, these should be assigned a risk factor depending on the severity of the deficiency.

The severity is usually determined by the deficiency type, the business unit, the contribution amount of the business unit to the specific line or account, etc.

ERRORS

Based on an analysis of the Finance Division Error Control Log, the team should establish the risk factor for each line based on a review of the Finance Division Error Logs.

This log must identify specific Financial Statement lines and the direct Significant Account (by Business Unit).

SIGNIFICANT CHANGES

We would recommend that the analysis team review any significant changes identified for specific accounts (which should have been documented in the sub certifications received from the functional business units in the previous quarter).

SIGNIFICANT ACCOUNT

Annotate this column if the account has been deemed significant or not by team based on a combination of all of the previous factors.

ADDITIONAL INFORMATION

In some companies, we would recommend the addition of a COMPENSATING CONTROLS column to the above work sheet, if an agreement has been reached with the External Auditors for definition and identification of compensating controls.

PROCESS OUTPUT

From this process, your company should develop the following output table:

	2005	SIGNIFICANT ACCOUNT	ANALYSIS TEAM COMMENTS
CURRENT ASSETS		The designation of whether an account is significant or not is entered into this section. NON significant accounts are excluded in later steps.	The analysis team comments – with primary focus on exclusionary reasons, should en included in this output.
Cash and cash equivalents	$1,290		
Restricted cash and cash equivalents	$28		
Accounts receivable - net	$893		
Inventories - net	$495		
Deferred income taxes - net	$89		
Other current assets	$125		
Investments	$2,920		
Plant and equipment - net	$56		
Goodwill	$578		
Intangible assets - net	$806		
Deferred income taxes - net	$27		
Other assets	$1,308		
CURRENT LIABILITIES	$250		

	2005	SIGNIFICANT ACCOUNT	ANALYSIS TEAM COMMENTS
Trade and other accounts payable	$5,944		
Payroll and benefit-related liabilities			
Contractual liabilities			
Restructuring liabilities			
Other accrued liabilities	$349		
Long-term debt due within one year	$180		
Long-term debt	$199		
Deferred income taxes - net	$89		
Minority interests in subsidiary companies	$988		
Guarantees, commitments and contingencies	$5		
SHAREHOLDERS' EQUITY	$1,810		
Issued and outstanding shares:	$1,352		
Additional paid-in capital	$50		
Accumulated deficit	$116		
Accumulated other comprehensive loss	$4,328		

ARCHIVAL INFORMATION

All worksheets should be maintained for each quarter within the repository. In addition, all notes on the rationale for excluding a financial statement line from the significant account balance should also be documented and maintained within the Repository by period.

STEP 2 – ASSIGNMENT OF DEFAULT FINANCIAL ASSERTIONS

We would recommend that you review each Financial Statement Line and Disclosure and assign default minimum assertions for each line.

PCAOB REFERENCES

PCAOB outlines its recommendations in the following paragraphs

68. Identifying Relevant Financial Statement Assertions. For each significant account, the auditor should determine the relevance of each of these financial statement assertions:[28]
- Existence or occurrence;
- Completeness;
- Valuation or allocation;
- Rights and obligations; and
- Presentation and disclosure.

69. To identify relevant assertions, the auditor should determine the source of likely potential misstatements in each significant account. In determining whether a particular assertion is relevant to a significant account balance or disclosure, the auditor should evaluate:
- The nature of the assertion;
- The volume of transactions or data related to the assertion; and
- The nature and complexity of the systems, including the use of information technology by which the company processes and controls information supporting the assertion.

ASSIGNMENT PROCESS

Using the worksheet below, the Analysis team should then assign the basic Financial Assertions to each line. Total and Sub Total lines should be excluded from this assignment process.

---

[28] See AU sec. 326, *Evidential Matter*, which provides additional information on financial statement assertions.

	2004	2003	EXISTENCE OR OCCURRENCE	COMPLETENESS	VALUATION OR ALLOCATION	RIGHTS AND OBLIGATIONS	PRESENTATION AND DISCLOSURE
Assets							
CURRENT ASSETS							
Cash and cash equivalents	$1,290	$1,399					
Restricted cash and cash equivalents	$28	$22					
Accounts receivable - net	$893	$877					
Inventories - net	$495	$338					
Deferred income taxes - net	$89	$129					
Other current assets	$125	$142					
TOTAL CURRENT ASSETS	$2,920	$2,907		DO NOT ASSIGN			
Investments	$56	$85					
Plant and equipment - net	$578	$580					
Goodwill	$806	$807					
Intangible assets - net	$27	$30					
Deferred income taxes - net	$1,308	$1,189					
Other assets	$250	$209					
TOTAL ASSETS	$5,944	$5,807		DO NOT ASSIGN			
LIABILITIES							
CURRENT LIABILITIES	$349	$307					
Trade and other accounts payable	$180	$267					
Payroll and benefit-related liabilities	$199	$186					
Contractual liabilities	$89	$72					
Restructuring liabilities	$988	$877					
Other accrued liabilities	$5	$42					
Long-term debt due within one year	$1,810	$1,751					
TOTAL CURRENT LIABILITIES	$1,352	$1,362		DO NOT ASSIGN			
Long-term debt	$50	$67					
Deferred income taxes - net	$116	$31					
OTHER LIABILITIES	$4,328	$4,210		DO NOT ASSIGN			
TOTAL LIABILITIES	$221	$216		DO NOT ASSIGN			
Minority interests in subsidiary companies							
Guarantees, commitments and contingencies							
SHAREHOLDERS' EQUITY							
	$1,440	$1,400					
Issued and outstanding shares:	$1,149	$1,169					
Additional paid-in capital	$0	$0					
Accumulated deficit	($193)	($188)					
Accumulated other comprehensive loss	$2,396	$2,381					
TOTAL SHAREHOLDERS' EQUITY	$5,944	$5,807		DO NOT ASSIGN			
TOTAL LIABILITIES AND SHAREHOLDERS' EQUITY				DO NOT ASSIGN			

The assignment of these Financial Assertions provides the Analysis team with the basic tool that will be used to determine the *minimum default* Financial Assertions for each significant account.

OUTPUT OF THIS SECTION

The output for this section is the previous table combined with the table designating significant accounts from the previous section as illustrated below.

2004		SIGNIFICANT ACCOUNT	EXISTENCE OR OCCURRENCE	COMPLETENESS	VALUATION OR ALLOCATION	RIGHTS AND OBLIGATIONS	PRESENTATION AND DISCLOSURE
ASSETS							
Current assets							
Cash and cash equivalents	$1,290						
Restricted cash and cash equivalents	$28						
Accounts receivable - net	$893						
Inventories - net	$495						
Deferred income taxes - net	$89						
Other current assets	$125						
Total current assets	$2,920						
Investments	$56						
Plant and equipment - net	$578						
Goodwill	$806						
Intangible assets - net	$27						
Deferred income taxes - net	$1,308						
Other assets	$250						
Total assets	$5,944						
LIABILITIES AND SHAREHOLDERS' EQUITY							
Current liabilities							
Trade and other accounts payable	$349						
Payroll and benefit-related liabilities	$180						
Contractual liabilities	$199						
Restructuring liabilities	$89						
Other accrued liabilities	$988						
Long-term debt due within one year	$5						
Total current liabilities	$1,810						
Long-term debt	$1,352						
Deferred income taxes - net	$50						
Other liabilities	$116						
Total liabilities	$4,328						
Minority interests in subsidiary companies	$221						
Guarantees, commitments and contingencies (notes 12, 13 and 21)							

This table will be used to generate the detailed Significant Accounts by Business Unit Lists that are discussed in the following section. These lists are communicated to the Business Units for their feedback and objections.

Like all other worksheets, this should be filed within the repository by period in order to support Management's assumptions on designating the significant accounts.

STEP 3- DECOMPOSITION INTO SIGNIFICANT ACCOUNTS

Depending on the Chart of Accounts, the decomposition process is actually a *reverse financial consolidation process*[29].

This process uses the *account to financial statement line consolidation* cross reference table in reverse for decomposition into significant accounts. The decomposition map table should be constructed based on the example below for each period (consolidation mapping may change

---

[29] Most organizations usually execute a specific *financial consolidation process* as a part of their Financial Closing cycle. This process summarizes all accounts into the Financial Statement Lines based on a cross reference table that is maintained and developed within the Finance Division.

at the end of fiscal period; therefore the Analysis team should always ensure that they receive and archive every quarter's consolidation).

FORMAT OF DECOMPOSITION MAP

FINANCIAL STATEMENT LINE	SIGNIFICANT ACCOUNT DESCRIPTION	CONSOLIDATION / SIGNIFICANT ACCOUNT NUMBER	BUSINESS UNIT SYSTEM	BUSINESS UNIT SYSTEM ACCOUNT NO	COMMENTS
Cash And Cash Equivalents	Account No 1	10001-11	GL1 – Europe	GL1_001	Management Comments
	Account No 2	10002-11	GL2 – SA	GL2987	Management Comments
	Account No 3	10003AB1	GL3 USA	DB279	Management Comments
Restricted cash and cash equivalents	Account No 4	10006-11	GL1 – Europe	GL1_002	Management Comments
	Account No 5	10009-11	GL2 – SA	GL287987	Management Comments
	Account No 6	100012CD21	GL3 USA	DB15236	Management Comments

The format of the map should be customized based on the following:

1. If the Business Units are aware of the Consolidation Account used in the main General Ledger for consolidation purposes, these should be provided as the Significant Account (please refer to diagram on the next page),

2. In the example above, we have assumed that the Business Units do not know the primary General Ledger codes and we have therefore illustrated the local General Ledger codes (the grey columns).

You will need to establish the format to be used in this section after consultation with the Finance Division in order to determine which Accounts should be provided to the Business Units.

PROCESS STEPS

The output of the previous section is the listing of the *deemed* significant Financial Statement Lines and their Quarter end (or Fiscal Yearend) balances.

For the *deemed* significant financial statement lines, you should then cross reference these lines to their significant accounts (using either the central general ledger chart of accounts or the regional chart of accounts) for each line.

In order to ensure that Management Guidelines are complied with for coverage purposes, the Analysis team would then decompose these financial statement lines into their respective Significant Account lines.

After decomposition into the significant account lines, the team should then ensure that the materiality thresholds are being complied with by totaling the balances in each significant account to see whether it reconciles with the total in the financial statement line.

RECONCILIATION CAPABILITIES

We have based the following steps on a disparate accounting system model. In this model, we have assumed that your company maintains multiple versions of financial accounting software within each business unit. *We have further assumed that the Chart of Accounts used in the centralized Corporate General Ledger is not the same as in the subsidiary General Ledgers.*

We have further assumed that a conversion process transports all data into the central General Ledger (in most companies– this process is executed daily). This process also usually includes a reconciliation process to ensure that there are no conversion/ transportation errors.

The diagram below illustrates this model. In this diagram, we display multiple business locations utilizing disparate accounting financial accounting systems. On a periodic basis (daily, weekly or other) the balances are imported into the primary general ledger. The activities and balance are stored into conversion accounts (your company may have a different nomenclature for these accounts).

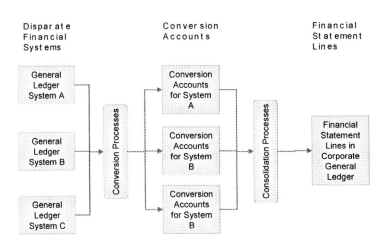

DISPARATE FINANCIAL SYSTEMS CONSOLIDATION MODEL

It is these conversion accounts that are usually consolidated into the Financial Statement Lines. These conversion accounts are usually be maintained by Business Unit or by originating general Ledger system to facilitate reconciliation processes. In some companies, there is a further step where all Business Units are further *summarized* into a corporate set of accounts before consolidation into the financial statement lines.

Depending on the methods used by your company, Significant Accounts may be identified at the Conversion Account Level or at the Source (originating) Financial System level. This needs to be determined in collaboration with your Finance Division.

The diagram further implies that the sum of the conversion accounts, when mapped to the Financial Statement Lines, will equal what is reported in your Financial Statements.

Obviously, there must be a managed reconciliation process between the originating subsidiary ledgers and the primary general ledger to ensure that all balances are reconciled at the end of each import / conversion cycle and that any errors are corrected promptly.

SIGNIFICANT ACCOUNT PROCESS OUTPUT

Using the cross Financial Statements to Significant Account Coverage cross reference table, the Analysis team should then construct the interim table used for the Significant Account Process.

This table, illustrated below, ensures that the Management Guidelines for Balances are being complied with. As you will note in the example below, the balances in the Significant Accounts are totaled and compared against the Financial Statement Line to ensure that the cross reference is accurate and that the coverage is within Management Guidelines

The first line (Cash and Cash Equivalents) meets and exceeds the management guideline of 90%. *The second line (restricted Cash and Cash Equivalents) does not meet management guidelines because it falls beneath the 90% threshold (arbitrarily established to provide an illustration for this example).*

FINANCIAL STATEMENT LINE	SIGNIFICANT ACCOUNT DESCRIPTION	SIGNIFICANT ACCOUNT NUMBER BUSINESS SYSTEM	SYSTEM	SIGNIFICANT ACCOUNT BALANCE	FINANCIAL STATEMENT BALANCE 2004	SIGNIFICANT ACCOUNTS TOTAL	% COVERAGE	COMMENTS
Cash And Cash	Account No 1	10001-11 GL1_001	GL1 – Europe	$1,220	$3,686	$3,586	97.28	Management Comments

Equivalents	Account No 2	10002-11 GL2987	GL2 – SA	$643					Management Comments
	Account No 3	10003AB1 DB279	GL3 USA	$1,723					Management Comments
Restricted cash and cash equivalents	Account No 4	10006-11 GL1_002	GL1 – Europe	$55	$80	$70	87.50		THIS LINE HAS FAILED GUIDELINES
	Account No 5	10009-11 GL287987	GL2 – SA	$10					Management Comments
	Account No 6	100012CD21 DB15236	GL3 USA	$5					Management Comments

IDENTIFICATION OF SIGNIFICANT BUSINESS UNITS

The next step in the process is to identify which Business Units are required to document their internal controls for specific significant accounts or processes.

This is usually simply accomplished by use of the output from the previous step together with the subdivision by Business Unit. In the example below, we have used Country or Region names to identify Business Units.

Referring to the Cash and Cash Equivalent line, each System has been subdivided into the specific Business Units. Assuming that your company has a comprehensive General Ledger that can identify Business Unit balances for significant accounts, the Analysis teams should be populate the balances for each business unit.

For ease of reference, we have colored these columns in a light grey shade.

The inclusion of Italy from the Business Locations for this Financial Statement Line and for Significant No 1 would not have an impact on the management threshold tolerance. Therefore, Italy could be excluded from documenting this significant account, at the analysis team's discretion.

FINANCIAL STATEMENT LINE	SIGNIFICANT ACCOUNT DESCRIPTION	SIGNIFICANT ACCOUNT NUMBER BUSINESS SYSTEM	SYSTEM	SYSTEM SIGNIFICANT ACCOUNT BALANCE	BUSINESS UNIT	BALANCE	FINANCIAL STATEMENT BALANCE 2004	SIGNIFICANT ACCOUNTS TOTAL	% COVERAGE
Cash And Cash Equivalents	Account No 1	10001-11 GL1_001	GL1 – Europe	$427.00	France	$169.75	$1,290.10	$1,255.10	$34.05
					Germany	$183.05			
					UK	$71.75			
					Italy	$2.45			
	Account No 2	10002-11 GL2987	GL2 – SA	$225.05	Brazil	$74.20			$451.50
					Argentina	$61.25			
					Chile	$89.60			
	Account No 3	10003AB1 DB279	GL3 USA	$603.05	USA	$207.20			
					North East	$166.60			
					Midwest	$89.25			
					West Coast	$61.60			
					South East	$78.40			
Restricted cash and cash equivalents	Account No 4	10006-11 GL1_002	GL1 – Europe	$19.25	France	$3.85	$28.00	$24.50	$30.63
					Germany	$4.20			
					UK	$7.00			
					Italy	$4.20			
	Account No	10009-11	GL2 –	$3.50	Brazil	$3.50			

Financial Statement Line	Significant Account Description	Significant Account Number Business System	System	System Significant Account Balance	Business Unit	Balance	Financial Statement Balance 2004	Significant Accounts Total	% Coverage
	5	GL287987	SA						
					Argentina	$0.00			
					Chile	$0.00			
	Account No 6	100012CD21 DB15236	GL3 USA	$1.75	USA	$1.75			
					North East	$0.00			
					Midwest	$0.00			
					West Coast	$0.00			
					South East	$0.00			

MANAGEMENT JUDGMENT

Business Unit and Finance Management may be aware of significant changes that may change the significant account requirements for the next Quarter. Typical examples of this type of change may be:

5. Increases or decreases to revenues,
6. Increases or decreases to expense, and
7. Potential contingent liabilities etc.

We would strongly recommend that significant accounts be added to the Business Unit responsibility lists and not removed from these lists despite any management factors that may be identified in this stage. We have usually found it is better to err on the side of prudence by having additional significant accounts than the opposite course of action.

STEP 4 - COMMUNICATION OF BUSINESS UNIT RESPONSIBILITIES

As outlined in the *Communications* chapter, the Business Units should be advised of their Significant Account coverage requirements at the beginning of each quarter using the illustrated report. In addition, a listing of all Financial Statement Note requirements and Qualitative Accounts should also be provided in a similar format.

The communication to the Business Units should comprise of the following:

QUANTITATIVE ACCOUNT LISTING

The Quantitative Significant Account List as outlined in the previous section in Business Unit sequence so that each Business Unit receives a listing of the Quantitative Significant Accounts it is required to cover.

Examples for France and USA are provided in the following sections

FRANCE QUANTITATIVE ACCOUNT LISTING

This listing only provides the examples of the Cash Accounts.

Financial Statement Line	Significant Account Description	Significant Account Number Business System	System	System Significant Account Balance	Business Unit	Balance	Financial Statement Balance 2004	Significant Accounts Total	% Coverage
Cash And Cash Equivalents	Account No 1	10001-11 GL1_001	GL1 – Europe	$1,220	France	$485	$3,686	$3,586	97.28

Financial Statement Line	Significant Account Description	Significant Account Number Business System	System	System Significant Account Balance	Business Unit	Balance	Financial Statement Balance 2004	Significant Accounts Total	% Coverage
Restricted cash and cash equivalents	Account No 4	10006-11 GL1_002	GL1 – Europe	$55	France	$11	$80	$70	87.50

USA QUANTITATIVE ACCOUNT LISTING

This listing only provides the examples of the Cash Accounts.

Financial Statement Line	Significant Account Description	Significant Account Number Business System	System	System Significant Account Balance	Business Unit	Balance	Financial Statement Balance 2004	Significant Accounts Total	% Coverage
Cash And Cash Equivalents	Account No 3	10003AB1 DB279	GL3 USA	$1,723	USA	$592	$3,686	$3,586	97.28
Restricted cash and cash equivalents	Account No 6	100012CD21 DB15236	GL3 USA	$5	USA	$5	$80	$70	87.50

QUALITATIVE ACCOUNT LISTING

The Qualitative Significant Account List may be provided by the Analysis team in two formats. Most companies provide the guidelines for identifying qualitative accounts and permit Business Units to identify the accounts that meet these qualification attributed.

Other organizations perform an analysis of their General Ledgers based on type of class of accounts and provide this listing to the Business Units. The analysis is usually based on identifying suspense, reconciliation, clearing and other transitory accounts.

We would recommend that you provide both the guidelines for identifying Qualitative Accounts and, at the same time, a listing of all suspense and other accounts (based on a GL account analysis) for Business Unit review and consideration.

NOTES AND DISCLOSURE LISTINGS

Similar to the Balance Sheet and Income Statement sections, the notes and disclosures sections should be analyzed to determine the Business Units responsible for contributing information necessary for the preparation of these notes. This is referenced throughout this volume as the Notes Matrix.

At the end of this chapter, we have provided an example in Appendix A.

SECTION II - RECONCILIATION OF FINANCIAL STATEMENT COVERAGE

At the end of each quarter, we recommend that you review your entire company's Financial Statement coverage for Quantitative, Qualitative and Financial Statements Notes.

RECONCILIATION OF FINANCIAL STATEMENT COVERAGE

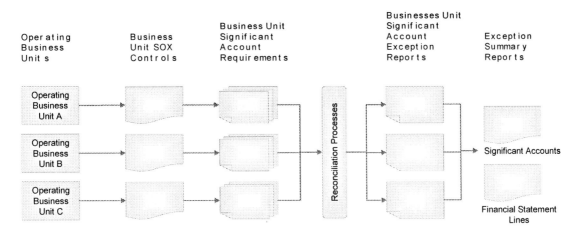

In order to ensure that the Business Units have met their requirement for documenting and assessing their controls for the significant accounts that have been assigned to them, the steps illustrated in the diagram above should be executed on a quarterly basis.

1. Documentation should be assembled, validated and deposited into the Repository on a quarterly basis as outlined in the Repository report,

2. From the documentation, you should extract from only the *validated* controls all significant accounts that have been documented within these controls,

3. These extracted Significant Accounts should be compared versus the Business Unit list of required Significant Accounts (that you communicated to the Business Units in the previous section of this paragraph) and an Exception Listing produced of all undocumented Significant Accounts,

4. The Significant Account exceptions and their balances should be summarized into a corporate summary,

5. These should then be consolidated, using the financial statements cross reference, to determine the impact on the Financial Statements (percentage of each financial statement line that has been covered by the internal control framework), and

6. Finally, your SOX Department and Corporate Management should take the necessary remedial action to ensure that the Business Units meet their Significant Account coverage requirements before fiscal yearend..

STEP 5 - REPOSITORY DOCUMENTATION AND EXTRACTION

As outlined in the *Repository* chapter, you should assemble all Business Unit documentation on a quarterly basis.

From this documentation, you should extract from the assessed controls all Significant Accounts that have been documented and the financial assertions that have been documented within each control.

SIGNIFICANT ACCOUNT EXTRACTION REPORT

Assuming that your company adopts our recommendation for use of a standard control ID number in its documentation, the extraction should provided the following minimum information

SIGNIFICANT ACCOUNT EXTRACTION REPORT FOR Q1 2006												
Business Unit	Control ID	Cycle	Process	Sub Process	Control Description	Significant Account	EXISTENCE OR OCCURRENCE	COMPLETENESS	VALUATION OR ALLOCATION	RIGHTS AND OBLIGATIONS	PRESENTATION AND DISCLOSURE	Comments
BU1	12345-1	Revenue	Process1	Sub Process 1	Control Description 1	GL1_001	Y	N	Y	N	Y	
BU1	12345-1	Revenue	Process1	Sub Process 1	Control Description 1	GL1_002	Y	Y	Y	N	N	
BU1	12346-1	Revenue	Process1	Sub Process 1	Control Description 2a	GL1_001	N	Y	Y	N	Y	
BU1	12347-1	Revenue	Process1	Sub Process 1	Control Description 3b	GL1_001	Y	N	Y	N	Y	

This analysis extracts each significant account identified with the documented controls. The information should be stored in a format similar to that in the table above.

STEP 6 - COMPARISON TO SIGNIFICANT ACCOUNT REQUIREMENTS

With the Significant Account Extract information, you should then compare the Significant Accounts that have been documented (including the financial assertions for each significant account) to the Business Units Significant Accounts requirements lists that were communicated at the beginning of the quarter.

Detailed below is an example of the USA Quantitative Account requirement that should be compared to the documentation extract. In this table we will focus on the Cash and Cash Equivalent Line only.

We will assume that this line, for illustrative purposes, has all five financial assertions set to YES. Normally, the Cash Line does not have the Valuation assertion to yes unless a conversion is required.

FINANCIAL STATEMENT LINE	SIGNIFICANT ACCOUNT DESCRIPTION	SIGNIFICANT ACCOUNT NUMBER BUSINESS SYSTEM	SYSTEM	SYSTEM SIGNIFICANT ACCOUNT BALANCE	BUSINESS UNIT	BALANCE	FINANCIAL STATEMENT BALANCE 2004	SIGNIFICANT ACCOUNTS TOTAL	% COVERAGE
Cash And Cash Equivalents	Account No 3	10003AB1 DB279	GL3 USA	$1,723	USA	$592	$3,686	$3,586	97.28
Restricted cash and cash equivalents	Account No 6	100012CD21 DB15236	GL3 USA	$5	USA	$5	$80	$70	87.50

For illustrative purposes, we will assume that we have extracted from the repository the following information for the same Business unit for these specific significant accounts.

SIGNIFICANT ACCOUNT EXTRACTION REPORT FOR Q1 2006 FOR USA												
Business Unit	Control ID	Cycle	Process	Sub Process	Control Description	Significant Account	EXISTENCE OR OCCURRENCE	COMPLETENESS	VALUATION OR ALLOCATION	RIGHTS AND OBLIGATIONS	PRESENTATION AND DISCLOSURE	Comments
USA	12346-1	Cycle 1	Process 10	Sub Process 15	Control Description 1123	10003AB1	Y	N	N	N	N	
USA	98562-1	Cycle 2	Process 32	Sub Process 17	Control Description 1434	10003AB1	N	Y	Y	N	N	
USA	12346-1	Cycle 3	Process 123	Sub Process 1948	Control Description 346456	10003AB1	N	Y	N	Y	N	
USA	12347-1	Cycle 4	Process 109	Sub Process 1635	Control Description 34746	10003AB1	Y	N	Y	N	N	

In the extract from the Repository, we have identified four controls for the specific significant Account (grey column).

Assuming that this significant account requires all five financial assertions, we can determine that the USA Business unit did not document a control (or is missing a control) for the *Presentation and Disclosure* Financial Assertion (second grey column).

BUSINESS UNIT COVERAGE EXCEPTION REPORT

There are two logical coverage exceptions that should be provided to the Business Units.

1. MISSING SIGNIFICANT ACCOUNTS – the Significant Account was not documented and assessed for a specific Significant Account

2. PARTIALLY COVERED EXCEPTION REPORT – the Significant Account and its financial assertions was only *partially documented and assessed* in the Business.

For each of these, the SOX Department should request the Business Unit to take remedial action and to apprise the SOX Department of its remediation efforts on a periodic (we recommend fortnightly) basis.

CORPORATE MANAGEMENT EXCEPTION REPORT

The initial Corporate Management Report should provide Senior Management, Board and Board Committees with the following information.

We have only provided illustrative data for the first two rows of data.

		2004	2003	Documented and Assessed	EXISTENCE OR OCCURRENCE	COMPLETENESS	VALUATION OR ALLOCATION	RIGHTS AND OBLIGATIONS	PRESENTATION AND DISCLOSURE	Not Documented and Assessed	Action Plan
Assets											
CURRENT ASSETS											
Cash and cash equivalents		$3,686	$3,997	$1,968	$1,350	$1,268	$1,350	$0	$1350	$368	Yes
Restricted cash		$80	$63		$80	$80	$80	$80	$80		

	2004	2003	Documented and Assessed	Existence or Occurrence	Completeness	Valuation or Allocation	Rights and Obligations	Presentation and Disclosure	Not Documented and Assessed	Action Plan
and cash equivalents			$80						$0	
Accounts receivable - net	$2,551	$2,505								
Inventories - net	$1,414	$967								
Deferred income taxes - net	$255	$369								
Other current assets	$356	$405								
TOTAL CURRENT ASSETS	$8,342	$8,306								

APPENDIX A– FINANCIAL STATEMENT NOTES / DISCLOSURES WORKING PAPERS

In this section, we provide an example of the Financial Statements Notes Matrix for a fictitious company.

2005	PRIMARY RESPONSIBILITY	NO ASSIGN (This column is used to designate No Assignment)	FRANCE	GERMANY	UK	ITALY	BRAZIL	ARGENTINA	CHILE	USA
1. General Corporate Financial and Overview	Legal Department	NO								
2. Significant accounting policies	Finance Department	NO								
(a) Principles of consolidation	Finance Department	NO								
(b) Use of estimates	Finance Department	NO								
(c) Translation of foreign currencies	Finance Department	NO								
(d) Revenue recognition	Finance Department	NO								
(e) Research and development	Finance Department	NO								
(f) Income taxes	Finance Department	NO								
g) Earnings (loss) per common share	Finance Department	NO								
(h) Cash and cash equivalents	Finance Department	NO								
(i) Restricted cash and cash equivalents	Finance Department	NO								
(j) Provision for doubtful accounts	Finance Department	NO								
(k) Inventories	Finance Department	NO								
(l) Receivables sales	Finance Department	NO								
(m) Investments	Finance Department	NO								
(n) Plant and equipment	Finance Department	NO								
(o) Impairment or disposal of long-lived assets (plant and equipment and acquired technology)	Finance Department	NO								
(p) Goodwill	Finance Department	NO								
(q) Intangible assets	Finance Department	NO								
(r) Warranty costs	Finance Department	NO								
(s) Pension, post-retirement and post-employment benefits	Finance Department	NO								
(t) Derivative financial instruments	Finance Department	NO								
(u) Stock-based compensation	Finance Department	NO								
(v) Recent accounting pronouncements	Finance Department	NO								
3. Accounting changes										

2005	PRIMARY RESPONSIBILITY	NO ASSIGN THIS COLUMN IS USED TO DESIGNATE NO ASSIGNMENT	FRANCE	GERMANY	UK	ITALY	BRAZIL	ARGENTINA	CHILE	USA
(a) Guarantees										
(b) Asset retirement obligations										
(c) Accounting for costs associated with exit or disposal activities										
(d) Consolidation of variable interest entities										
(e) Accounting for certain financial instruments with characteristics of both liabilities and equity										
(f) Accounting for revenue arrangements with multiple deliverables										
4. Consolidated financial statement details										
5. Segment information										
6. Special charges										
7. Income taxes	Finance Department		Y	Y	Y	Y	Y	Y	Y	Y
8. Employee benefit plans										
9. Acquisitions, divestitures and closures										
10. Long-term debt, credit and support facilities		,								
11. Financial instruments and hedging activities										
12. Guarantees										
(a) Business sale and business combination agreements										
(b) Intellectual property indemnification obligations										
(c) Lease agreements										
(d) Third party debt agreements										
(f) Other indemnification agreements										
13. Commitments										
14. Financing arrangements										
15. Capital stock										
16. Earnings (loss) per common share										
17. Accumulated other comprehensive loss										
18. Stock-based compensation plans										
19. Discontinued operations										
20. Related party transactions										
21. Contingencies										
22. Subsequent events										

SUMMARY

In this chapter, we have provided you with a step by step approach to the Financial Risk Assessment process.

If your company has already certified, it is likely you have already successfully executed Section I of this chapter. Section II may or may not have been performed, depending on your company's size and complexity and the requirements of your External Auditors.

We would recommend that you review each of the steps in Section II and incorporate these into your final assessment process at the end of each fiscal year.

Chapter 8 – Reporting and Metrics for SOX

If you cannot measure it, you (usually) cannot manage it!

This maxim definitely applies to SOX. While many areas of SOX require management judgment and interpretation, to successfully manage the internal control framework requires tangible metrics and reporting.

Intent of this Chapter

The intent of this chapter is to provide you with the processes and methods by which you should report the status and progress of your certification efforts within any fiscal period.

Several areas of SOX require management judgment, but we suggest that these judgments should be based on metrics that are derived from accurate, validated data securely stored in your SOX Repository (refer to Chapter 6)

The recommendations are based on our experience and research on the information required to assess and manage an internal control framework in a proactive, sustainable series of processes throughout the life cycle and also applies to control requirements other than Sarbanes Oxley 404.

The success of a comprehensive reporting system depends on the maturity of the framework design and processes within the organization.

In the initial phase, there is no prioritization placed on the more advanced reports as your company will be "*feeling its way through*" the reporting necessary to establish and implement an internal control framework. Usually after the initial certification, it is common practice to provide the more basic reports to the Business Unit management of your company, with the company's executive management receiving only Summary, Exception and Escalation reports.

Importance of Valid, Accurate Data

The importance of the processes mandated in the Repository functions cannot be over emphasized. *Without accurate data, the entire recommended reporting process can be invalidated.* It is therefore imperative that you implement the Repository processes we recommend in Chapter 5 for mitigating the risks of invalid or questionable data.

Prerequisites for Reporting and Metrics

Prior to proceeding into the implementation of the Reporting and Metrics processes in this chapter, we have assumed that your company has implemented all the preceding chapters. To recap, these are:

Basic Prerequisites

The following prerequisites (refer to Chapter 2) should have been implemented and tested:

1. SOX Policies, Procedures and Guidelines (aka Methodology) is required for these processes to function. We have therefore assumed that these have been designed, approved by the Board, trained and implemented throughout the SOX community – or your company is proceeding along this path.

2. REPOSITORY. Implementation of a Repository (and all the related data processes) is critical to the reporting process. Please refer to Chapter 6 – SOX Repository.

COMMON KEYS (THREADS) THROUGHOUT DOCUMENTATION

The reports and analyses that are used to prepare the assessment of your company's internal control framework will require the use of a variety of different types of documents or data. For example, the reporting and analysis processes will use data from process, control, assessment and deficiency documents and data to provide company management with a comprehensive analysis of the overall environment.

This applies to both the entity level controls and the process/transaction level controls.

In order for these reporting and analysis processes to be performed, the documents and data must be organized to ensure that there are *common keys* linking the various documents. These common keys provide the necessary relationships by which you can perform a comprehensive analysis of the framework. These interrelationships are usually represented by foreign keys or indices within a relational database management system.

In Volume II, of this series, we provide detailed information on the data requirements for a SOX Management System. It includes the definitions of the keys and indices referenced in the previous paragraph.

Therefore, we have assumed that your company has adopted the following cross references or methods provided in the previous chapters

1. FINANCIAL STATEMENTS TO SIGNIFICANT ACCOUNTS CROSS REFERENCE – with the significant account inheriting, at a minimum, the financial assertion requirements for the parent Financial Statement line (refer to chapter 7 on Financial Statements Risk Assessment),

2. PROCESS / CONTROL SIGNIFICANT ACCOUNT LINKAGE - All processes / controls should have the capability to be linked to multiple significant accounts and also have the capability of documenting financial assertions by significant account individually. This must be incorporated into your design of the process and control documentation formats outlined in Chapter 6 – the SOX Repository.

3. CONTROL ID - Each control has been assigned a unique control ID that is validated by a tested, automated program when being received into the Repository for storage. The Control ID should comprise of:

    a. THE BUSINESS UNIT ID – the Business unit responsible for designing and operating this control,
    b. THE SIGNIFICANT PROCESS ID – identifying which the process this control is a part of,
    c. A CONTROL SEQUENCE NUMBER – which together with the Business Unit ID and the Process ID provides the control its unique ID, and

4. SYSTEM IDs – The systems on which the process or control is reliant on.

CRITICAL INFORMATION PREREQUISITES

In order for the reporting processes to operate effectively, the data and derived information on which the reports and presentations are prepared are based on three critical processes:

1. ACCURACY OF DATA. All the information has met the standards defined within the SOX methodology and have successfully passed the SOX validation process,

2. VALIDITY OF INFORMATION. The entire data set has been cross validated to the each other to ensure that there are "no rotten apples in the barrel" or inconsistent data in the data sets (e.g. invalid process to process connectors), and

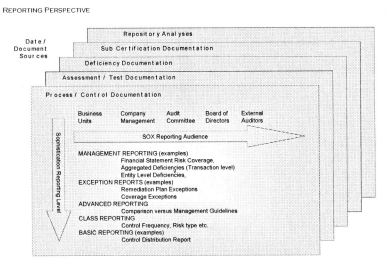

3. COMPLETENESS OF DATA. The final reports are provided based on a *complete* data set. Exceptions are stored and escalated on a timely basis. For example, you cannot complete a company wide analysis unless all documentation *for the entire company* is received within the Repository. In unusual circumstances, company management may request an ad hoc analysis with data substituted from a previous period substituted for current data – *but this is highly unusual and risky.*

REPORTING AND METRICS OVERVIEW

The approach to developing your reporting requirements should be based on a phase by phase sequence as illustrated in the above diagram.

The Vertical axis designates the Sophistication Level of reporting. In this diagram, we have illustrated five levels of your reporting viz.

- Basic Reporting,
- Class Reporting,
- Advanced Reporting,
- Exception Reporting, and
- Management Reporting

The Horizontal axis designates the various SOX audience members to whom the reports and metrics will be distributed e.g. Board, CEO, CFO etc.

The third axis is used to provide examples of the data sources (Objects) that should be covered in the SOX analyses and reports e.g. Controls, Control Assessments, etc.

REPORT LEVELS

The reporting process is usually an incremental process that increases with the organization's sophistication in assessing the control framework and the maturity of the framework itself. We recommend the step sequence outlined below, but at your discretion, this sequence can be modified to meet more immediate demands or priorities.

These report levels apply to all report objects (the third axis of the diagram) e.g. controls, tests, and deficiencies.

BASIC REPORTING

Basic reporting is usually *quantitative* (versus qualitative or more advanced reporting) providing summaries and metrics that are usually "*stand alone*" and do not necessarily provide management a comprehensive perspective into the state of the internal control framework because it is usually focused on one of the elements that comprise the internal framework.

We have reviewed several major corporations whose basic reports provide diametrically opposite metrics based on their implementations of internal control frameworks.

The following examples highlight the need for a comprehensive reporting perspective and management capability in order to properly assess an internal control framework.

Corporation A has 1,800 processes and 6,000+ key financial controls. They perform approximately 12,000 tests of these controls in a fiscal year. They have approximately 300 deficiencies. These were aggregated into no material weaknesses, 4 significant deficiencies and 250 deficiencies.

Corporation B has 60 standardized processes and 400+ centralized, standardized key financial controls. They perform approximately 40,000 tests of these controls in a fiscal year. They have approximately 200 deficiencies. These were aggregated into no material weaknesses, 3 significant deficiencies and 180 standard deficiencies.

Which corporation manages and assesses its internal financial control process better?

Neither corporation has an advantage or disadvantage in reporting – they are providing accurate quantitative reports.

However, these basic reports provide a quantitative measure that is of limited use unless combined with some other reference data or material. *It's just that – a set of numbers – with no reference points or guidelines!*

Each corporation uses a different methodology. The basic statistics, in a *stand alone,* basic report provides no insight into the state of either corporation's internal control framework. Instead, the metrics provided merely provide raw data on some of the elements of the framework without any references to plans or other data that may provide management with the capability to analyze or assess the state of the framework.

CLASS REPORTING

Controls in an internal control environment need to be analyzed from multiple perspectives. Classification codes are a *family* of codes that are assigned to a control by the business unit and confirmed by the central Finance Division or other authority. Within this family of classification codes, most organizations subdivide the controls into classifications that provided management insight into different aspects of their control framework e.g.:

1. FREQUENCY OF CONTROLS e.g. daily, weekly, monthly, etc.,

2. The MECHANISM OR PROCESSES used to perform the controls e.g. manual methods, automated methods, IT dependent methods, etc., and

3. RISK TYPE designates the risk that the control mitigates (assuming that you maintain standard set of risk codes),

ADVANCED REPORTING

Advanced Reports are based on the advanced metrics that are prepared from comparing management's expectation guidelines versus the internal control documentation within the repository. As outlined in the section on advanced metrics later in this chapter, this requires you to develop and establish guidelines for the implementation and assessment of the internal control framework.

ASSESSMENT REPORTING

Assessment reporting generally focuses on:

1. Whether the required walkthroughs, tests and other assessment processes have been performed,

2. Comparing the test methods versus established management guidelines (sample sizes, thresholds, frequencies, etc.), and

3. The test results and reviews.

EXCEPTION REPORTING

Management must be cognizant of any variations or exceptions of the assessment data versus the standards and guidelines prescribed for the internal control framework. Exception reporting should display all exceptions that require corrective action to be taken.

Typical examples are:

- Process documentation that fails company standards,
- Control documentation that fails company standards,
- Test results that are not in compliance with company test guidelines, etc.

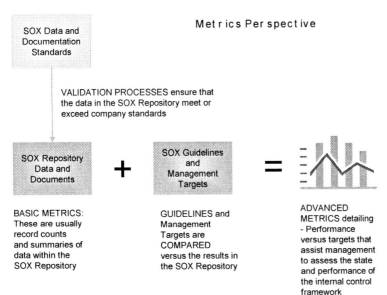

METRICS

Within the SOX Department, *properly designed* metrics will provide SOX Management and Senior Management with some of the information necessary for assessing the state of the internal control framework on an ongoing basis

As outlined in the previous chapters, we recommend that you adopt the guidelines and thresholds that outline (and in some instances, mandate) management's expectations and objectives for the internal control framework within the organization on a periodic and *continued* basis.

These guidelines should not be confused with *documentation* standards which are instructions on *how to* complete the variety of documents that are required to provide the evidence of the existence and operating effectiveness of a SOX framework.

With these management guidelines, the department can measure, assess and report on the performance of the internal control framework versus management's expectations and objectives. These usually are delivered by:

1. BASIC METRICS – these are usually summaries and counts of the documents by type of documentation, class, risk factors, Business Units and other management criteria.

2. ADVANCED / COMPOUND METRICS – these usually comprise of

    - COMBINATION of data sources to provide management with a comprehensive overview of the framework, e.g. measuring deficiencies versus controls by risk factors,

    - COMPARISONS of the framework versus management guidelines and targets – e.g. management expectations for financial statements risk assessment coverage, and

    - OTHER metrics covered in this chapter.

BASIC REPORTS

Basic Reports usually provide environmental type information, which on a stand alone basis, is *quantitative* in nature. The illustrated reports provide you with a distribution perspective of the processes, controls and deficiencies and other data.

PROCESS / CONTROL REPORTS

1. CONTROL DISTRIBUTION REPORT - This report should report on the distribution of controls by Type of Control and Business Unit. The report should contain the following headers. The vertical Axis of the report should be the Business Units.

    The intent of the report is to provide your management with a high level perspective of their controls and the distribution of these controls within your company. A high level of manual controls in some organizations may indicate a higher risk dependency and potentially higher costs.

    - DISTRIBUTION - No of Processes, No. of Controls, etc.,
    - ATTRIBUTES - PREVENTATIVE – Manual, Automated, IT Dependent, etc.,
    - ATTRIBUTES - DETECTIVE – Manual, Automated, IT Dependent, etc.

		CONTROL DISTRIBUTION REPORT								
	DISTRIBUTION			ATTRIBUTES						
				PREVENTATIVE				DETECTIVE		
BUS UNIT	PROCESSES	SUB PROCESSES	CONTROLS	MANUAL	AUTOMATED	IT DEPENDENT		MANUAL	AUTOMATED	IT DEPENDENT
BU1	10	45	135	35	22	12		45	6	15
BU2	25	26	51	14	5	11		9	0	12
BU3	15	78	172	58	11	0		98	5	0
Totals	50	149	358	107	38	23		152	11	27

2. CONTROL RISK DISTRIBUTION REPORT - This report assumes that you use a standard method for classifying control risks. Usually the High Risk controls are estimation or provisioning controls. *We would recommend that you display percentages which we have removed because of space limitations.*

	CONTROL RISK DISTRIBUTION REPORT										
	HIGH RISK				NON ROUTINE				ROUTINE		
BUS UNIT	NO OF CONTROLS	TESTED	DEF NO.		NO OF CONTROLS	TESTED	DEF NO.		NO OF CONTROLS	TESTED	DEF NO.	TOTAL
BU1	45	10	15		50	25	32		40	40	2	**135**
BU2	10	2	5		15	15	1		26	22	9	**51**
BU3	42	22	19		59	45	3		76	47	22	**172**
	97	34	39		124	85	36		142	109	33	**358**

3. CONTROL FREQUENCY REPORT - This report assumes that you use a standard method for identifying the frequency of controls (e.g. daily, monthly, weekly, etc.). *Again, we would recommend that you display percentages which we have removed because of space limitations.*

	CONTROL FREQUENCY DISTRIBUTION REPORT									
BUS UNIT	DAILY	WEEKLY	FORTNIGHTLY	MONTHLY	QUARTERLY	SEMI ANNUALLY	ANNUAL	FISCAL YEAREND	ON DEMAND	TOTAL
BU1	18	4	12	22	32	10	20	7	10	**135**
BU2	8	2	0	10	11	0	20	0	0	**51**
BU3	42	30	19	31	25	5	15	5	0	**172**
	97	34	39		124	85	36		142	**358**

4. BUSINESS UNIT CONTROL DISTRIBUTION REPORT - Illustrated is an example of a business unit control distribution report which displays the basic count of controls by Business Unit and their distribution between preventive and detective controls.

   Some organizations use this report to determine, and change where necessary, the distribution between preventive and detective controls.

	BUSINESS UNIT CONTROL DISTRIBUTION REPORT									
	DISTRIBUTION			ATTRIBUTES						
				PREVENTIVE				DETECTIVE		
BUS UNIT	PROCESSES	SUB PROCESSES	CONTROLS	MANUAL	AUTOMATED	IT DEPENDENT		MANUAL	AUTOMATED	IT DEPENDENT
BU1	10	45	135	35	22	12		45	6	15
BU2	25	26	51	14	5	11		9	0	12
BU3	15	78	172	58	11	0		98	5	0
Totals	50	149	358	107	38	23		152	11	27

5. PROCESS CONTROL DISTRIBUTION REPORT - Illustrated is an example of a process control distribution report which displays the basic count of controls by Significant Process and their distribution between preventive and detective controls.

   If your organization uses Standardized processes and controls, this report would highlight the variances between the standard requirements and the actual implementation.

PROCESS OR CYCLE CONTROL DISTRIBUTION REPORT											
	DISTRIBUTION			ATTRIBUTES							
				PREVENTIVE				DETECTIVE			
PROCESS	BUSINESS UNITS	CONTROLS		MANUAL	AUTOMATED	IT DEPENDENT		MANUAL	AUTOMATED	IT DEPENDENT	
PROC 1											
PROC 2											
PROC 3											
TOTALS											

6. **SYSTEM CONTROL DISTRIBUTION REPORT** - Illustrated is an example of a system control distribution report which displays the basic count of controls by System and their distribution between preventive and detective controls. Depending on the design of the control record, your management should be able to identify their critical control systems and their dependencies by system.

NOTE CAREFULLY: Most organizations are usually unpleasantly surprised by the high degree of dependency on spreadsheets and desktop databases and use this report to attempt to alter the environment where possible.

SYSTEM CONTROL DISTRIBUTION REPORT											
	DISTRIBUTION			ATTRIBUTES							
				PREVENTIVE				DETECTIVE			
SYSTEM	PROCESSES	CONTROLS		MANUAL	AUTOMATED	IT DEPENDENT		MANUAL	AUTOMATED	IT DEPENDENT	
SYS 1											
SYS 2											
SYS 3											
TOTALS											

TEST (ASSESSMENT) REPORTS

Basic test reports are intended to provide you with an overview of the testing activities / results on the internal control framework.

1. **BUSINESS UNIT TEST REPORT** - This report requires that you have an established test calendar for testing activities within a specific quarter. With this established calendar, the report can therefore provide

BUSINESS UNIT TEST PROGRESS REPORT											
			THIS QUARTER				PRIOR QUARTER				
BUS UNIT	PROCESSES	CONTROLS	PLANNED TESTS	ACTUAL TESTS	% COMPLETE	% INCOMPLETE	PLANNED TESTS	ACTUAL TESTS	% COMPLETE	% INCOMPLETE	
BU1											
BU2											
BU3											
TOTALS											

2. **BUSINESS UNIT ANNUAL CONTROL TEST REPORT** - A subset of the previous report should provide information based only on annual controls. This report would highlight to management any *missed* annual control testing requirements which can be critical to certification since an annual control (by definition) has only one opportunity to be tested,

3. RISK CATEGORY TEST REPORTS - Customarily, SOX and Corporate Management should focus on the high risk and non-routine control test activities. A high incidence of untested controls should trigger the escalation processes within your company.

   Based on your experience with this report, the report may need to be modified to include four quarters to provide a wider trend line for analysis.

RISK CATEGORY TEST PROGRESS REPORT										
			THIS QUARTER				PRIOR QUARTER			
RISK FACTOR	BUSINESS UNITS	CONTROLS	PLANNED TESTS	ACTUAL TESTS	% COMPLETE	% INCOMPLETE	PLANNED TESTS	ACTUAL TESTS	% COMPLETE	% INCOMPLETE
HIGH RISK	BU1									
	BU2									
	BU3									
NON ROUTINE	BU1									
	BU2									
	BU3									
ROUTINE	BU1									
	BU2									
	BU3									
TOTALS										

DEFICIENCY REPORTS

The basic deficiency reports should focus on the distribution of deficiencies across the business units, processes, systems and risk categories.

In the future with these four basic reports, you should have a perspective of the potential or possibility of aggregated deficiencies before the aggregation process commences. This will permit you to focus the resources necessary to remediate key *"leverage point"* deficiencies that can reduce the possibility of significant deficiencies or material weaknesses.

1. BUSINESS UNIT DEFICIENCY REPORT - The intent of this report is to provide a perspective of the distribution of deficiencies across the Business Units. Obviously, Business units with higher absolute or percentage values should cause remedial action to be taken.

BUSINESS UNIT DEFICIENCY REPORT								
BUS UNIT	PROCESSES	CONTROLS	TESTS EXECUTED	IDENTIFIED DEFICIENCIES	% DEFICIENCIES	DESIGN DEFICIENCIES	% OF TOTAL DEFICIENCIES	OPERATIONAL DEFICIENCIES	% OF TOTAL DEFICIENCIES
BU1									
BU2									
BU3									
TOTALS									

2. RISK TYPE DEFICIENCY REPORT - This report will provide your management with a risk perspective of their deficiencies. The intent is to focus management's attention to the high risk and non routine controls that are reporting deficiencies. The report also displays information on the distribution of deficiencies between design and operating deficiencies

CONTROL RISK DEFICIENCY REPORT									
RISK FACTOR	BUSINESS UNIT	CONTROLS	TESTS EXECUTED	IDENTIFIED DEFICIENCIES	% DEFICIENCIES	DESIGN DEFICIENCIES	% OF TOTAL DEFICIENCIES	OPERATIONAL DEFICIENCIES	% OF TOTAL DEFICIENCIES
HIGH RISK	BU1								

	BU2									
	BU3									
NON ROUTINE	BU1									
	BU2									
	BU3									
ROUTINE	BU1									
	BU2									
	BU3									
TOTALS										

REMEDIATION PLANS

The reports in this section are intended to provide you with a comprehensive perspective on the remediation efforts within your company.

1. BASIC REMEDIATION PLAN REPORTING – Based on the data displayed by this report, you should focus on all *missing* remediation plans. In addition, you should provide n alternate view displaying the time span between deficiency identification date and proposed remediation date so that management is aware of the average time lapse.

BUSINESS UNIT REMEDIATION PLAN REPORT										
BUS UNIT	PROCESSES	CONTROLS	DEFICIENCIES	REMEDIATION PLANS FILED	MISSING PLANS	Q1 2006	Q2 2006	Q3 2006	Q4 2006	2007
BU1										
BU2										
BU3										
TOTALS										

2. RISK TYPE REMEDIATION PLANS - This report provides a distribution across the risk categories allowing you to focus on the risk categories that are of importance to their efforts. Missing plans should trigger escalation processes. Missing plans for *high risk* and *non routine* deficiencies must be given the highest priority.

SOX Management must communicate these priorities to the Business Units and require fortnightly or monthly updates from the responsible Business Units.

RISK TYPE REMEDIATION PLAN REPORT										
RISK	BUSINESS UNIT	CONTROLS	DEFICIENCIES	REMEDIATION PLANS FILED	MISSING PLANS	Q1 2006	Q2 2006	Q3 2006	Q4 2006	2007
HIGH RISK	BU1									
	BU2									
	BU3									
NON ROUTINE	BU1									
	BU2									
	BU3									
ROUTINE	BU1									
	BU2									
	BU3									
TOTALS										

3. PROCESS REMEDIATION PLANS - When used correctly, the report will provide you with one of the first indications of the possibility of an aggregated significant deficiency or material weakness by indicating any processes with a significantly number of deficiencies versus controls.

The Report can, at your option be further expanded to indicate a further subdivision between high risk and other controls

PROCESS REMEDIATION PLAN REPORT										
PROCESS	BUSINESS UNIT	CONTROLS	DEFICIENCIES	REMEDIATION PLANS FILED	MISSING PLANS	Q1 2006	Q2 2006	Q3 2006	Q4 2006	2007
PROC 1	BU1									
	BU2									
	BU3									
TOTALS										
PROC 2	BU1									
	BU2									
	BU3									
TOTALS										
PROC 3	BU1									
	BU2									
	BU3									
TOTALS										
REPORT TOTALS										

OTHER DOCUMENTATION

This section covers all external audit issues, sub certifications, significant changes, and error log data.

1. EXTERNAL AUDIT ISSUES DETAILED REPORT - External Audit issues do not always relate to processes and controls. In some instances, they may not be attributed to a specific business unit, region, process or test. Where process, control and business unit cross references do not exist, they should be classified jointly by the External Auditor and the SOX Department.

   Therefore, there are usually three reports – a detailed report, an exception report and a summary report. It is recommended that the exception report be used for management escalation. Because of space limitations, we have not been able to display all the columns required for this report, only the key columns.

EXTERNAL AUDIT ISSUES REPORT								
PRIORITY LEVEL	EXTERNAL AUDIT ID	PROCESS ID	CONTROL ID	BUSINESS UNIT	DESCRIPTION	ID DATE	TARGET DATE	ASSIGNED TO:
HIGH	EXT123-8	Revenue			This is an example of a description	2005/01/05	2005/11/30	Mr. A. Jones
	EXT 6545							
	EXT 987-8							
MEDIUM	EXT 1456							
	EXT 9856							
	EXT 2541							
LOW	EXT 8745							
	EXT 3652							
	EXT 1452							
TOTALS								

The following minimum *additional* columns are usually required

- Status of item e.g. in progress, delayed, cancelled, etc.

- Your company's response,
- Update columns by date detailing progress of report,
- Cross references to Entity Controls,
- External Audit contact, and
- Business Unit contact,

2. EXTERNAL AUDIT SUMMARY / EXCEPTION REPORTS - Summary and Exception Reports should be provided based on Priority of items, Business Units, Late Target dates, and Audit requirements.

3. ERROR LOG REPORTS – these are designed to report on all Finance Division Error Logs on a quarterly basis. Similar to the External Auditor Issues, these should comprise of detail, exception and summary reports.

This report should be provided to all Senior Management and the Audit Committee at the end of each quarter. The intent is to focus Management's attention to the areas that will require additional attention in the next quarter.

A pattern in Financial Statement Lines may also indicate the possibility of an aggregated significant deficiency or material weakness and should be analyzed by SOX Management with their recommendations

Exception reports should state clearly all errors for which there are no existing controls.

All Error Log reports must display at a minimum the following information:

- Financial Statement Line,
- Identifier of Error,
- Business Unit that was source/originator of error,
- Whether a Control Exists to prevent or detect this error,
- Control ID,
- Description of error,
- Amount of error,
- Whether the Business Unit has been notified of the error caused by the Unit,
- Whether a Remediation Plan has been received,
- Remediation date?
- Deficiency Listing updated? and
- Deficiency ID number,

Exceptions Reports should list:

- Log Errors for which there are no controls,
- Log Errors for which there are no remediation plans, and
- Log Errors with late remediation plans.

4. ERROR LOG SPECIAL PROCESSING - In some organizations, if an error is identified for a control that has previously passed normal testing, the control is added to a special management approval list for future review and approval.

This list requires the control and its future tests to pass special SOX Department or Internal Audit review prior to any future test results that designate the control as operating effectively being accepted. In some instances, the test is re performed by internal audit before the control is accepted as being properly designed and operating effectively.

ADVANCED / COMPOUND REPORTING

This section assumes that you have established the guidelines for the design, implementation and assessment of your internal control framework in tangible, pragmatic terms. These guidelines should have been reviewed and approved by the audit committee and external auditors. In addition, they have been published to the Business Units for implementation in the current fiscal year.

CONTROLS, TEST AND DEFICIENCY PERSPECTIVE

Usually, we recommend that these reports be designed for use by:

- BUSINESS UNIT MANAGERS – these reports are an aid to assist the manager in their design, implementation and assessment efforts. These reports should be provided quarterly or as requested by the Business Unit Managers,

- CHIEF FINANCIAL OFFICER – to provide an overall comprehensive status of the internal control framework and its assessments. The CFO should be concentrating on the coverage and deficiency areas in Q2 and Q3.

- BOARD AND COMMITTEES – provides an overall status of the internal control framework, the aggregated deficiencies, the remediation plans for material weaknesses and significant deficiencies.

    1. BUSINESS UNIT ADVANCED REPORTS – ENVIRONMENT - The Report provides a Business Unit Manager with a comprehensive view of their unit's SOX documentation, assessment, deficiency identification and other critical results. This enables the manager to focus and concentrate necessary resources on the critical areas identified.

    This summary should be supported by a detailed report listing all the information summarized in the above example.

BUSINESS UNIT SOX ADVANCED REPORT FOR BUSINESS UNIT BUS 1								
SIGNIFICANT ACCOUNT RECAP								
SIGNIFICANT ACCOUNT COVERAGE	REQUIRED ACCOUNTS	42	DOCUMENTED ACCOUNTS	32	APPROVED CHANGES	-2	MISSING ACCOUNTS	18
SIGNIFICANT ACCOUNT RECAP								
PROCESS RECAP	REQUIRED PROCESSES	14	DOCUMENTED PROCESSES	12	MISSING PROCESSES	2		
CONTROLS RECAP FOR FISCAL YEAR TO DATE								
CONTROL TYPE	COUNT	REJECTED CONTROLS	TESTED	TESTS NOT MEETING GUIDELINES	NOT TESTED	DEFICIENCIES	REMEDIATION PLANS	REQUIRING MANAGEMENT ACTION
HIGH RISK	33	2	30	14	3	5	4	This cell should contain the sum of all errors
NON ROUTINE	21	9	19	4	2	12	6	
ROUTINE	45	15	33	5	12	8	1	
TOTALS	99	26	82	23	17	25	11	

   2. CFO AND BOARD ADVANCED REPORTS – ENVIRONMENT - The CFO, Board and Committees' Reports should be the same information recapped at the Corporate Level.

   3. ADVANCED REPORTS – FINANCIAL STATEMENT PERSPECTIVE - We provide this report as an example of a "*best in breed*" type of report that your company should aspire to.

We are however assuming in presenting this report, that you have a mature and tested internal control framework with robust SOX operating procedures.

The intent of the report is to provide the Senior Management, Board and all Committees with a comprehensive perspective of the Internal Control framework and its direct coverage of the financial Statements.

In this illustration, we have used only the Current Assets section of a fictitious corporation's Financial Statements. The entire Financial Statements, including Notes should also be covered in this report.

For each of columns in the illustration, detailed support information should be provided to support the Financial Statement Line summary above. This detailed information should be provided by Financial Statement line and by Business Unit so that Management can determine the remedial action required to cover any inadequacies or gaps in coverage.

In addition, we have also excluded the following columns for space limitations

- Error Log occurrences and Amounts,
- Amounts covered by Controls from Business Units,
- Deficiency dollar amounts,
- Remediation Dollar Amounts, and
- Aggregated Deficiencies for Financial Statement lines.

FINANCIAL STATEMENT / INTERNAL CONTROL FRAMEWORK SUMMARY REPORT.										
FINANCIAL STATEMENT LINE	BALANCE	RISK LEVEL	% COVERAGE	CONTROLS - ACCEPTED REJECTED	TESTS	NON GUIDELINE TESTS	NOT TESTED	DEFICIENCIES	REMEDIATION PLANS	MISSING REDEMPTION PLANS
Cash and cash equivalents	$ 3,686	High	42%	42 16	35	4		22	10	5
		Other		145 22						
Restricted cash and cash equivalents	0	High								
		Other								
Accounts receivable - net	$2,551	High								
		Other								
Inventories - net	$1,414	High								
		Other								
Deferred income taxes - net	$ 255	High								
		Other								
Other current assets	$356									
TOTALS										

TIME LINE PERSPECTIVES

Assuming that you adopt a prudent time line as outlined in the SOX *Calendar* chapter, the activities should be *front ended* in the fiscal year. Typically, the calendar should operate on the following basis:

QUARTER 1 – all documentation and tests should be performed for all annual controls, one half of all high risk controls and one third of all other controls.

QUARTER 2 – all documentation and tests should be performed for all annual controls, the remainder of the high risk controls and one third of all other controls. *Remediation activities for all high risk deficiencies, identified in Q1, should immediately commence with a targeted end date of Q3.*

QUARTER 3 – all documentation and tests should be performed for all annual controls, the remainder of the other controls. Coverage exceptions for Significant Accounts should be identified and reported back to the Business Units for correction. *Remediation activities for all high risk deficiencies, identified in Q2, should immediately commence with a targeted end date of Q3 (or with management approval Q4).*

QUARTER 4 – All remediated items should be jointly tested with External Auditors or Internal Audit. All incomplete coverage exceptions should be remediated.

The time line reports should therefore reflect all tardy items by Business Unit, Period and Risk factor.

EXCEPTION REPORTING

The Exception Reporting in this section is intended for use by Business Unit Management, SOX Department Management and Senior Management. The Senior Management reports should also be used for the Audit Committee and the Board of Directors.

In developing exception reports, there must be a standard or other control feature against which the data being examined is measured or compared. Based on this comparison to a standard, exceptions can be simply identified.

BASIC STANDARDS REQUIRED FOR EXCEPTION REPORTING

In order for a sound exception process to operate, you must develop at a minimum the following *classes* of standards:

1. SOX DATA COMPLETENESS refers to the presence or absence of information based on the individual record,

2. SOX DATA ACCURACY asks whether data values have been entered into the Repository correctly and whether data values have been distorted during the processing. We have provided additional information on this area within the Repository chapter,

3. SOX DATA AUTHORIZATION looks at whether transactions are authorized by appropriate personnel for proper accountability. We usually recommend that there are quarterly representations (sub certifications) in which Business Unit Managers explicitly state that they have reviewed and approved the processes, controls and all other related activities.

4. SOX DATA CONSISTENCY asks whether policies, procedures, and standards have been uniformly applied.

5. SOX DATA TIMELINESS means that data is current for its intended use and that has been provided based on the prescribed timeline.

6. SOX COVERAGE COMPLETENESS requires that the Business units ensure that their portions of the framework cover the required subject areas identified by Significant Account and

Processes assigned to each Business Unit. This coverage must be designed to ensure that both the accounts and their relative financial assertions are covered entirely.

7. SOX PERFORMANCE STANDARDS are required in the assessment (test) functions and other related areas. Management mandates the performance level required based on the risk profile of the process or control. For example, high risk controls can only be tested at the re performance level.

8. EXTERNAL AUDITOR GUIDELINES are usually mutually agreed at the beginning of the fiscal year in order to ensure that the audit is conducted in a coordinated and cost effective manner.

DATA STANDARDS EXCEPTION REPORTING

All data submitted to the Repository must be subjected to a validation routine that we have previously described in the Repository chapter.

Records not meeting the validation requirements must be identified on an exception listing and returned to the Business Units for correction. It is integral to the design of the report that the cause for rejection is clearly identified for each record. In most instances, from our experience, there are usually multiple causes for failure and the first validation will require a minimum of three occurrences.

1. INVALID RECORDS REPORT - The report may be produced by Business Unit, or by file submitted. For each file that is validated, the following report should be produced. We have not displayed all the columns due to space limitations.

VALIDATION REPORT FOR FILE 125487.xls							
CONTROL ID	CONTROL DESCRIPTION	OTHER CONTROL DETAILS	DUPLICATE?	COLUMN 1	COLUMN 2	NO OF ERRORS FOR CONTROL	RESPONSIBILITY
BUS1 PROC1_ CTL 523	Controls for ABC	This section should be used for other columns used to identify the Control that has Failed Validation	No	This section is an illustration of all the columns that are validated within the program. For each column that is validated a pass or fail code should be displayed. Where the validations interrelated between columns, combination column headings should be used.			
BUS1- PROC1_ CTL 524	Controls for DEF		No				
BUS1- PROC1_ CTL 525	Controls for Synchronized Step 1		No				
BUS1- PROC1_ CTL 526	Logical Access control		No				
TOTALS							

2. SUMMARY VALIDATION REPORT BY BUSINESS UNIT - produced by Business Unit and Quarter. The intent of the report is to provide SOX Department Management with the capability to identify patterns in the validation process.

Typically, repeat offenders in the Business Units usually signify the need for retraining. A pattern of consistent errors in specific columns usually signifies the need to change the methods used to train this specific item.

VALIDATION REPORT by BUSINESS UNIT for Q1 2006								
BUSINESS UNIT	FILES	PROCESSES	CONTROLS	REJECTED RECORDS	COLUMNS PER CONTROL	NO OF INVALID COLUMNS	CONTROLS % FAILED	COLUMNS % FAILED
BUS 1								
BUS 2								

VALIDATION REPORT by BUSINESS UNIT for Q1 2006								
BUSINESS UNIT	FILES	PROCESSES	CONTROLS	REJECTED RECORDS	COLUMNS PER CONTROL	NO OF INVALID COLUMNS	CONTROLS % FAILED	COLUMNS % FAILED
BUS 3								
BUS 4								
TOTALS								

RULES

Assuming that you have predefined the documentation, testing and sub certifications rules then all documentation that is submitted to the repository must *meet or exceed* these rules or be subject to Senior Management intervention. We have used the Testing environment to provide the illustrations

1. TEST RULE – LEVEL/ FREQUENCY ETC.- All controls are to be tested as per the prescribed chart. We have provided a typical example. We have not completed the sections for Semi Annual or Annual as these should be self explanatory.

	VALIDATION REPORT by BUSINESS UNIT for Q1 2006							
	LESS THAN QUARTERLY		QUARTERLY		SEMI ANNUAL		ANNUAL	
CONTROL LEVEL	LEVEL	NO OF TESTS PER ANNUM	LEVEL	NO OF TESTS PER ANNUM	LEVEL	NO OF TESTS PER ANNUM	LEVEL	NO OF TESTS PER ANNUM
HIGH RISK	Re Performance	2	Re Performance	2				
Non Routine	Examination	2	Examination	2				
Routine	Examination	2	Examination	2				
IT GENERAL	Re Performance	4	Re Performance	4				
TOTALS								

2. TEST RULE EXCEPTION REPORT – TEST LEVEL - This report will display all test exceptions that were not performed at the prescribed level by Business Unit. These reports should be provided to the Business Units for corrective action and for follow up by the SOX Department.

3. TEST RULE EXCEPTION REPORT – FREQUENCY - The report should identify all controls that have not been tested for the required frequency.

COMPLETENESS

SOX Management should ensure that the internal control framework is complete in its coverage of the Financial Statements and significant processes within the Corporation.

Usually this is subdivided into three sections for completeness checks:

- QUANTITATIVE ACCOUNTS as reflected on the Financial Statements

- QUALITATIVE ACCOUNTS represented by clearing accounts, off balance sheet items, offset accounts, transfer accounts, etc., and

- FINANCIAL STATEMENT NOTES where these notes and their supporting schedules are supported by input from Business Units and are not necessarily always directly reflected on the Financial Statements.

1. **QUANTITATIVE ACCOUNTS EXCEPTION REPORT** - The intent of this report is to identify whether the Business Units assigned have covered the Significant Accounts assigned to them at the beginning of the quarter.

   You must have a *Significant Account to Financial Statement cross reference file* that is maintained on a quarterly basis in order for this report to be produced. The Report quantifies the differences based on the amounts that are attached to each significant account for the period.

| QUANTITATIVE ACCOUNTS EXCEPTION REPORT ||||||||||||
| FINANCIAL STATEMENT LINE | BUSINESS UNIT | FINANCIAL STATEMENT | COVERAGE REQUIRED | COVERAGE DOCUMENTED | % | ASSERTIONS ||||||
						EXIST	OCCUR	COMP	RIGHTS	VALUE	PRESENT
Cash and cash equivalents	BUS 1	$ 3,686	$2,654	1954		Yes	Yes	Yes			
	BUS 2		$150	150			Yes				
	BUS 3		$462	314							
TOTAL		$ 3,686	$3,266	$2,418	65						
Restricted cash and cash equivalents	BUS 1	0									
	BUS 2										
	BUS 3										
TOTAL											
Accounts receivable - net	BUS 1	$2,551									
	BUS 2										
	BUS 3										
TOTAL											
Inventories - net	BUS 1	$1,414									
	BUS 2										
	BUS 3										
TOTAL											
Deferred income taxes - net	BUS 1	$ 255									
	BUS 2										
	BUS 3										
TOTAL											

2. **QUALITATIVE ACCOUNT EXCEPTION REPORT** - Qualitative Accounts are more nebulous to attribute to specific Business Units.

   Assuming that these will be attributed from a central area, you should maintain a schedule on a quarterly basis of all Business Units and their coverage requirements. If this schedule is maintained, then the previous report format, without dollar amounts, will provide the exception coverage report.

3. **FINANCIAL STATEMENTS NOTES EXCEPTION REPORT** - You should maintain a *Notes Coverage Matrix* by Business Unit as outline in the Financial Statements Risk Assessment chapter. The Financial Notes Exception Report should be in the same format as the Qualitative Accounts Exception Report.

DETAILED METRICS

We would recommend that the following metrics be maintained on a period over period basis within the repository.

1. QUARTERLY ARCHIVE METRICS - These basic metrics should be maintained by Period, by Category below, by Business Unit.

    - Number of Processes,
    - Number of Controls,
    - Number of Systems,
    - Number of Auditor issues,
    - Number of Regulator deficiencies, and
    - Number of Internal Audit Issues.

2. YEAREND METRICS - These basic metrics should be maintained by Period, by Category below, by Business Unit.

    - Number of Yearend Controls,
    - Number of Error Log entries – Preventive,
    - Number of Error Log – Detective,
    - Number of Auditor Error Log, and
    - Number of Auditor Deficiency reconciliation

3. DEFICIENCY MANAGEMENT METRICS - These basic metrics should be maintained by Period, by Category below, by Business Unit.

    - New deficiencies for this quarter
    - Design deficiencies,
    - Operational deficiencies,
    - Deficiencies by deficiency Type,
    - Deficiencies by deficiency Classification,
    - Deficiencies by deficiency Category,
    - Modifications, and
    - Quarter over quarter reconciliations

4. REMEDIATION ANALYSES - These basic metrics should be maintained by Period, by Category below, by Business Unit.

    - Action Plan tracking,
    - Business Unit Reporting, and
    - Management Reporting

5. CALENDAR REPORTING -These basic metrics should be maintained by Period, by Category below, by Business Unit.

    - Documentation Submission metrics,
    - Validation metrics,
    - Period over Period Adds, and
    - Period over period deletions

6. TESTING STATUS - These basic metrics should be maintained by Period, by Category below, by Business Unit.

    - Cycle Reports,
    - Threshold exception reports, and
    - Guideline exception reports

SUMMARY

In this chapter, we have provided a organized, but diverse, perspective of the reports and metrics that should be used in SOX Reporting. For additional information, please refer to our website at **www.sustainedsox.com**.

Chapter 9 – Sarbanes Oxley Assessment (test) Processes

Intent of this Chapter

The intent of this chapter is to provide you with the methods and tools that should be used in the assessment of an internal control framework.

The assessment of the internal control framework requires your company to evaluate the design and operating effectiveness of the entire framework as implemented within your company. The approach should always be *top down* and not the bottom up approach several companies used in their initial certification.

The words assessment, evaluation and test are used frequently in SOX books, manuals and documentation with varying meanings.

For purposes of this chapter, we define all of these terms as follows:

Assessment / Evaluations and Tests are defined as *"a series of processes that are executed to ensure that your internal control framework is designed correctly, implemented and operating effectively. These processes must be performed based on management or regulatory guidelines and thresholds."*

Objectives of the Assessment/Evaluation Processes

The objectives of the assessment processes are fourfold:

1. DESIGN AND OPERATIONAL EFFECTIVENESS: An overall examination of the entire framework to ensure that as a whole it has the correct design and operating capabilities,

2. COMPLETENESS: To ensure that the internal framework is complete in its coverage – that it includes all the relative entity and transaction processes and controls required to maintain control over the financial reporting,

3. COMPONENTS: To deconstruct the framework into its components e.g. processes, points of focus, controls etc. and to *collectively* ensure that these are designed, implemented and operating effectively,

4. REASONABLE ASSURANCE: To provide the CEO and CFO with the reasonable assurances for them to confidently certify the effectiveness of the internal control framework.

Therefore, the assessment process must:

- Review and ensure the framework for overall design effectiveness,
- Ensure that all key elements are implemented as designed,
- Collectively and singularly, all elements operate effectively, and
- The Framework covers all pertinent requirements for financial reporting.

The link between the assessment processes and the risk identification processes must be considered to be immutable when designing your firm's assessment processes.

Overview

In this chapter, we outline the eight basic steps for a comprehensive assessment program. These eight basic steps are as follows:

1. Establish your corporate guidelines and thresholds for both the entity and transaction level program assessment processes,

2. Review the entire framework for completeness – based on this review you can determine whether the framework is complete by executing the following steps,

    - Review the Entity Level program and compare for completeness versus the COSO model (or other model being used), and

    - Review the transaction level program to ensure it addresses all Significant accounts and processes,

3. Design and execute the Entity Control assessment program (using the information in the detail section of this chapter and Chapter 3) to evaluate the design and operations of the program,

4. Design and Execute the Transaction Level assessment program (using the information in this chapter) to evaluate the design and operations of this program,

5. Compare the results of these assessments versus the Management Guidelines and Thresholds to ensure integrity of the assessment program,

6. Identify deficiencies and execute the steps outlined in the Deficiency Management chapter,

7. Execute the sub certification program in Chapter 11 – which requires all SOX personnel to certify that they have complied with all requirements, and

8. Summarize all the activities for the inclusion into the management certification report that is outlined in a later section of this chapter for management and board for review and approval

GROUND RULES

For an effective assessment process, these are the basic rules that you should implement within your company as prerequisites to starting the assessment process.

ASSESSORS / TESTERS

All personnel are involved in these activities are required to attend and *successfully pass* your company's training for assessing entity level and transaction level controls.

The SOX Department should maintain a master file for all personnel that have attended and successfully passed these training courses. The External Auditors may request this information in order to determine the level of reliance to be placed on some of the testing efforts. This file should contain the following basic information.

- Name of individual,
- Name of Company (you may be using external consultants for some activities),
- Internal Business Unit (if an employee),
- Years of accounting/ finance experience,
- Accounting/ Finance designations,

- Date of training class and subject of training class,
- Business Unit and Processes individual has been assigned to that individual has been assigned, and
- Objectivity Levels based on assigned processes.

EVIDENCE MAINTENANCE

For transaction level control tests, Business Units are required to maintain all supporting evidence of the test for the minimum period established by your company. This evidence should be maintained in special digital directories that are subdivided by fiscal year and quarter.

Where evidence is in a physical format, the Business Unit SOX Manager should be responsible for maintaining all files for audit or regulatory review.

OBJECTIVITY LEVEL

When any of the assessment processes is performed the objective is to achieve the maximum level of objectivity possible.

The *objectivity* of assessments is one of the qualifying factors used by External Auditors to determine whether they can rely on these assessments. Objectivity is assigned based on the following table.

OBJECTIVITY LEVEL	ASSESSMENT PERFORMER
Unacceptable	• The process or the control owner performing the assessment of processes and controls that are owned by them.
Minimal Level	• Individuals within the same Business Unit performing assessments on processes or controls which they do not own
Moderate Level	• Individuals from outside the Business to which the process or control owner reports that are assigned to asses the processes or controls, or • Internal Audit or qualified external third party assesses controls and reports to Company Management
High Level	• Internal Audit or qualified external third party assesses controls and reports to Audit Committee

SAMPLE SIZES

Sample sizes are usually based on a mutual agreement between your company and its Auditors. The table below illustrates an example of Sample Sizes and Test periods. The table, like the rest of examples in the volume, assumes a fiscal yearend of December 31, 2006:

CONTROL FREQUENCY	SAMPLE SIZES	USUAL QUARTERLY TEST PERIOD	MIN. REMEDIATION TIME
Annual at Fiscal Yearend	1	Usually in January or February 2007 on the performance date of the control	1 year
Annual not at Fiscal Yearend	1	Upon anniversary date of the control	1 Year
Semi-Annual	1	Q1 or Q2 – if this control has had a deficiency previously or this is your initial certification – this will provide you the opportunity to fix in the second half of the year. Based on your judgment, you may perform the test in the second half of the year.	At least half a year.
Quarterly	2	Q1 or Q2 – if this control has had a deficiency previously or this is your initial certification – this will provide you the	2 Quarters

Control Frequency	Sample Sizes	Usual Quarterly test period	Min. Remediation Time
		opportunity to fix in the second half of the year. Based on your judgment, you may perform the test in the second half of the year.	
Monthly	2	Q2 – if this control has had a deficiency previously or this is your initial certification – this will provide you the opportunity to fix in the second half of the year.	2 months
Weekly	5	In Q2 and Q3 of the fiscal year.	5 weeks
Daily	20	In Q2 and Q3 of the fiscal year.	15 days
Multiple times a day	25	In Q2 and Q3 of the fiscal year.	30 days
Event-driven	10% of events (min=1, max=10)	From Q2, Q3, or Q4 (At least 50% from Q3 and Q4)	N/A

In selecting samples, the tester should be observing the following guidelines:

- The sample selected should be *representative* of the population of normal transactions,

- Every item in the population should have an *equal chance* of selection except when required to select the most recent occurrences. There should be no bias or judgment applied in the selection of sample items,

- If an item selected for sampling cannot be located for testing - the unavailable sample item must be noted as a test exception. *Testers should not select another item*, and

- Corrected controls must be operating effectively for the minimum amount of time displayed in the last column before retesting is attempted.

Test Methods - Entity Level Controls

There are four types of tests used in entity level controls viz.

1. INTERVIEWS of key personnel e.g. CEO, CFO, Senior Managers, etc.

2. ANONYMOUS EMPLOYEE SURVEYS that are used to ascertain the effectiveness of entity controls,

3. REVIEWS OF KEY DOCUMENTS to determine the design and operational effectiveness of these controls.

4. SUMMARY EVALUATIONS based on the above three items to determine whether the control has been designed and is operating effectively.

Test Methods - Transaction Level Controls

There are four ypes of tests used in transaction level control assessments, listed from most reliable to least reliable.

1. RE-PERFORMANCE TEST: The independent execution of controls by the tester. The tester should know the results anticipated prior to the actual re performance.

   This level of testing is usually required for all high risk controls by prudent company management.

2. INSPECTION / EXAMINATION: Obtaining testing evidence by examining records or documents, whether internal or external, in paper form, electronic form, or other media based on the Business Unit's testing. The tester should establish the authenticity of all test material,

3. OBSERVATION: Obtaining testing evidence by looking at a process or procedure being performed by others – usually the control performer. The tester should request that specific tests be performed using data or examples provided by the tester, and

4. INQUIRY: Obtaining testing evidence by seeking information of knowledgeable persons from within the company or external to the company..

TIMETABLES - TRANSACTION LEVEL CONTROLS

Because of the inter reliance between some types of tests, the timing and coordination is critical.

The SOX Department must have a comprehensive view of the entire framework in order to efficiently organize the testing. The basic rules used in developing the time table are as follows:

1. Determine all processes and controls that "*hand off*" to another process or control – these should be tested simultaneously in order to have a complete end-to end test. Coordinate these activities with the relevant Business Units.

2. Determine where there is a reliance on other processes and controls that require coordination of the test activities. These are usually in the IT and other centralized areas. For example, the security features of an IT application (controlled centrally by the IT Department) is included as part of a control in the transaction level program – it requires IT assistance in order to complete any testing activities.

   These activities can be coordinated by the SOX Department or the centralized departments can provide the SOX Department with their "testing windows" and contacts for publication in the SOX Calendar.

3. The SOX Departments should mandate that all key or high risk controls be tested earlier in the fiscal year in order to have the necessary remediation time in the event of a deficiency,

ENTITY CONTROLS

Entity Control Assessment processes focus on three primary areas: interviews, surveys and evidence reviews. Please reference Chapter 3 for detailed information on the Entity Level program

INTERVIEWS

Interviews are usually designed or modified in Q1 of the fiscal year. This provides the SOX Department (assuming that it will be the SOX Department that will be conducting this assessment) with the lead time to assemble the interview documents for a Q2 assessment process.

The development of interview forms and other documents require all entity control owners to prepare their questions or interview points within the first 60 days of the new fiscal year.

These should be forwarded to the SOX Department for sorting into the requisite interview forms. The following are the minimum interview forms that should be prepared within your organization

- Chief Executive Officer (an example of this interview form is provided in Chapter 3),
- Chief Financial Officer,
- Chief Operations Officer,
- Chairperson of the Board,
- Chairperson of Audit Committee,
- Chairperson of Disclosure Committee,
- Board Member (a random sample of board members is usually used for this interview),
- Audit Committee Member (other than Chairperson)
- Chief Administrative Officer,
- Senior Human resources Manager,
- Chief Information Officer,
- Controller,
- Chief Legal and Compliance Officers,
- Chief Risk Officer, and
- Chief Internal Auditor.

ANONYMOUS EMPLOYEE SURVEY

Nothing in the regulations requires this survey to be anonymous. However, in our experience, if this survey is anonymous, we have tended to receive more frank responses when compared with open surveys.

The Survey should cover all pertinent elements of the Entity Control Framework. We have provided a sample of this survey in Chapter 3 – please refer to it.

The population selected for the survey should focus on critical areas of the organization. In our experience we tend to weigh 65% of the surveys to Finance, Accounting, IT and Management candidates. The remaining 35% is focused on all other areas of the organization (including external vendors).

SUPPORTING EVIDENCE

To support the existence and operational effectiveness of entity controls, the testers must acquire and review the necessary evidence to ensure that it meets the standards. The acquisition of this evidence is done through

- The interviews as noted in the first section,
- The employees surveys as noted in the second section, and
- The "paper trail" of documents that support the entity control structure.

This paper trail comprises of the following:

1. Policies that have been reviewed and approved by management and the board,

2. Company procedure manuals,

3. Evidence of enforcement of company policies and procedures when non compliance has been detected,

4. Evidence of mechanisms within the company to assist in the identification of non compliance – the most obvious being the whistle blower program

5. The management communications that are used to disseminate these policies and procedures an the remedies taken when there is an infraction,

6. The training and orientation processes used to make employees aware of the requirements and to educate them on their roles and responsibilities, and

7. The formal documentation of the company's organization hierarchy including the table of authorities and responsibilities, performance measurements, compensation plans and formal job definitions.

A properly designed entity level control assessment program provides guidance to the tester on what are the key objectives and elements that should be incorporated into the review. This should reduce the reliance on an individual's judgment and place emphasis on definitive company guidelines.

In Chapter 3, we provide examples of the preparation work required for this assessment. The table below expands on one of the components – the Control environment, its points of focus and related controls.

For each of these controls, we display a pragmatic assessment process for each control. The judgmental elements cannot be totally eliminated, but as you can note from this table, we have established the minimum standards for assign a control as being designed properly and operating effectively.

ASSESSMENT CHECK LIST FOR THE CONTROL ENVIRONMENT

This is an example of the assessment checklist that should be constructed for the Control Environment. We have provided only the Code of Conduct (Ethics) to illustrate the assessment steps that should be used in this process.

CONTROL	CONTROL ASSESSMENT GUIDELINES
POINT OF FOCUS: CODE OF CONDUCT	
CC 001 - A code of conduct and other policies regarding acceptable or permitted business practices, conflicts of interest, and expected standards of ethical behavior is developed and maintained on an ongoing basis in your company,	1. Determine whether a code of Conduct or Ethics exists in a formal document.. Obtain copy of latest code of conduct and ethics, 2.. Review document to ensure that it includes the minimum following information: • Our company's conduct towards employees – ensure health, safety, discrimination and harassment policies/processes are covered,, • Employees Conduct required toward company, • Conflicts of Interest, Confidential Information policies and prohibition of personal benefit from these activities, • Compliance with Laws, Rules and Regulations – including all securities, national, regional and other laws,, • Accounting, Record Keeping and Financial reporting policies and necessity to comply with the e policies, • Conduct with Clients – respect, client complaints, etc., • Conduct with Suppliers – arms length, prohibition of bribes, non solicitation, etc., • Conduct required for Company Assets, • Communications about Business Ethics concerns – grievances, complaints, channels, etc., • Fraud Policies, • Intellectual Property and copyrights • Conduct with Investors, • Conduct with Creditors, • Conduct with Auditors,

CONTROL	CONTROL ASSESSMENT GUIDELINES
	• Conduct toward/within Industry, • Conduct as member of Society and Community – including environmental laws etc. • Implementation and Enforcements policies and procedures for this Code of Conduct • Waiver process for this policy (not all companies have this section) • Communications of any infraction of this Code of conduct 3. Include in interviews questionnaires for all Senior Officers/Managers of company, and **4. Determine whether Code of Conduct meets the minimum requirements in item 2.**
CC 002 - The communications and training processes that your company employs to inform all employees of the policies regarding acceptable behavior and what they are required to do when they encounter improper or non compliant behavior,	1. Obtain Training and orientation material – including manuals, presentations, HR exception file detailing employees who have not attended and their positions / titles within the firm. 2. Review Training material to ensure that it covers all items in item 2 of previous section, 3. Review most current update to Code of Conduct and one other randomly selected update. Determine whether these updates were communicated to all employees. Determine whether Managers were required to acknowledge receipt of these updates. 4. Request evidence of Senior Management's latest communications on importance of ethics and code of conduct, 5 Sample interview personnel across several locations on Code of Conduct using pertinent questions on acceptable practices, etc., and **6. Assess this control based on:** • **Completeness of training courses – does it cover all the topics?,** • **Attendance percentage of personnel – use the HR Exception list to determine whether high risk areas adequately covered,** • **Review Update communications processes– determine whether or not they were communicated to employees on a timely basis, and** • **Use the Interview results to determine employee absorption.**
CC.003 – All new employees are informed of the importance of ethics and good internal control at their initial orientation into the company This is required to be delivered at the original orientation session and employees should be required to acknowledge receipt of this training.	1. Same as above – with focus on new employee orientation, and 2. Focus only on new hires in last six months.
CC.004 - Company Management follows ethical guidelines in dealing with all parties. This must include employees, suppliers, investors, creditors, competitors, external counsel and auditors,	1.. Review representative sample of the external parties files (on the left) together with the pertinent sections of the Code of Conduct (CC 001- Item 1) 2. Based on these samples and the code ascertain if management follows these guidelines, 3. Include as part of External Vendor's survey, 4. Include as part of anonymous employees survey. **5. Assess this control based on the results of items 2 through 4.**
CC.005 -Management removes incentives or temptations that might cause personnel to engage in dishonest or unethical acts. Management reviews all	1. Review all reward programs (including compensation programs), 2. Discuss plans, metrics of rewards, changes to plans, etc. with responsible Human Resource personnel, 3. Review compensation strategy to determine impact on fraud considerations,

CONTROL	CONTROL ASSESSMENT GUIDELINES
incentives, etc. on a regular periodic basis.	4. Review if any complaints filed with Whistle Blower program, 5. **Assess this control based on the results of items 1 through 4.**
CC.006 -Compensation processes, such as bonuses, granting of options, stock ownership etc., are designed and implemented to promote an appropriate ethical tone (e.g. bonuses are not granted to those who circumvent established policies, procedures, or controls),	1.Review Executive Compensation Policy, 2. Discuss the executive compensation plans with the Executive Compensation HR committee, 3. Include as part of Senior Executives Interviews, and 4. **Assess this control based on the results of items 1 through 3.**
CC.007 - When management becomes aware of non compliance with policies and procedures, they respond to such violations in an appropriate and timely manner based on established company guidelines. If there is a variation versus company guidelines that can be construed as favoritism, Management is obligated to explain any mitigating circumstances without violating any other company policies.	1. Review HR records for disciplinary actions taken over last fiscal year, 2. Review Whistler Blower programs for complaints and management actions based on these complaints, 3. If possible, conduct anonymous survey of employees based on employee survey outlined later in this chapter,, 4. Include in Senior Company Management interviews, and 5. **Assess this control based on the results of items 1 through 4.**
CC.009 - All changes to established relationships with external parties (e.g., attorneys, auditors, bankers) are approved at an appropriate level of management on a timely basis. If possible, all such changes should be subject to a 30 day review that is performed by Internal Audit or a qualified third party – that present their findings to management., and	1. Review a representative sample of changes in relationships over the last year. From this sample 2. Determine Review and Approval process and documentation used for evidence these processes, 3. **Assess this control based on the results of items 1 through 4.**
CC.009 -Relationships with professional third parties are periodically reviewed to establish that the entity maintains associations only with reputable third parties.	1. Request files for significant third party relationships with emphasis on legal counsel, consulting firms, Auditors and other professional organizations 2. Review these files for regular periodic reviews by Managers other than those with direct relationships to the organizations 3. Determine whether management has et review parameters (quantitative or qualitative for these reviews) 4. **Assess this control based on the results of items 1 through 3.**

TRANSACTION LEVEL CONTROLS

Entity Control Assessment processes focus on three primary areas: Walkthroughs, Tests and Test Result reviews.

WALKTHROUGHS

A Walkthrough is the review of a process (or control) from initiation (e.g. order entry) to process end (e.g. revenue recognition). In this review, a single, *representative* transaction is selected and is traced from the beginning to the end of the process to verify that the process and its related controls are accurately documented and that the controls are operating as designed.

All walkthroughs should be performed in the operating Business Unit in order to observe whether the process or control has been implemented properly.

The objectives of performing a walkthrough are:

1. To confirm the logical flow of transactions in the process or control documentation,
2. To ensure completeness of the process, control and other required documentation,
3. Evaluate and Confirm the design of the control activities themselves or within the process, and
4. Confirm the implementation of the process and controls within the operating Business Unit.

Upon completion of the walkthrough, the Tester should complete a Walkthrough Evaluation form and file with the other testing documentation resulting from the following.

PROCESS TESTING

Whilst the walkthrough was performed on a representative sample, the process testing will require additional samples to test key controls within the process. *The walkthrough sample process should be the first process that is tested.*

Process testing should focus on the steps below. This is a sample Process Test form highlighting the key areas:

DATE TEST COMMENCED		YOUR FULL NAME	
DATE TEST ENDED		YOUR EMAIL ADDRESS	
HAVE YOU READ THE GUIDELINES REQUIRED FOR THIS TEST?	☐ YES ☐ No	YOUR TELEPHONE NUMBER	
WAS THIS TEST PERFORMED ON SITE?	☐ YES ☐ No	YOUR CELL NUMBER	
ARE YOU AN EMPLOYEE?	☐ YES ☐ No	YOUR JOB TITLE	
IF NO – PLEASE STATE YOUR EMPLOYER'S NAME		YOU BUSINESS UNIT	
IF NO – PLEASE PROVIDE YOUR FINANCIAL OR ACCOUNTING PROFESSIONAL DESIGNATIONS		ARE YOU AFFILIATED WITH THIS BUSINESS UNIT?	
IF NO, PLEASE STATE YOUR YEARS OF EXPERIENCE IN FINANCE OR ACCOUNTING		IF YES, STATE RELATIONSHIP:	
HAVE YOU ATTENDED ANY TRAINING CLASSES FOR THE INTERNAL CONTROL FRAMEWORK?	☐ YES ☐ No	YOUR IMMEDIATE SUPERIOR'S NAME	
IF YES, PLEASE STATE WHICH CLASSES YOU HAVE ATTENDED		YOUR IMMEDIATE SUPERIOR'S TITLE	
		YOUR IMMEDIATE SUPERIOR'S EMAIL ADDRESS	

	PROCESS TEST STEP	ASSESSMENT REQUIREMENTS
1.	FREQUENCY OF PROCESS	State frequency of process:
2.	INITIATION OF PROCESS – What action initiates this process – it is a standard process that is executed as part of normal business? Is it an exception process? Is it a receiving process?	Process initiation is base on:
3.	ACCOUNTING TRANSACTIONS – how many different type of accounting transactions are within this process?	☐ YES ☐ No - Initiation ☐ YES ☐ No - Approval ☐ YES ☐ No - Recording

Process Test Step	Assessment Requirements
	☐ Yes ☐ No - Reconciliation ☐ Yes ☐ No – other processes (e.g. estimation, etc.)
4. COMPLETENESS – does the process documentation reflect all the steps in the process accurately based on the sample used?	☐ Yes ☐ No If no, please identify missing steps and your opinion of criticality of these steps in a separate document. Are any of the missing steps a control? ☐ Yes ☐ No
5. CONTROL IDENTIFICATION – have all key controls been identified?	☐ Yes ☐ No If no – what are the missing controls other than those identified in Step 1.
6. PROCESS CONNECTORS – if there are process connectors within the sample – please execute the following steps:	
• Are the receiving processes within this business unit?	☐ Yes ☐ No
• Are the data values or other information required to initiate the receiving process passed correctly – is the origination step passing the information a control? Is the step receiving the information in the receiving process a control?	☐ Yes ☐ No
• Are the frequencies of the two processes the same?	☐ Yes ☐ No
• *If not, is the receiving process operated more frequently than the originating process?*	☐ Yes ☐ No
• If the receiving process is not in the same business unit, how does the originating unit receive notification of end of process? *Ensure that there is a loop back of information,*	PROVIDE EXPLANATION:
• If there is an end-to end process connector (the process passes at the end of its steps to another process) ensure that it consistently passes to the same process. Consistently passes to same process?	☐ Yes ☐ No
• If it does not consistently pass to the same process, determine the method (condition) by which the originating process determines which receiving process it passes control to. Are these conditions synchronized?	☐ Yes ☐ No
• Ensure that the originating process *ends* in a control and the receiving process *starts* with a control – this ensures that the connection is controlled,	☐ Yes ☐ No
• Determine who is testing the receiving unit's process and provide them with the results of above. Request them to provide you with their assessment results.	
7. Please provide Process IDs that are connected to this process	
8. SEGREGATION OF DUTIES – have the guidelines been complied with?	☐ Yes ☐ No If No, please state exceptions (this will be cross checked to Item 3)
ASSESSMENT STEPS PERFORMED	
9. How did you perform this assessment?	☐ RE PERFORMANCE?

Process Test Step	Assessment Requirements
	☐ Examination? ☐ Observation? ☐ Inquiry?
10. What is the control objective(s) for this process?	Please state:
11. In your opinion, did this process achieve its objectives?	☐ Yes ☐ No If no, please advise exceptions
12. Did you receive the control objectives, significant accounts and financial assertions that this process covers from the Repository or the process Owner?	☐ Repository ☐ Process Owner
13. Did this process and controls cover all the required significant accounts and their financial assertions?	☐ Yes ☐ No
This section should be expanded based on your internal control framework design and operating procedures.	
Documentation – Process Documentation review	
14. Is the Documentation you are using from the repository or the process owner?	☐ Repository ☐ Process Owner
15. Does the documentation accurately reflect the process steps?	☐ Yes ☐ No
16. Does the Documentation accurately reflect all significant accounts and financial assertions?	☐ Yes ☐ No
Conclusion – Design Effectiveness	
17. Does the process activity either alone or in conjunction with other documented processes adequately support the stated assertion or mitigate the related risk?	☐ Yes ☐ No
18. Conclusion on the design effectiveness based on the following ratings:	☐ Pass ☐ Fail
Conclusion – Operational Effectiveness	
19. Please state your conclusion on the operating effectiveness of this process	☐ Pass ☐ Fail
20. If you have failed this process, please describe the reason for failure and your recommendations for correction.	

Depending on your environment and methodology, you may need to expand the specific test questions outlined in the control form below for the various test types.

Transaction Level Control Testing

We have assumed due to space limitations that the tester of the processor is the control tester and have not required all the personal and other information on this form (refer to process form for an example).

Control Test Step	Assessment Requirements
1. Process ID:	The tester should have completed a personal profile as outlined in the Process form.
2. Control ID:	
3. Business Unit ID:	
4. Name of Control Performer:	This information is specific to the control being tested.
5. Title of Control Owner:	
6. Frequency of Control	State frequency of process: ☐ Yes ☐ No - Many times daily ☐ Yes ☐ No - On Demand ☐ Yes ☐ No - Daily, etc.
7. Method used for Control	☐ Yes ☐ No - Manual

CONTROL TEST STEP	ASSESSMENT REQUIREMENTS
	☐ Yes ☐ No - IT enabled
	☐ Yes ☐ No - Automated
8. Is this control an IT control?	☐ Yes ☐ No
9. Which IT control area does it focus on?	☐ Access - General ☐ Access – Application ☐ Data Conversion ☐ Infrastructure ☐ Interface ☐ Application
10. Does this control use any End User Computing Applications?	☐ Yes ☐ No
11. If yes, please list the names of the applications and their current directory locations within the Business Unit (this can also be included in the Process Test form)	
12. Please state how many End User Computing Application Test forms are attached to this form	State number:
13. Risk level of Control	☐ Yes ☐ No - High ☐ Yes ☐ No - Medium ☐ Yes ☐ No - Low
14. Accounting transactions – which accounting transaction type does this control perform?	☐ Yes ☐ No - Initiation ☐ Yes ☐ No - Approval ☐ Yes ☐ No - Recording ☐ Yes ☐ No - Reconciliation ☐ Yes ☐ No – other processes (e.g. estimation, etc.)
15. Does this control perform more than one transaction type?	☐ Yes ☐ No
16. Completeness – does the control documentation reflect all the steps in the control accurately based on the sample used?	☐ Yes ☐ No If no, please identify missing steps and your opinion of criticality of these steps in a separate document.
17. Control connectors – if this control directly connects to another control – please execute the following steps:	
• Please provide the receiving Control ID	Control ID:
• Is the receiving control within this business unit?	☐ Yes ☐ No
• Have you determined whether the control ID provided is an active, valid control?	☐ Yes ☐ No
• Do the two controls (originating and receiving) cover the *same significant account and all its financial assertions*?	☐ Yes ☐ No If no, please state the Significant account and financial controls that the receiving control covers:
• Are the data values or other information required to initiate the receiving control passed correctly?	☐ Yes ☐ No
• Are the frequencies of the two controls the same?	☐ Yes ☐ No
• *If not, is the receiving control operated more frequently than the originating control?*	☐ Yes ☐ No
• If the receiving control is not in the same business unit, how does the originating unit receive notification of end of control functions? *Ensure that there is a loop back of information,*	Provide explanation:
• If it does not consistently pass to the same control, determine the method (condition) by which the originating control determines which	☐ Yes ☐ No

CONTROL TEST STEP	ASSESSMENT REQUIREMENTS
receiving control it passes control to. Are these conditions synchronized?	
• Determine who is testing the receiving unit's control and provide them with the results of above. Request them to provide you with their assessment results.	
18. SEGREGATION OF DUTIES – have the guidelines been complied with?	☐ YES ☐ NO If No, please state exceptions (this will be cross checked to Item 3)
ASSESSMENT STEPS PERFORMED	
19. How did you perform this assessment?	☐ RE PERFORMANCE? ☐ EXAMINATION? ☐ OBSERVATION? ☐ INQUIRY?
20. What is the control objective(s) for this control?	PLEASE STATE:
21. In your opinion, did this control achieve its control objectives?	☐ YES ☐ NO If no, please advise exceptions
22. List all Significant Accounts and their assertions that this control covers?	
23. In your Opinion – did this control achieve these objectives?	☐ YES ☐ NO
This section should be expanded based on your internal control framework design and operating procedures.	
RE PERFORMANCE TESTS	
24. Describe what steps were re performed – you may use the control documentation to assist you	
25. List inputs (transactions, formulae, etc.) used to start the test	
26. Did you select the samples to be used in this test?	☐ YES ☐ NO
27. Describe method used to select samples (e.g. random, etc.)	
28. What was sample size used for this test?	
29. Please provide location of evidence.	
30. List output of test (web pages, reports, screen names, etc.)	
31. Did you perform this test? Or was it done under your supervision?	☐ SELF ☐ SUPERVISION
EXAMINATION	
32. Describe what was examined	Provide a description that can be used by a third party to duplicate your examination. Attach a full sheet.
33. Inputs examined	Please state where evidence of input is maintained:
34. Did you select the sample that was used for input?	☐ YES ☐ NO
35. Outputs examined (screens, reports, etc.) provide system name and full screen number or report number	Please state what section of reports or screens that were examined:
36. How did you verify the results were accurate?	
37. Please provide location of examination	
38. What was the sample size used for the examination?	
39. Please provide location of this test's evidence	
40. Pleas describe method used to select sample (e.g. random, etc.)	

Control Test Step	Assessment Requirements
41. Please describe source of sample (e.g. date, time, batch, etc.)	
42. Please provide Business Unit personnel Name and Title who maintains the documentation for examination:	
Observation	
43. Where was control observed	
44. Who performed control that was observed? Name and title please.	
45. Did you select the sample for this observation test?	☐ Yes ☐ No
46. Describe sources of sample (date, time, batch, etc.)	
47. Describe how sample was selected (e.g. random, etc.	
48. Were all the control steps that are contained in the documentation followed?	☐ Yes ☐ No
49. Did the results of the control equal to the computations performed by you?	☐ Yes ☐ No
50. How did you verify the results?	
51. What was sample size used for this observation?	
52. Please provide location of evidence	
This section can be further expanded for different test types allowed by your company e.g. inquiry, etc.	
Documentation – Control	
53. Is the Documentation you are using from the repository or the control owner?	☐ Repository ☐ Control Owner
54. Does the documentation accurately reflect the control steps?	☐ Yes ☐ No
Conclusion – Design Effectiveness	
55. Does the control activity either alone or in conjunction with other documented control activities adequately support the stated assertion or mitigate the related risk?	☐ Yes ☐ No
56. Conclusion on the design effectiveness based on the following ratings:	☐ Unreliable - a control that does not perform as designed and returns unpredictable results. *This should be reported as a deficiency.* ☐ Informal – these are controls that are inadequately documented and are dependent on manual intervention, ☐ Standardized – the control is in place and documented but undetected deviations may occur, ☐ Monitored – standardized controls are in place and periodic testing is conducted which evaluate their design and operation, ☐ Optimized – standardized controls are in place with automated monitoring systems.
57. Does this control have a separate monitoring control	☐ Yes ☐ No Please provide Control ID:
Conclusion – Operational Effectiveness	
58. Did this control on its own achieve its control objective?	☐ Yes ☐ No
59. Did this control require other controls to achieve its control objective?	☐ Yes ☐ No

Control Test Step	Assessment Requirements
60. Please advise the other Control IDs	Control ID:
61. Did this control have a control connector documented?	☐ Yes ☐ No
62. Please state your conclusion on the operating effectiveness of this control	☐ Pass ☐ Fail
63. If you have failed this control, please describe the reason for failure and your recommendations for correction.	

End User Computing Application form

End User Applications are usually spreadsheets, desktop databases or similar applications. This is a general definition that should be further refined to meet your company's environment.

Description of End User Computing Application	
1. Name of End User Computing Application (EUCA)	
2. Location of EUCA – provide full path	
3. Version of EUCA tested	
4. Is this EUCA maintained on a version control basis?	☐ Yes ☐ No
5. Is this EUCA subject to end user testing?	☐ Yes ☐ No
6. Are the developer and user functions separate for this EUCA?	☐ Yes ☐ No
7. Is this EUCA a Complex or Simple EUCA?	☐ Complex – this EUCA supports complex calculations, valuations and modeling tools. It uses macros and multiple supporting subordinates where cells, values and other end user computing applications are linked Typical examples are spreadsheets used for fixed asset calculation of amortization, preparation of annual budgets, etc. ☐ Simple
8. Description of functions performed by EUCA – detail each processing step	
9. Did the Business Unit provide you with any documentation to support this application	☐ Yes ☐ No
10. Please attach this documentation to this form.	
11. Provide primary User Name and Title for this application	
12. Provide Manager's name and title for this application	
13. Are the results of this EUCA used by other than this Business Unit?	☐ Yes ☐ No
14. Please provide IDs for other Business Units	

Test Result Form Review

Test results are submitted, *by the tester(s),* to the Repository in a complete package that must comprise of:

- Process Documentation,
- Control documentation,
- Test working papers (forms above) including working papers, and

- Deficiency forms, (if any of above has failed).

The package should contain all these items in order to ensure that the Repository receives a complete, synchronized set of documentation used by the Tester. We have seen instances where the documentation used by the Tester did not reconcile to the documentation submitted by the Business Unit to the repository– *this could automatically invalidate the test results.*

Test results should be quality assured promptly. This process can be automated if the formats, rules and other guidelines have been incorporated into you SOX Management System.

Remediation plans should be filed promptly. These should be forwarded either

- With the Tester submission package, or
- One week after receipt of the Tester package.

The Repository should ensure that all Test packages are received by the submission dates. These submissions should be compared versus the Documentation Inventory established in Chapter 6 – The Repository. This should identify all missing documentation packages that have not been received.

In addition, we recommend that the Repository perform a fiscal period versus prior fiscal period (e.g. Q1 vs. Q2) comparison. This comparison establishes the following:

- Processes and Controls that have been *deleted or are missing* from this period's archives, and
- New Processes and controls that have been *added* this period.

The Repository should confirm these deletions and additions with the Business Unit as a fail safe measure.

CROSS CHECKS OF TEST RESULTS

As test result forms are received, the Repository commences the following analyses (this is a sample list of the processes we normally recommend):

1. CONFLICT IN EUCA TESTS – two or more tests (for different controls) are in conflict. Control A reported the EUCA to be operating effectively, Control B has reported the EUCA to be not operating effectively. There is therefore a conflict between the two test results,

2. INVALID CONTROL TO CONTROL CONNECTORS – connectors for controls that "hand off" to another control to achieve a control objective. The receiving control may be invalid for a variety of reasons (e.g. incorrect significant account, etc.)

3. INVALID PROCESS TO PROCESS CONNECTORS – connectors for processes that "hand off" to another process to achieve a control objective. The receiving process may be invalid for a variety of reasons (e.g. receiving process does not exist),

4. DEFICIENT RECEIVING CONTROL – the receiving control in a hand off is deficient,

5. DEFICIENT RECEIVING PROCESS – the receiving process in a hand off is deficient,

6. SEGREGATION OF DUTIES REVIEW REQUIRED – Tester has indicated that process or control is operating effectively but Segregation of duties guidelines have not been complied with

7. INVALID SAMPLE SIZE – the test results are non compliant with test guidelines,

8. INVALID TEST DATE – an annual control was not tested on its date of performance

9. INVALID TEST TYPE – the process or control tested was not executed at the right level e.g. a high risk control was tested by inquiry. Management guidelines state that all high risk controls must be tested by re performance or examination,

10. INVALID SIGNIFICANT ACCOUNT – the significant account is invalid (e.g. does not exist, etc.),

11. CONTROL DID NOT ACHIEVE CONTROL OBJECTIVE – self explanatory,

12. CONTROL OR PROCESS DID NOT ACHIEVE ALL FINANCIAL ASSERTIONS – self explanatory,

Based on your methodology and management guidelines, this list should be developed for use within the Repository.

IT Control Assessments

IT controls are an extensive subject that is covered in Volume II of this series. However, for purposes of this volume, we would recommend that you develop the following processes:

1. GENERAL CONTROLS – that review the controls established for the entire IT environment that include infrastructure, Data Management policies, Interface, security, etc.

2. SECURITY ACCESS CONTROLS – these are usually part of the suite of synchronized controls that require special assessment procedures. The following are usually the assessment steps used to assess these controls. In this example, we are assuming an application sample of one application.

    Special emphasis is usually placed on segregation of duties when granting accesses.

    The process should apply to all critical centralized applications.

    - Ensure that Business has a control for completing and reviewing applications to the central IT Department for User security access,
    - Central IT has a control for reviewing and approving application based on their security criteria (e.g. internal employee, external vendor, etc.),
    - IT has an operating control for IT Security System updates,
    - IT has a control to advise HR of new or changed security access for inclusion in personnel file,
    - HR has a control to update and maintain processes in individual's HR file. (If external Vendor – the External Vendor Manager should be advised)
    - IT has a monthly control for requiring all Business Units to confirm the security accesses
    - HR has an additional control to advise IT of any terminations together with the individuals complete security profile.

3. APPLICATION CONTROLS – these controls are usually subdivided into the following classes of controls:

    - CHANGE MANAGEMENT - The controls used to manage the entire application change management process,
    - TESTING – the controls used in the testing of applications,
    - SEGREGATION OF DUTIES, and

- PRODUCTIONS DATA CONTROLS,

These processes and their related controls are covered in Volume II of this series.

TEST RESULTS ANALYSIS

Upon receipt, test result forms should be analyzed for:

1. COMPLETENESS – is all required information included in the firm?

2. ACCURACY – as you will note in the examples of the forms there are several self checking mechanisms built into the form,

3. SYNCHRONIZATION of tests – some tests need to be synchronized in order for the entire control objective to be achieved. In other words the same sample(s) should be used in testing all the synchronized controls in sequence.

A typical example would be the controls used for accounts payable.

Assuming that your company has a central Accounts Payable function and that all invoices are authorized at the Business Unit where the goods or services were received, the following would be the controls that would need to be synchronized.

BUSINESS UNIT	CONTROL	CONTROL PASSED TO	COMMENTS
Operating Business Unit	• Approves Invoice and Forwards to Accounts Payable Department • Designates Account(s) to be charged expense, asset, etc.)	Account Payable – receipt of approved invoices	This is the initial first step
Accounts Payable Department	• Check invoice for approval • Checks approval limit for authorizer • If within limits, proceed to invoice processing • If not within limits, reject for non approval, • Checks extensions on invoices for accuracy • Checks validity of account for type of goods or purchases received • If asset, proceeds to Asset processing • If expense, proceeds to Expense processing, etc.	Accounts Payable – Asset processing, or Accounts Expense Processing	This can be subdivided into multiple controls – but we have maintained as a single control for space limitations
Accounts – Asset processing	• Inputs into fixed asset ledger with all pertinent information (individual A) • Processes payment through payable system (Individual B) • Note segregation of duties	Accounts Payable Reporting	Alternatively, the next control would be used for expense processing
Accounts – Expense processing	• Processes payment through payable system (Individual B)	Accounts Payable Reporting	Alternatively, the previous control would be used for expense processing
Accounts Payable Reporting	• Business Unit checks Accounts Payable register for the Unit provided by Accounts Payable Department, and		

Business Unit	Control	Control Passed To	Comments
	• Business unit verifies its General Ledger journal entries.		

SUMMARY

The Entity Level Control Assessments worksheets have been provided for the Code of (Conduct) Ethics to provide you with a starting point for developing your assessment work packages.

Additional Assessment work packages are provided in the other volumes in this series. However

CHAPTER 10 – SARBANES OXLEY DEFICIENCY MANAGEMENT PROCESSES

INTENT OF THIS CHAPTER

This chapter focuses on the processes that should be used to implement a Deficiency Management Process. The detail steps included in this chapter are:

- IDENTIFICATION AND COMPILATION of deficiencies from all sources e.g. entity level program, transaction level program, external auditors, internal auditors, etc.

- COMBINATION AND ELIMINATION of duplicate deficiencies

- AGGREGATION of deficiencies,

- Deficiency ANALYSIS AND REPORTS

- REMEDIATION PLANS and status reporting,

The chapter provides the detail process steps and the analyses/reports that should be implemented. .

DEFICIENCY MANAGEMENT OVERVIEW

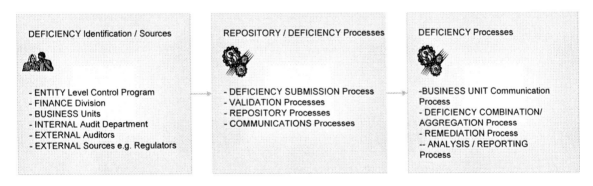

OVERVIEW

The objectives of any Deficiency Management Process is to ensure that deficiencies are

1. IDENTIFIED promptly and submitted to the SOX Department for further analysis and processing,

2. STORED AND ANALYZED by the SOX Department resulting in a comprehensive, validated list of deficiencies which are then

3. REPORTED promptly to the CEO, CFO, the Board, Board Committees and External Auditors, and

4. REMEDIATION PLANS and activities are monitored and reported to Management and the Board on a regular, periodic basis

SOX Deficiency Management is usually the responsibility of the Repository Unit that resides within the SOX Department. When there are a large number of material weaknesses or significant deficiencies, the Deficiency Management function may be assigned to a special organization unit to manage which reports directly to the SOX Department Manager.

In the diagram on the previous page, we illustrate the key components of the Deficiency Management process. The processes in the middle are usually classified as General SOX Department processes that are not specific to the deficiency management process itself, but are used throughout the SOX Department.

We have assumed that you have implemented the steps outlined in the previous chapters which will serve as a foundation for the deficiency management steps outlined in this chapter. To recap, you should have already completed the following items from the previous chapters:

1. CHAPTER 1 – Organizing for Sarbanes Oxley – which identifies the roles and responsibilities for all SOX participants,

2. CHAPTER 2 – The prerequisites required for Sarbanes Oxley, most of which are further expended in later chapters, and

3. CHAPTERS 3 THROUGH 8 and include the development of the Entity Level Program, the Repository, Communications Infrastructure, Plans & Calendars, etc.

DEFICIENCY IDENTIFICATION / SOURCES

The identification and submission of deficiencies usually originates from the following sources:

1. OPERATING BUSINESS UNIT – these usually identify deficiencies based on the testing contacted on the transaction (process) level controls within their operating units.

   For purposes of deficiency Identification, we have assumed that External Vendors will be required to file their deficiency notifications as if they were internal operating business units or that an individual will be appointed within your firm to perform this function and to coordinate activities with the External Vendors.

   These are usually submitted to the repository on a quarterly or monthly basis. New deficiencies are submitted with full documentation and a proposed remediation plan. Previously identified deficiencies are resubmitted with *updates* on their remediation plans.

   The deficiencies identified by the Business unit usually include the following deficiency classes:

   - Design deficiencies identified from Process Walkthrough and Assessments,
   - Operational defects identified from Assessments (tests),
   - Internal Audit deficiencies (based on Internal Audit Reports received by the Business Unit, if any),
   - External Audit deficiencies (based on External Audit Assessments within the Business Unit),
   - External Audit Issues that have been promoted to deficiencies (based on External Audit Issue Lists),
   - Regulators' deficiencies (that have been attributed to the Business Unit by the Regulators or by Company Management)

2. INTERNAL AUDIT – Internal Audit deficiencies are usually identified in the course of their normal auditing duties within the company. Some of the Internal Audit identified deficiencies may already be included in the deficiencies submitted by the operating Business Units from their

transaction level testing or from the Entity Level Program. In the Deficiency combination process discussed later in this chapter, these duplicates will have to be identified and cross referenced.

The Internal Audit Department, in most organizations, performs periodic audits of the internal control framework on behalf of the Audit Committee and Company Management.

These audits may result in four classes of deficiencies:

- Design Defect for a activity level or transaction level control,
- Operational ineffectiveness for a activity level or transaction level control,
- Missing Control, and
- Business Unit or Entity Level Control Defect.

The Internal Audit deficiencies are subject to the same submission and validation processes (as outlined in the next section). We have assumed that the Internal Audit advises the Business Units of any deficiencies that are directly attributed to the Business Unit.

For Entity Level Control Deficiencies, we have assumed that Internal Audit will advise both the Entity Level Control Program Manager and the SOX Department Manager of any deficiencies.

3. EXTERNAL AUDIT – External Auditors will also identify deficiencies in the course of their assessment activities. Many of these deficiencies should already be identified by the operating Business Units to the SOX Department.

    In both the Internal Audit and External Audit listings, they will identify controls that they consider essential to the operation and integrity of the internal control framework.

    During the fiscal year, External Auditors will also advise you of *issues* that they may arise during the course of their review. The issues may cover *broad based* topics and may not always be linked to a specific control, process, business unit or line of business.

    Depending on the agreement between you and your External Auditors, these issues may not have been communicated to any parties other than the SOX Department. Therefore, it should be the responsibility of the SOX Department to communicate and coordinate all activities for the External Auditor's Issue List.

4. ENTITY PROGRAM – the department or unit responsible for the Entity Level Control program will also identify deficiencies. Usually, the Entity Level Program is not responsible for the development of remediation plans. These are the responsibility of the individual Entity Level Control owners who are required to forward this information to the SOX Department.

5. FINANCE DIVISION – The Finance Division identifies deficiencies from three processes – its walkthroughs of its internal processes, its internal control testing processes and its Financial Statement Error Logs. The first two (walkthroughs and testing) are standard to all internal Business Units within your company and are reviewed in the Business Unit section above.

    The Financial Statement Error Log process is a unique process that is usually resident only in the Finance Division.

    At the end of each fiscal quarter, most Finance Departments carefully scrutinize the financial statements with its consolidation and other processes to ensure accuracy and validity prior to Board review and public publication. During this process, errors may be identified and corrected. Statements may also be reviewed by the External Auditors and errors identified and corrected prior to publication.

Depending on the source of the error and the individual identifying, controls are deemed deficient based on the following table.

IDENTIFICATION OF CONTROL	CONTROL FAILED	COMMENTS
Internal Personnel	• Preventive Control	Since an error was discovered at the Financial Statement preparation level, it should be presumed that the preventive control within the Business Unit or Finance Division did not operate effectively. The determination whether the monitoring control operated effectively is a judgment call that will need to be supported by a management assessment.
External Auditor	• Preventive Control • Detective Control • Monitoring Control	Since the error has been identified by an external party, it can be presumed that both the Preventive and Monitoring controls have failed and operationally effective. If the Monitoring and/or detective controls had operated effectively, the error would not have been present in the Financial Statements.

6. EXTERNAL REGULATORY AGENCY - External Regulatory Agencies, in the course of their inspections or audits, may identify deficiencies in your internal control framework. Depending on the Agency, this correspondence may be routed to various Departments (usually the Legal or Compliance Departments) within your company.

An organized mechanism should be established to ensure that all these deficiencies are submitted to the Repository on a regular, periodic basis.

REPOSITORY DEFICIENCY PROCESSES

As illustrated in the diagram, all deficiencies, regardless of source or originator, should be submitted to the Repository on a periodic, regular basis. Upon receipt into the repository, deficiencies must follow the same processes as all other SOX documentation and evidence.

SUBMISSION PROCESSES

Submission deadlines for deficiencies should be published within the SOX Quarterly Bulletin and Calendar.

The required format for deficiency submissions will vary by source/ originator and it is the responsibility of the Repository or Deficiency Management Team to establish and enforce these standards for all submissions.

Wherever possible, the formats should meet the following minimum guidelines:

1. DEFICIENCIES – MANDATORY REQUIREMENTS

    - UNIQUE DEFICIENCY ID – Every deficiency should be assigned a unique deficiency ID that is based on a combination of the Control ID and the Date identified. As previously noted, the Control ID should be based on the Business Unit ID, Process ID and Control Sequence number. The Repository team should review the deficiency records by control ID periodically in order to ensure that there are no duplicate records within the repository for the same date or deficiency occurrence[30]. .

---

[30] A control may be deficient at different periods for different reasons. For example, a control can be deficiency in Quarter 2 of Year 1 and is corrected and retested. It may pass all audits and assessments but in Q3 of Year 2, in re assessing this control an operational deficiency is discovered. This control therefore has two deficiencies in the database – *but from different periods*.

Where a deficiency is reported for a missing control, a control ID does not exist and therefore the Repository should designate a special series of deficiency ID numbers for these missing controls,

- SOURCE / ORIGINATING UNIT - All deficiencies must be identified with a Source or Originating Unit.,

- IDENTIFICATION DATE - All deficiencies must have the original date of identification,

- SUBMISSION DATE – Date submitted to the Repository for processing,

- COMPANY PERSONNEL ID - The individual who identified the deficiency must be identified,

- EXTERNAL VENDOR PERSONNEL ID – In the event the source is an External Vendor, the name of the individual to contact at the External Vendor should be included in this record,

- DEFICIENCY TYPE - The type of deficiency must be identified from the various types previously identified e.g. Activity Level, Entity Level, External Auditor issue, etc.

- DEFICIENCY CLASS – Design, Operating, Missing control, etc.,

- STATUS - The status of the deficiency whether open, closed, etc., and

- DESCRIPTION – A description of the deficiency must be provided.

2. DEFICIENCIES – OTHER INFORMATION - In addition, the following segments should also be populated depending on the type or class of deficiency.

- CONTROL ID – the control that is deficient and should be auto generated from the control record – as previously noted not all deficiencies may be linked to an existing control (e.g. regulatory / external agency deficiencies). Validation routines should be constructed to examine the deficiency type or class before examining this field,

- PROCESS ID – should be auto-generated from the control record in Repository (if referencing an existing control),

- BUSINESS UNIT – the deficiency may be attributed to a specific business unit instead of a specific control (e.g. Internal Audit, External Audit and Regulatory Agencies who may not identify specific controls). This field is not required if a control ID is provided since the control Id, by default, will identify the Business Unit,

- SIGNIFICANT ACCOUNT(S) – the Significant Account(s) for which the deficient control was responsible. If the deficiency is for a missing control, the Significant Account(s) the deficiency impacts should be entered ,

- PRIORITY – In some organizations Internal Audit, Regulatory and External Audit Issues are assigned a priority code after discussions with the originators. These priority codes are used to determine the dates or terms in which issues become deficiencies,

- REMEDIATION PLAN REFERENCE – Deficiencies should have a remediation plan appended to their records. If none exists, these should be viewed as exceptions subject to management escalation.

Remediation Plans should be identified by the Deficiency ID and the Date of Plan in order to provide a unique reference.

3. FINANCE ERROR LOG SUBMISSION FORMAT - An illustration for the spreadsheet or data format is provided below. In addition, this format may also include the following fields.

- Whether the BUSINESS UNIT(S) responsible for the error has been identified (the error may occur in a decentralized finance function, a centralized function, combination of both) has been notified,

- The INDIVIDUAL notified within the Business Unit(s),

- The REMEDIATION PLAN ID,

- JOURNAL or other references, and

- Repository ACCEPTANCE DATE,

Financial Statement Line or Significant Account Impacted	Source of Error (Business Unit or Finance Division)	Description of Error	Preventive Control for this Unit / Line	Monitoring Control for this Unit / Line	Amount (Thousands)	Identified by Internal Personnel (Yes / No)	Internal Personnel	Identified by External Auditor (Yes / No)	External Auditor	Deficiency(ies) generated
Cash and Cash Equivalents	USA	A full, complete description should be provided	1232435-AB	8978935-AC	$1,250	No	None	Yes	Mr. A. Schwartz	Preventative: 1452-1 Monitoring: 1422-8

4. ACTIVITY LEVEL DEFICIENCY SUBMISSION FORMAT - We have illustrated only the deficiency elements and not the assessment (test), control, processes elements that normally constitute a part of the deficiency submission. We have illustrated only the *critical* elements that are used in Deficiency Management processing and not all other deficiency elements.

Financial Statement Line or Significant Account Impacted	Control ID	Process	Individual Identifying Deficiency	Deficiency Type	Deficiency Class	Remediation Plan ID	Description of Deficiency	Date of Deficiency	Deficiency Status	Deficiency(ies) generated
Cash / Equiv	58778-AC	Proc 1	Mr. M Brown	Operating	Activity level	Not assigned	Description 1	1/1/2005	Active	1965-1

5. INTERNAL AUDIT ISSUE SUBMISSION FORMAT - The Internal Audit Issue and Deficiency Log should always include the Internal Audit reference Number or Internal Audit Report for references purposes.

In the table below, we have provided the most *critical* elements that are required and have excluded other elements that may be included with this record e.g. Business Unit Contact, Internal Audit Coordinator, etc.

A separate update file should be submitted, on a quarterly basis, to the repository to ensure that the most current information is monitored on existing issues and deficiencies. A procedure between the SOX Department and the Internal Audit Department should be developed for updates and closed items.

Financial Statement Line or Significant Account Impacted	Control ID, if available	Internal Audit Reference No.	Individual Identifying Deficiency	Deficiency Type	Deficiency Class	Remediation Plan ID	Description of Deficiency	Date of Deficiency	Deficiency Status	Deficiency(ies) generated	Business Unit Advised?
Cash / Equiv	58778-AC	INT-87-235	Mr. M Jones	Missing Control	Activity level	Not assigned	Missing Control for Bank Reconciliations	1/1/2005	Active	1965-1	No

6. EXTERNAL AUDIT ISSUE SUBMISSION FORMAT - THE External Audit Issue and Deficiency Log should always include the External Auditor's reference Number or External Audit Report for references purposes.

In the table below, we have provided the most *critical* elements that are required and excluded other elements that may be included with this record e.g. Business Unit Contact, External Audit Coordinator, External Auditor references for working papers, etc.

A separate update file should be submitted on a quarterly basis to the repository so that the current information on existing issues and deficiencies can be monitored.

Financial Statement Line or Significant Account Impacted	Control ID, if available	External Audit Reference No.	Individual Identifying Deficiency	Deficiency Type	Deficiency Class	Remediation Plan ID	Priority	Description of Deficiency	Date of Deficiency	Deficiency Status	Deficiency(ies) generated	Business Unit Advised?
Cash / Equiv	58778-AC	EXT-87-235	Mr. M Kengla	Missing Control	Activity level	Not assigned	HIGH	Missing Control for Cash Suspense Reconciliations	2/1/2005	Active	1965-1	Yes

7. ENTITY LEVEL DEFICIENCIES SUBMISSION FORMAT – The Entity Level format should be similar to the Transaction Level Deficiency report. The only difference between the two formats is the Entity Level deficiency should reference the COSO component and the point of focus for which the deficiency was identified in addition to the other information in the transaction level format.

8. REGULATOR'S ISSUE SUBMISSION FORMAT -This log is normally assembled by *one* of three Departments – Internal, Legal or Compliance Departments. We assume that you have assigned this responsibility to *one* of these departments.

This central coordination department will be responsible for coordinating the activities of the other departments. These activities include the input of data into a central Regulator's log for submission quarterly into the Repository. The central coordinator will also assume responsibility of issuing and maintaining a unique Deficiency ID for each item.

On a quarterly basis, this department is also required to obtain the most current status from each of the contributing departments.

Financial Statement Line or Significant Account Impacted	Control ID, if available	Regulator's Reference No.	Individual Identifying Deficiency	Deficiency Type	Deficiency Class	Remediation Plan ID	Priority	Description of Deficiency	Date of Deficiency	Deficiency Status	Deficiency(ies) generated	Business Unit Advised?
Cash / Equiv	58778-AC	EXT-87-235	Mr. R. Reyes	Ineffective Design	Activity level	Not assigned	HIGH	Missing Control for Cash Suspense Reconciliations	2/1/2005	Active	1965-1	Yes

VALIDATION PROCESSES

The validation processes for deficiencies submitted to the Repository varies based on the deficiency type. The table below provides the basic validation requirements for deficiencies usually employed in Repository validation processes.

Validation Requirement	Finance Error Logs	Activity Level or Transaction Deficiencies	Entity Level Deficiencies	Internal Audit Issues	External Audit Issues	Regulator Issues	Outsourced Issues or Deficiencies	Comments
Unique Deficiency ID	Yes	Yes	Yes	Yes	Yes	Yes	Yes	
Source	Yes	Yes	Yes	Yes	Yes	Yes	Yes	
ID Date	Yes	Yes	Yes	Yes	Yes	Yes	Yes	
Submission Date	Yes	Yes	Yes	Yes	Yes	Yes	Yes	
Identifier	Yes	Yes	Yes	Yes	Yes	Yes	Yes	
Type	Std	Std	Std	Std	Std	Std	Std	
Deficiency Class								
Deficiency Status								
Deficiency Description								
Control ID	Yes	Yes	Yes – if control IDs are assigned	Yes – if can be linked to a specific control	Yes – if can be linked to a specific control	Yes – if can be linked to a specific control	Yes – if can be linked to a specific control	
Process ID								
Business Unit								
Significant Account								
Priority								
Remediation Plan Reference								

NORMAL REPOSITORY PROCESSES

All processes outlined in Chapter 6 should be executed.

COMMUNICATION PROCESSES

The Deficiency Management Process has three communications objectives to achieve:

1. It must notify all operating Business Units of the deficiencies for which they are responsible (remember – some deficiencies may originate from sources that did not notify the Business Unit e.g. Regulators),

2. It must communicate with the originators of deficiencies identifying any conflicting deficiencies that need to be resolved. During the process of evaluating deficiencies, the Deficiency Management team will be presented with conflicting information on some occasions. One of the deficiency reporting parties may report an item as operating effectively and a different source may report this same item as NOT operating effectively. Every attempt must be made to reconcile this difference.

3. It must keep Management and the Board (and its committees) apprised of deficiencies and their remedial status.

Chapter 4 outlines the communications processes that should be used for deficiency communications.

DEFICIENCY PROCESSES

BUSINESS UNIT COMMUNICATION PROCESS

Business Units are required to *confirm* the deficiency records that are attributed to them since records may originate from other sources external to the Business Unit (e.g. External Audit, Regulators, etc.). Business Units should be required to validate all non-Business Unit originated deficiencies on a regular, periodic basis.

These confirmation communications must be bilateral and the entire bilateral cycle should be completed at least once per quarter.

The communications are required to ensure that Business Units:

1. Confirm their deficiency statuses regularly,
2. Update their action / remediation plans,
3. Confirm any closing tests, and
4. Confirm auditor (internal or external) verification of closures.

DEFICIENCY COMBINATION / AGGREGATION PROCESS

After compilation of deficiencies from multiple sources, the Deficiency Management Unit should review all in order to determine:

- DUPLICATE CONTROLS – these should be cross referenced and only one instance report carried forward into the aggregation process below,

- COMPENSATING CONTROLS – in some instances, the Business Unit may have a compensating control that is designed and operating effectively. With the agreement of your External Auditor, deficiencies may be eliminated from the following aggregation process if a compensating control has been identified and the identified control is designed and operating effectively.

The deficiencies that have been eliminated from the combination / aggregation process should be clearly documented with the elimination reasons and necessary supporting documentation.

The aggregation process requires significant judgment by the deficiency management team.

The Framework published on December 10, 2004, provides the following guidance:

"Deficiencies are considered in the aggregate by significant account balance, disclosure and COSO component to determine whether they collectively result in significant deficiencies or material weaknesses.

Aggregation of control activities deficiencies by significant account balance and disclosure is necessary since the existence of multiple control deficiencies related to a specific account balance or disclosure increases the likelihood of misstatement.

Aggregation by the control environment, risk assessment, information and communication, and monitoring components of COSO is more difficult and judgmental. For example, unrelated control deficiencies relating to design ineffectiveness in other COSO components could lead to the conclusion that a significant deficiency or material weakness in the risk assessment component exists.

Similarly, unrelated control deficiencies in other COSO components could lead to a conclusion that a significant deficiency or material weakness in the control environment or monitoring component exists. "

We would recommend that you review your deficiencies in aggregate by the following minimum aggregation attributes:

- COSO component (refer above),
- Financial Statement Line,
- Significant Account,
- Business Unit Location,
- IT System (and related impact to Financial Statement Lines),
- Outsourcer, and
- Significant Processes.

For each of these analyses, the related account balance at the period end should also be included.

Deficiencies should be reviewed and aggregated from multiple perspectives to determine, whether in aggregate some deficiencies collectively comprise a significant deficiency[31] or material weakness[32]

A single deficiency can be used on the aggregation process many times based on the control having multiple contributing factors.

For example, a control has a significant account of Cash and is a part of the New York Business Unit.

This control may be aggregated with other controls that each has a significant account of Cash.

---

[31] PCAOB AU2 Paragraph 9: A *significant deficiency* is a control deficiency, or combination of control deficiencies, that adversely affects the company's ability to initiate, authorize, record, process, or report external financial data reliably in accordance with generally accepted accounting principles such that there is more than a remote likelihood that a misstatement of the company's annual or interim financial statements that is more than inconsequential will not be prevented or detected.

[32] PCAOB AU2 Paragraph 10: A *material weakness* is a significant deficiency, or combination of significant deficiencies, that results in more than a remote likelihood that a material misstatement of the annual or interim financial statements will not be prevented or detected.

At the same time, the control may also be aggregated with other controls for the New York Business location.

REMEDIATION PLANS

The SOX Department should require the submission of a remediation within 14 days of the identification of a deficiency.

This plan must contain basic information about the deficiency including the following:

1. The individual(s) responsible for the remediation of the deficiency,
2. The detailed action plan documenting the corrective steps being taken and their proposed implementation dates,
3. The final correction date,
4. Any dependencies for this plan (including other departments),
5. Any corporate support required to assist in this plan

Business units should be required to provide a quarterly status report outlining:

1. Activities performed to date,
2. Additional activities required to fully remediate the deficiency,
3. Target dates for remediation
4. Optionally, you may require for some key deficiencies specific target dates for each key activity – so that management can monitor the activities in greater detail. We would recommend that you use this option in all of its high risk controls,
5. Some organizations request a percentage completion estimate. We do not recommend requesting this information unless you can establish tangible metrics for measuring this activity e.g. task hours, budgetary amounts.

The status reports should be validated, similar to any other documentation received into the Repository. These reports should be analyzed for variances versus the original plans filed and also for any changes versus the prior update.

CLOSING OF A DEFICIENCY

You should give special consideration to implementing a deficiency closing process that requires Internal Audit to approve the closing of the Deficiency after an internal audit review has been performed. This should be reviewed with the External Auditors prior to implementation as the External Auditors may have special requirements for some deficiencies.

The retesting of these corrected controls should be subject to the assessment guidelines in Chapter 9.

ANALYSIS / REPORTING

The analysis / reporting of deficiencies is required for three primary purposes:

1. To ensure that all responsible parties are aware of the deficiencies that are attributed to them and their remediation responsibilities,

2. To apprise management of the assessment status of the internal control framework and related deficiencies

3. To ensure that remediation efforts are managed throughout the corporation in order to achieve management's goals for the effective operation of internal control framework.

It should also be recognized that Business Unit management may sometime identify compensating controls that are not evident to the central SOX Department. These will subsequently have to be confirmed by the original source of the deficiency and the deficiency report withdrawn or modified.

Example: External Auditors identify a deficiency. Business Unit identifies a compensating control. Sox Department communicates to External Audit. External Audit agrees/ disagrees. Results of agreement / disagreement communicated to Business Units and Management.

BUSINESS UNIT DEFICIENCY REPORTS

The Business Unit Deficiency Reports should be provided on a monthly basis. These reports should request updates from Business Unit Management on the following:

- Confirmation whether the deficiency exists (if an item has been closed – a full explanation of why the deficiency was closed and whether External Audit or Internal Audit has confirmed closure),
- Identification of compensating controls, if any,
- Status of remediation plans,

REPORT SAMPLES

As outlined in Chapter 8, Corporate Management should receive reports that provide summarized information on the deficiencies. We would recommend that the following basic reports be provided.

1. COMPREHENSIVE FINANCIAL STATEMENT OVERVIEW - For each of the columns, detailed support information should be provided to support the Financial Statement Line summary above. This detailed information should be provided by Financial Statement line and by Business Unit so that Management can determine the remedial action required to cover any inadequacies.

FINANCIAL STATEMENT / INTERNAL CONTROL FRAMEWORK SUMMARY REPORT.										
FINANCIAL STATEMENT LINE	BALANCE	RISK LEVEL	% COVERAGE	CONTROLS - ACCEPTED REJECTED	TESTS	NON GUIDELINE TESTS	NOT TESTED	DEFICIENCIES	REMEDIATION PLANS	MISSING REDEMPTION PLANS
Cash and cash equivalents	$ 3,686	High	42%	42 16	35	4		22	10	5
		Other		145 22						
Restricted cash and cash equivalents	0	High								
		Other								
Accounts receivable - net	$2,551	High								
		Other								
Inventories - net	$1,414	High								
		Other								
Deferred income taxes - net	$ 255	High								
		Other								
Other current assets	$356									
TOTALS										

2. REMEDIATION PLAN EXCEPTION REPORT

The SOX Department should report exceptions for remediation plans that are based on the following:

- Remediation plans that have been extended from prior update or where the "*status completed*" is less than the previous update.

    Example 1: Deficiency was previously stated as being 62% completed. In recent update, the deficiency status completed was changed to 40%.

    Example 2: The previous date for correcting the deficiency was December 1, 2005. In the most recent update, the remediation plan has been extended to January 31, 2006. This constitutes an elongation of the remediation period by two months and corporate management should be informed. If in the SOX Department's management's view, the elongation is justified, the report foes not need to include inconsequential items.

- Remediation plans have not achieved the completion date. The item is late and needs to be escalate

CHAPTER 11 – OTHER SOX SUBJECTS

INTENT OF THIS CHAPTER

This chapter focuses on five major subjects:

1. DISCLOSURE COMMITTEE – the purpose, role, responsibilities and processes of the Disclosure Committee

2. SEGREGATION OF DUTIES – an explanation of the policies and procedures for segregating duties in your company,

3. SUB CERTIFICATION PROCESS – the process by which the various organization levels certify to the CEO and CFO that the deign, implementation and assessment of their section of the internal control framework meets your internal control guidelines,

4. EXTERNAL AUDITOR COORDINATION – the coordination required to ensure that your internal control framework audit is conducted as expeditiously as possible, and

5. SPECIAL YEAR END PROCESSES – the 13th month processes required in the fiscal year post closing cycle for SOX assessment.

DISCLOSURE COMMITTEE OVERVIEW

The Disclosure Committee shall assist the CEO and CFO in fulfilling their oversight responsibility for the accuracy, completeness and timeliness of our company's disclosure requirements. This will be achieved by the promotion of consistent disclosure practices which ensure that there is accurate, complete, timely and broadly disseminated disclosure of material information about our company to the market in accordance with applicable laws and exchange requirements.

ROLES AND RESPONSIBILITIES

The Disclosure Committee is responsible for the following:

1. DISCLOSURE CONTROLS AND PROCEDURES - The Disclosure Committee shall oversee the design and operating effectiveness of the disclosure controls and procedures and ensure that financial and non-financial information required to be disclosed, or *that may potentially required to be disclosed* is communicated to management to allow timely management decisions for disclosure.

   The chairperson (or designate) of this committee is the customary owner of these controls and is usually responsible for ensuring their operational effectiveness on a company wide basis,

   The conclusions based on evaluations of these controls shall be reported directly to the CEO and CFO and should include:

   - Any significant deficiencies or material weaknesses identified in the aforementioned processes and controls,

- Any significant or material changes made to these processes and controls since the last Committee report,

- Any changes that need to be made to the processes and controls based on new regulations together with the committee's plan to address these requirements,

- Business Units and all related personnel have provided timely, accurate required information – *identifying any exceptions requiring CEO / CFO intervention,*

2. The Committee shall consider determinations of MATERIALITY of information and required disclosure, with regards to applicable securities laws and SEC rules,

3. The Committee shall be responsible for the APPOINTMENT OF AUTHORIZED SPOKESPERSONS responsible for external communications (optional based on your company's processes) to the Regulatory Agencies, Investors, Clients, Suppliers and other pertinent third parties.

DISCLOSURE DOCUMENTS:

In the normal course of business, The Disclosure Committee should designate specific working groups to be responsible for preparation, review and approval of specific disclosure documents viz.

- annual and interim financial reports to shareholders and related earnings releases;
- annual information forms required by regulation,
- management proxy circular,
- prospectuses and registration statements,
- press releases containing financial information,
- earnings guidance,
- information about material acquisitions or dispositions or other material information, and
- other current and periodic reports or other information filed with securities regulators (SEC, NYSE, etc.)

Initially, the sub-committees shall be as set out below:

DISCLOSURE DOCUMENT	RESPONSIBLE SUB-COMMITTEE
Annual and interim financial report to shareholders	CFO, Controller, Chief Legal Officer, Investor Relations Department Manager and other personnel as required.
Annual information form, prospectuses, registration statements, other offering documents	CFO, Chief Risk Officer, Chief Legal Officer, Chief Compliance Officer, Investor Relations Department Manager, External Counsel and other personnel as required,
Proxy circular	CEO, Chief Administrative Officer, Chief Legal Officer, Chief Compliance Officer and other personnel as required.
Earnings releases, earnings guidance, release of other material information	CEO, CFO, Controller, Chief Administrative Officer, Chief Legal Officer, Investor Relations Department Manager, Chief Compliance Officer, External Counsel and other personnel as required.
Other periodic reports or disclosure documents filed with securities regulators	CEO, Chief Administrative Officer, Chief Legal Officer, Chief Compliance Officer and other personnel as required.

MEMBERSHIP

Membership in the Committee should comprise of the CEO, CFO, Controller (and/or other Senior Financial/ Accounting Officer), Chief Legal Officer, Chief Compliance Officer, Investor Relationships Department Manager, Senior Business Unit Managers as selected by the CEO.

At the invitation of the CEO, Board and Committee members may be invited to attend key meetings. The External Auditor should be invited whenever the Financial Statements or the Internal Control Framework is discussed.

SEGREGATION OF DUTIES

The Segregation of Duties Policies and Procedures direct your Business Units on the methods to be used to ensure that separate individuals perform key functions within the unit and its transaction processes.

Business Unit SOX Managers are usually assigned the primary responsibility to design and structure the internal controls and responsibilities in order to ensure that there is an appropriate segregation of duties *built into the performance of key functions or processes within the Business Unit.*

This responsibility must be achieved by implementing and executing a formal evaluation process, which ensures that all functions are assessed on a regular, periodic and timely manner *and that incompatible functions are performed by separate individuals.*

ROLES AND RESPONSIBILITIES

As part of the SOX testing, Control Responsibility Officers and Business Unit SOX Managers are required to evaluate the segregation of duties for the internal control framework under their control and to document any deficiencies. They are further required to certify that they have reviewed all processes and controls within their business units and that they all comply with the segregation of duties policy.

In general, the basic tenet underlying appropriate segregation of duties is that *controls over financial reporting should be designed such that no one employee or group of employees should be in a position both to perpetrate and conceal errors or irregularities in the normal course of their duties.*

The primary incompatible functions to be segregated are:

- Authorization
- Custody of Assets
- Recording or reporting of transactions
- Monitoring of Control Effectiveness

TIMING

The scope and frequency of evaluations to ensure that there is an appropriate segregation of duties should be performed:

- At least *once per quarter* and be part of the sub certification process by the Business Unit SOX Manager,

- If there is any *restructuring* within the Business Unit, as part of the restructuring exercise, a segregation of duties evaluation should be performed, or

- If there is a *significant change* within the Business Unit or Company e.g. an acquisition or divesture of another company.

SEGREGATION OF DUTIES GUIDELINES

Adequate segregation of duties reduces the likelihood that errors (intentional or unintentional) will remain undetected by providing for separate distinct processing by different individuals at various stages of a transaction and for independent reviews of all work performed.

The table illustrates an overview of the guidelines and standards that should be used as a template within your company:

SEGREGATION OF DUTIES OVERVIEW TABLE		
TRANSACTION CLASS	MINIMUM SEGREGATION PROCESSES	COMMENTS / DESCRIPTION
ASSETS	Different individual must be responsible for executing the following transaction steps:<ul><li>initiating asset transactions,</li><li>funding the transactions (person authorizing release of funds),</li><li>recording the transaction,</li><li>reconciling the related general ledger and subsidiary accounts, and</li><li>approving write-offs of any assets.</li></ul>	Where the required segregation does not exist, the Business Unit SOX Manager and Control Responsibility Officer must note this exception in their sub certification forms (outlined in other sections of this chapter)
LIABILITIES	<ul><li>initiating liabilities (e.g., purchases and commitments),</li><li>funding the transactions,</li><li>recording the transactions, and</li><li>reconciling the related general ledger and subsidiary records.</li></ul>	
CAPITAL	<ul><li>issuance or repurchase of stock,</li><li>dividend distributions,</li><li>collections or disbursement of related funds,</li><li>recording of equity transactions, and</li><li>reconciling general ledger accounts.</li></ul>	
REVENUE AND EXPENSES	<ul><li>initiating other transactions,</li><li>receipt of funds / disbursement of funds,</li><li>recording the transactions, and</li><li>reconciling subsidiary records.</li></ul>	
SPECIAL CATEGORIES		
JOURNAL ENTRIES	<ul><li>An individual different from the individual that approves the required journal entries enters journal entries into the general ledger application system.</li><li>Different individuals are assigned for the approval and deletion of new general ledger accounts</li></ul>	
RECONCILIATIONS	<ul><li>Reconciliations are reviewed by an individual that is *not the preparer,*</li><li>Reconciliations are prepared and reviewed by individuals who *do not have unrestricted access to assets or liabilities*</li></ul>	
INFORMATION TECHNOLOGY	<ul><li>Segregation of duties in the IT Department is *modular* and separates development, operational and security personnel.</li><li>Business Unit personnel and IT personnel do not commingle functions or accesses,</li><li>Severe restrictions and authorization requirements are placed on access to live production data and usually requires a two-person access code and is only permitted on an exception basis (e.g. to correct system failure).</li><li>General ledger application system users will only be granted access to those functions and data required for their specific job functions (e.g., individuals who are responsible for transaction processing should not maintain General Ledger master files).</li></ul>	

EXEMPTIONS

Exemptions may be applied for, in unusual circumstances, by formal application to the CFO. These must be approved by the CFO in writing and copied to the Internal Audit Department and Audit Committee. Typical examples of these are small satellite offices that do not have a material impact on the financial statements.

Exemptions can be overridden by the CEO, Audit Committee or Board.

SUB CERTIFICATION PROCESS

The sub certification process is designed to provide company management with the assurance that all subordinate levels have performed their internal control duties.

PREREQUISITES

The sub certification process requires that the following prerequisites be established before implementation..:

1. Your organization has clearly defined the ROLES, AUTHORITIES AND RESPONSIBILITIES of each individual responsible for the internal control framework. We have provided this information in Chapter 1 with additional details in the Entity Level program.

    This Authorities / Responsibilities assignment clearly sets the Senior Management's expectations and should ensure that the responsible individuals clearly understand their responsibilities.

2. Your company has a process for reviewing the performance of these individuals periodically with appropriate rewards and penalties being applied based on the quality of the individual's work / results.

    By these performance evaluations, Management will set "*the tone at the top*" throughout the organization and clearly send a message to all personnel that the internal control framework and its processes are important to the organization – *and that no infractions will be tolerated.*

The two prerequisites are critical to ensuring the certifying officers understand their responsibilities and perform their duties in a responsible, prudent manner. Based on this, Management can be reasonably assured that their subordinates' certifications are accurate and complete.

SUB CERTIFICATION ORGANIZATION

The table below provides an overview of the sub certification requirements for each organizational level. We have provided a list of the most typical certifications usually required.

CERTIFICATION / ASSERTION POINTS	CONTROL RESPONSIBILITY OFFICER	BUSINESS UNIT SOX MANAGER	LEGAL ENTITY OFFICERS	REGIONAL BUSINESS MANAGERS	EXTERNAL VENDORS	INFRASTRUCTURE MANAGERS
1. All processes and controls have been accurately and completely documented based on company Guidelines.	Yes	Yes	Yes	Yes	Yes	Yes
2. All processes and controls have been assessed for design and operating effectiveness as at (date) based on the company's assessment guidelines. They have all been found to be designed and operating effectively except as	Yes	Yes	Yes	Yes	Yes	Yes

CERTIFICATION / ASSERTION POINTS	CONTROL RESPONSIBILITY OFFICER	BUSINESS UNIT SOX MANAGER	LEGAL ENTITY OFFICERS	REGIONAL BUSINESS MANAGERS	EXTERNAL VENDORS	INFRASTRUCTURE MANAGERS
noted in the deficiency schedule A attached to the sub certification.						
3. For all identified deficiencies, remediation plans have been prepared and filed with the Repository. These are all listed in Schedule A of this sub certification.	Yes	Yes	Yes	Yes	Yes	Yes
4. There are no fraudulent activities that have come to my attention that involved any employee or third party who have a significant role in the control activities under my accountability.	Yes	Yes	Yes	Yes	Yes	Yes
5. All significant changes to the internal control framework that have materially affected or are reasonably likely to materially affect the unit's control activities subsequent to (date) are disclosed in Schedule B.	Yes	Yes	Yes	Yes	Yes	Yes
6. For processes that are not started and completed within my Business Unit, I have reviewed the entire end to end process and the related controls to ensure that the entire process and controls have been designed and are operated effectively. Any exceptions are noted in Schedule A.	No	Yes	Yes	Yes	Yes	Yes
7. The accounting records supporting (underlying) the balance sheet, income statement and supporting schedules accurately and completely reflect the transactions of my business unit. They are in accordance with GAAP and are reported in the correct legal entity – except for items noted in the Schedule C.	No	Yes	Yes	Yes	No	No
8. All errors have been appropriately reported to the Finance Division, the Controller and the CFO as per the company's guidelines	No	Yes	Yes	Yes	No	No
9. All controls and procedures required by the Company's Disclosure Committee have been assessed and are operating effectively. All information required to be disclosed have been forwarded to the Disclosure Committee in the prescribed format and by the required date.	No	Yes	Yes	Yes	No	No

We would also recommend that certain Entity controls be included in these sub certifications e.g. compliance with code of ethics, etc.

Depending on the External Vendor relationships, an SAS 70 may substitute for this sub certification. However, please ensure that the vendor supplied SAS 70 meets your External Auditor's requirements / standards.

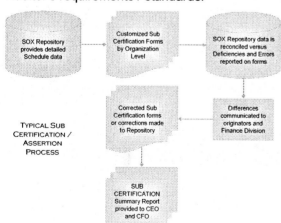

TYPICAL SUB CERTIFICATION / ASSERTION PROCESS

SUB CERTIFICATION PROCESS

The diagram on the left illustrates a typical sub certification process. The final objective of this process is to provide the CEO and CFO with a summary report detailing the results of all sub certification efforts.

The final summary report should provide the CEO and CFO, when combined with the other Senior Management reports, with a comprehensive view of the internal control network and its operating state in your company.

1. PREPARING THE SUB CERTIFICATION FORMS - The SOX Department should prepare the SOX Sub certification forms based on the preceding table.

    We would recommend that the sub certification forms should be customized with specific detailed schedules if your Repository system permits the production of these detailed schedules.

    The table outlines the contents of each sub certification package. These should be delivered electronically in a secure format or be input via an automated system – subject to validation.

    The entire sub certification process should not extend beyond 10 business days.

ORGANIZATION UNIT	CERTIFICATION / ASSERTION POINTS	LIST OF CONTROLS	LIST OF PROCESSES	SCHEDULE A - DEFICIENCIES	SCHEDULE B - SIGNIFICANT CHANGES	SCHEDULE C – ERRORS AND EXCEPTIONS
Control Responsibility Officer	Refer to preceding table	Yes	No	Yes	Yes	Yes
Business Unit SOX Manager		No	Yes	Yes	Yes	Yes
Legal Entity Officer		No	No	Yes	Yes	Yes
Regional Business Manager		No	Yes	Yes	Yes	Yes
External Vendors		No	Yes / No	Yes	Yes	Yes
Infrastructure Managers		Yes	Yes	Yes	Yes	Yes

2. Deliver the sub certification forms with staggered target dates for return of forms. Control Responsibility officers should be required to return their forms *before* Business Unit SOX Managers; Business Unit SOX Managers *before* Regional Business Managers, etc.

3. Upon receipt of forms, reconcile the Schedule A versus the deficiencies identified in the Repository. Any discrepancies must be immediately communicated to the originator with a request for correction or clarification by a specific date.

    These discrepancies are usually caused by non business unit identified deficiencies that are not known or recognized by the Business Unit or the Control Responsibility Officer.

    This step validates the information in the Repository before the final preparation of all management analyses and reports for the fiscal period.

4. Reconcile all errors in Schedule C to the Finance Division Error Logs. Any discrepancies must be communicated to both the Finance Division and the originator for correction and clarification.

    Differences are usually due to errors identified by the Business Unit that have not been captured into the Finance Division's Error Log due to a variety of reasons. The prime reason is usually materiality of the error.

5. Significant changes in Schedule B should be input into the Repository and should form a part of the overall company assessment (summary report) of the internal control framework that is conducted by the CEO, CFO and the SOX Department Manager.

6. The SOX Department is required to ensure that all sub certifications are received by the required due date. Any missing sub certifications should be escalated promptly for

management intervention.

7. The SOX Department, upon completing all reconciliations, should provide the CEO and CFO with sub certification report identifying:

- Sub certifications received on a summary level – highlighting any exceptions,

- A statement that all deficiencies have been accounted for and included in the Aggregation process. The results of which are provided in the Deficiency Aggregation Report from the SOX Department.

    Any exceptions should be highlighted with their materiality,

- All significant changes have been and are included in this report for review, and

- All errors and the impact on the financial reporting process. In addition, the steps being taken to ensure that the error does not recur in the future.

SAMPLE SUB CERTIFICATION FORM

Detailed below is a standard Sub Certification form for a Business Unit SOX Manager:

SUB CERTIFICATION FORM

NAME:	Smith, Abraham	PERIOD COVERED	Quarter ending March 31, 2006
BUSINESS UNIT:	Finance – Brazil	RETURN DATE	April 10, 2006

For all SOX activities within the Business Unit identified on this form, I attest to the following statements:

1. All processes and controls have been accurately and completely documented based on company guidelines.

2. All processes and controls within this business unit have been assessed for design and operating effectiveness as at (March 31, 2006) based on the company's assessment guidelines. They have all been found to be designed and operating effectively except as noted in the deficiency schedule A attached to the sub certification.

3. For all identified deficiencies, remediation plans have been prepared and filed with the Repository. These are all listed in Schedule A of this cub certification.

4. There are no fraudulent activities that have come to my attention that involved any employee who have a significant role in the control activities under my accountability.

5. All significant changes to the internal control framework that have materially affected or are reasonably likely to materially affect the unit's control activities subsequent to (date) are disclosed in Schedule B.

6. For processes that are not started and completed within my Business Unit, I have reviewed the entire end to end process and the related controls to ensure that the entire process and controls have been designed and operated effectively. Any exceptions are noted in Schedule A.

7. The accounting records supporting (underlying) the balance sheet, income statement and supporting schedules accurately and completely reflect the transactions of my business unit. They are in accordance with GAAP and are reported in the correct legal entity – except for items noted in the Schedule C.

8. All errors have been appropriately reported to the Finance Division, the Controller and the CFO as per the company's guidelines

9. All controls and procedures required by the Company's Disclosure Committee have been assessed and are operating effectively.

    All information required to be disclosed have been forwarded to the Disclosure Committee in the prescribed format

and by the required date.	
Business Unit SOX Manager	Date
Signature	Insert Date

Schedule A – Identified Deficiencies

Schedule A – Identified Deficiencies That Have Not Been Remediated

NAME	Smith, Abraham	PERIOD COVERED	Quarter ending March 31, 2006
BUSINESS UNIT	Finance Brazil	RETURN DATE	April 10, 2006

I confirm / attest that the following list of deficiencies are complete and that they are no other identified deficiencies within my Business Unit:

CONTROL ID	DESCRIPTION OF CONTROL ACTIVITY	TYPE OF DEFICIENCY	REMEDIATION PLAN ON FILE?	ETA REMEDIATION
FIN_BRAZL_PROC001_0045	Example text	Operational	Yes	5/12/2006

Schedule B – Significant Changes

Schedule B – Significant Changes to Internal Control Environment

NAME	Smith, Abraham	PERIOD COVERED	Quarter ending March 31, 2006
BUSINESS UNIT	Finance Brazil	RETURN DATE	April 10, 2006

I confirm / attest that the following significant changes are the complete list of changes impacting the internal control framework in my Business Unit.

TYPE	ID	DESCRIPTION OF SIGNIFICANT CHANGE	IMPACT ON INTERNAL CONTROL FRAMEWORK	COMMENTS
Environment	None	Control Responsibility Officer, Janet Jones, replaced in the quarter	None – Janet was the backup Officer. Her new back is Joseph Marques who has been trained in previous quarter	No impact

Schedule C – Errors and Exceptions

Schedule C – Schedule of Errors and Exceptions

NAME	Smith, Abraham	PERIOD COVERED	Quarter ending March 31, 2006
BUSINESS UNIT	Finance Brazil	RETURN DATE	April 10, 2006

I confirm / attest that the following errors and exceptions are the complete list impacting the internal control framework in my Business Unit.

PROCESS OR CONTROL ID	DESCRIPTION OF ERROR	NOTES AND DISCLOSURES	BALANCE SHEET	INCOME STATEMENT

EXTERNAL AUDIT COORDINATION

Coordination with your External Auditors is critical and should focus on the following key elements:

- Basic information exchange on your SOX environment – current policies, procedures, guidelines, etc.
- Scheduling and protocols,
- Assessment (test) guidelines for the fiscal year,
- Issue and Deficiency Management, and
- Management Escalation processes

BASIC INFORMATION EXCHANGE

At the beginning of each fiscal year, you should review formally with your External Auditors your internal control framework, your processes and your proposed plans for the next fiscal year.

1. You should commence this activity with a formal review and closing cycle of the previous fiscal year's SOX Audit. In this process, you should agree on all the issues, deficiencies and other audit requirements identified in the previous year's audit that will be carried over into the new fiscal year,

2. A review of all SOX Policies, procedures, guidelines and management thresholds that will be employed in *this* year's internal control framework assessment – all changes should be highlighted,

3. A review of any External Vendor or Third Party Procedural changes for the upcoming fiscal year,

4. Process improvements sought by the External Auditor for the forthcoming fiscal year – these originate with the External Auditors,

5. Appointment of an External Audit team member as the primary External Audit contact. This individual is responsible for:

    - Delivery and receipt of all data between the two organizations,
    - Jointly updating all External Auditor Issue Logs with the SOX Department contact,
    - Providing all calendar or other scheduling changes, and
    - Coordinating all External Audit activities within your company.

6. Appointment of a SOX Department Supervisor/Manager as the primary External Auditor coordinator. This individual is responsible for:

    - Ensuring that External Auditors receive all information requested,
    - Jointly updating all External Auditor Issue logs with External Auditor coordinator,
    - Communicating all External Audit calendar and scheduling changes to the SOX Department and Business Units, and
    - Coordinating all External Audit activities within your company.

7. Joint review and interpretations of any regulatory or environmental changes – the interpretation should be jointly developed so that both parties can take the appropriate actions within their organizations, and

8. A frank and open discussion on all proposed internal procedural changes from both perspectives – Auditors should voice any objections or concerns at these discussions. Items not jointly agreed upon should be added to the External Audit Issue List.

Scheduling and Protocols

The Schedules for the next fiscal year must be established at a high level for inclusion in the calendar.

Specific dates are not required at this stage, but indications of monthly activities should be requested from your Auditors. Prior to the beginning of each quarter, these should be assigned to specific dates for publication in the Quarterly SOX Bulletin and Calendar.

The operating protocols should also be established for the following:

1. Internal Audit's role, if any, in the assessment of the framework,

2. Operating Protocols for External Vendor's reviews – initial contact, coordination with your company's Supplier contact, Scheduling and timing, etc.

3. Whilst it is understood that the External Auditor has free and unrestricted access to the Audit Committee, Board and Senior Company Management, professional courtesy should provide the basis for frank and open discussions on future presentations by both the SOX Department and the External Auditors,

4. Review and operating processes for External Auditor Issues,

5. Access to Repository information and all derived analyses and reports, The Auditor will request information based on an established process.

Assessment (Test) Guidelines for the Fiscal Year

The Guidelines that will be issued to the Business Units should be reviewed with the External Auditors prior to the beginning and during the fiscal year.

Any unresolved issues should be added to the External Auditor Issue Log.

Issue and Deficiency Management

The processes for deficiency management must be finalized in the following areas:

1. External Audit Issue identification and communications must be established. Preferably, the External Auditor will communicate both to the SOX Department and the responsible Business Unit upon identification of a new issue or deficiency,

2. The list of issues and deficiencies will be reconciled and agreed on a regular, periodic basis in order to ensure that both parties are working with the same base data,

3. The SOX Department will exchange its list of aggregated deficiencies with the External Auditors and will reconcile with the External Auditors to determine any difference in either the processes or results, and

4. An operating protocol should to be established for disagreements on aggregation. How these items will be addressed, etc.

Management Escalation processes

Processes need to be established for the External Auditor to escalate to the Board, Committees and Senior Company Management.

Special Yearend Processes

The final quarter of the fiscal year requires the employment of special processes in a very limited time frame (usually 45 days or less)

The final quarter usually extends into the following fiscal year – we refer to this as the 13th month (even though the period may extend beyond a month). Depending on the automation level/features in your Repository, this period may also require special automation features as outlined in the sections below.

Issue cutoff dates

Depending on your External Auditor's processes, the issues raised by your Auditor and identified on the "Issues" list may be converted into deficiencies by a cutoff date imposed by your Auditors.

This date should be established by your Auditor before the beginning of the 4th quarter.

Usually your Auditor will designate which issues are being assigned as deficiencies (e.g. all controls that in the Auditor's opinion are required but are not present in your Repository)

Annual / Yearend Controls

Annual controls are controls that have a frequency of "*once per year*" as the name implies. Some are performed as part of the closing cycle and cannot be tested until the final stages of the closing period. Therefore, the assessment of these controls usually requires special processes:

The initial assessment review via a walkthrough can usually be performed before the fiscal yearend. However, the operation effectiveness of these controls is usually conducted within the 13th month.

You should discuss with your Auditors the most efficient process for these tests. In some instances, the business unit management will run their tests and immediately advise the Auditors of the results.

The Business Unit should immediately provide the Auditors with the means of running their tests independently, if required.

For some controls, the Auditor and Business Unit may perform their tests simultaneously and compare the results of their tests immediately after.

Since some of these processes have to be performed on a specific date in the closing cycle, it is important that these fiscal yearend controls be coordinated closely.

Sub certifications

Sub certifications are usually filed within 10 days(average in our experience) after a fiscal yearend close.

Auditors will need access to the certifications and their accompanying schedules.

This information should be provided in digital format. Auditors will usually request to see the physical documents based on their sampling model.

REPOSITORY DATA

The submission of Repository data is usually cut off on the last day the fiscal yearend or soon after (the longest elapsed time period we have seen to date is one business week).

Some of the yearend controls are assessed after these cutoff dates. Therefore, special processes need to be developed to ensure that the Auditors receive the test data as outlined in the previous section.

During the post closing phase, Business Units may also seek to update the Repository with corrected information.

Depending on your internal management and Auditor guidelines, you may or may not elect to receive these correction updates.

Most companies elect to receive these post closing updates in a controlled manner. The following are usually the processes by which they perform this function:

1. The yearend repository if backed up and stored as Archive 1 - Fiscal Year 2005 (2005 selected for illustrated purposes only. This version of the Repository is provided to the Auditors as Version 2005-1,

2. Business Units are only permitted to update specific controls and their related data. For example only Fiscal Yearend Controls (annual controls that occur as part of closing cycle) and high risk controls are permitted to be corrected.

3. This information is stored in a special version of the Repository – Archive 2 – Fiscal Year 2005.

4. Usually only two update sessions are performed.

5. All management and auditor reports must reference the archive that is being used to supply the data for the report.

6. Either your company or the Auditor may elect to "*roll back*" to an earlier version if the data in a later version is found to be inconsistent.

GLOSSARY

Aggregation of Deficiencies

The process by which all deficiencies are analyzed and assembled in groups or classes based on the attributes of the underlying control that is deficient.

The critical factor in the aggregation process is which control attributes should be used to group the deficiencies for analysis. We normally recommend the following as a minimum standard by which deficiencies are aggregated:

- Significant Account or Financial Statement Line,
- Business Unit or Location,
- Support Systems, and
- Underlying Processes

Refer to chapter on deficiency management processes for additional details

Assessment of processes and controls

The pre defined series of steps established by your company to review and audit the processes and controls implemented for your internal control framework. This series of steps usually requires walkthroughs, tests, etc.

Audit Committee

This committee should ideally consist of board members who are independent of the management of the entity and have a strong degree of financial literacy. Audit committees typically recommend the CPA or firm to be hired as independent auditors and have oversight responsibilities for both the internal audit function and the independent audit.

The SEC requires publicly-held companies to include reports by their audit committee in proxy statements. Auditing standards require certain communications between the audit firm and the audit committee.

Business Unit

The various operating and reporting organizational units that comprise your company. Included in this should be any outsourcing vendors with contractual arrangements that require them to implement your processes and controls.

Combination of Deficiencies

In this volume, we refer to the combination of deficiencies as the process by which deficiencies are collected from all possible sources viz. Business Units, Entity Level Program, Regulators, etc.

Upon assembling these deficiencies, they must be examined and all duplicates annotated as being duplicates. The result should be a collection of singular deficiencies that can then be used in the aggregation process.

Refer to chapter on deficiency management processes for additional details

Control

A control is usually the steps taken to achieve a specific control objective defined by your company for its internal control framework. Therefore, control activities are the actions of designated individuals carried out to ensure that management directives necessary to mitigate identified risks are executed as per your guidelines.

Control Automation

Usually one of the fields that is required in controls records (or forms) to be completed. This field is used in control framework analyses and should be a part of the master file collection.

- MANUAL – the control is performed manually,
- IT ENABLED – the control is performed manually with the aid of IT reports or analyses, and
- AUTOMATED – the control is fully automated and does not require manual intervention except in error resolution.

Control Classification	For analysis purposes, controls are usually classified into the following classes. This is usually a required field in all control forms and documentation. • PREVENTATIVE (some companies use the term – preventive) controls – controls that have been designed to prevent the occurrence of an error, and • DETECTIVE controls – controls that are designed to detect an error or non compliance with company guidelines, and • MONITORING controls e.g. a supervisor reviews all transactions over $1000 on a daily basis.
Control - Standardized	See *Standard Control*
Control Deficiency	PCAOB Auditing Standard 2, paragraph 8 defines: A CONTROL DEFICIENCY exists when the design or operation of a control does not allow management or employees, in the normal course of performing their assigned functions, to prevent or detect misstatements on a timely basis. • A deficiency in *design* exists when (a) a control necessary to meet the control objective is missing or (b) an existing control is not properly designed so that, even if the control operates as designed, the control objective is not always met. • A deficiency in *operation* exists when a properly designed control does not operate as designed, or when the person performing the control does not possess the necessary authority or qualifications to perform the control effectively.
Control Frequency	The operating frequency of a control within a process. The values permitted are usually part of the master files used for validating information submitted to the Repository. The following are the normal standard values: • On demand, • More than one per day, • Daily, • Weekly, • Fortnightly, • Monthly, • Quarterly, • Semi Annually, • Annually, and • Fiscal Yearend only.
Control ID	A unique ID that is assigned to each control employed in the internal control framework. We recommend that the Control should be a compound ID comprising of key identification attributes of your organization. For example, the control ID should comprise of the following elements at a minimum: • Business Units ID (e.g. BUS_001), • Process control ID (e.g. PROC_0011) , and • a unique sequence number (e.g. 00726) within the process its self. Alternately, your company could assign a unique sequential number to each control. However, in some advanced reporting this may limit the visual acuity of the report when attempting to identify business unit, or process (assuming you use standardized processes), etc.
Control Objective	The objective of a control is to eliminate the risk a misstatement or non disclosure in the company's financial statements and disclosures. It may require several controls within a process to eliminate this risk or to reduce the risk to an inconsequential level.

	A process may have one or more control objective. It may take one or more controls to achieve a control objective.
Control Type	Controls are usually subdivided into the following basic types: - Routine, - Non Routine - Estimation or Provisioning Some companies further expand these control types for analysis purposes into additional types viz. - Period end controls, - Dependent controls e.g. IT general controls, - Disclosure controls, etc. See *Routine, Non Routine and Estimation transactions*.
COSO	Committee of Sponsoring Organizations of the Treadway Commission. Commission provides a model for an internal control framework.
Deficiency	See *Control Deficiency*.
Deficiency ID	A unique ID assigned to identify each deficiency. Deficiencies usually refer to a control ID as either a part of the key or in the Body of the Record.
Disclosure Committee	Refer to *Section in Chapter 11*
Entity Level Controls	A series of controls that have a pervasive effect on the entire entity by their control over the entity's environment, policies, procedures, etc. The controls usually establish the five components of the COSO model into your company's operating philosophies viz. Control Environment, Control Activities, Information and communications, Monitoring and Risk Assessment. Refer to Chapter 3 for additional details.
Error Log **Escalation Process**	See *Finance Division Error Log* The PROCESS by which all errors, exceptions and non compliance events are reported to company management and the board. This process determines the level at which the report should be made based on the severity of the occurrence. All escalated items should be formally documented and logged together with the management directions received and the resolution of the item.
Estimation Transaction	ESTIMATION TRANSACTIONS are activities that involve management judgments or assumptions in formulating account balances in the absence of a precise means of measurement (for example, determining the allowance for doubtful accounts, establishing warranty reserves, assessing assets for impairment).
Finance Division Error Log	The FINANCE ERROR LOG is a collection of all errors identified during a period en closing cycle. These errors are usually identified in the consolidation phase. The Log should state whether these errors were identified by internal personnel or the Auditors. Depending on who identified the error, the SOX Department will have to automatically some of the controls for this specific account within the Business Unit responsible for the error.
Financial Statements	FINANCIAL STATEMENTS present information about an entity's economic resources and obligations at a point in time, the results of its activities during a particular period, and its sources and uses of cash during that period. They focus on information that is useful in making investment and lending decisions. Most

financial statements are prepared using a set of common ground rules, which have been developed over a period of many years, and are called generally accepted accounting principles (GAAP).

Financial Statement Assertions

For each financial statement line and related significant account, the risk assessment process should assign a risk factor for each of the following:

- Existence or occurrence;
- Completeness;
- Valuation or allocation;
- Rights and obligations; and
- Presentation and disclosure.

Refer to chapter of financial statement risk assessments for additional details

Generally Accepted Accounting Principles (GAAP)

GAAP encompasses the conventions, rules, and procedures necessary to define accepted practice in the preparation of financial statements in the U.S. The SEC has the statutory authority to set accounting standards for publicly held companies but historically has relied, without abdicating its responsibilities, on private sector bodies to set those standards. The Financial Accounting Standards Board (FASB) is currently the private-sector body with the primary authority to establish GAAP for all non-governmental entities.

Guidelines

A MANAGEMENT STATEMENT defining the required standard for the performance of specific tasks for the internal control framework. Management usually outlines the best practices and the minimum acceptable standards for these tasks in a series of documents to the SOX community.

Internal Control over Financial Reporting

INTERNAL CONTROL OVER FINANCIAL REPORTING is defined by Rules 13a 15(f) and 15d 15(f) of the U.S. Securities and Exchange Act of 1934 to mean a process designed by, or under the supervision of, the CEO and CFO, and effected by the board of directors, management and other personnel, to provide reasonable assurance regarding the reliability of financial reporting and the preparation of financial statements for external purposes in accordance with generally accepted accounting principles and includes those policies and procedures that: I) Pertain to the maintenance of records that in reasonable detail accurately and fairly reflect the transactions and dispositions of the assets of your company; ii) Provide reasonable assurance that transactions are recorded as necessary to permit preparation of financial statements in accordance with generally accepted accounting principles, and that receipts and expenditures are being made only in accordance with authorizations of management and directors; and iii) Provide reasonable assurance regarding prevention or timely detection of unauthorized acquisition, use or disposition of your company's assets that could have a material effect on the financial statements.

Issue

An item that requires resolution by company management or other individual within the company. Issues usually originate from External Auditors, Internal Audit Department and Regulators. Other Issues may originate in meetings.

Issues should be assigned to specific individuals for resolution by a specific data and should be tracked by SOX Department management.

Management Threshold(s)

These are METRICS / STANDARDS established by management against which they will measure the internal control framework results.

A typical example of this is the test level that is prescribed by management whereby they may designate that all high risk controls can only be tested by re performance.

Another example is the sample sizes or frequency of tests of the internal control framework.

Material Weakness	PCAOB Auditing Standard 2 Paragraph 10 defines a material weakness as: A MATERIAL WEAKNESS is a significant deficiency, or combination of significant deficiencies, that results in more than a remote likelihood that a material misstatement of the annual or interim financial statements will not be prevented or detected.
Non Routine transactions	NON ROUTINE TRANSACTIONS are activities that occur only periodically (for example, taking physical inventory, calculating depreciation expense, adjusting for foreign currencies). A distinguishing feature of non routine transactions is that data involved are generally not part of the routine flow of transactions.
PCAOB	See *Public Company Accounting Oversight Board*
Process	The series of steps employed to produce the desired outcome for a financial transaction.
Process - Standardized	See *Standardized Process*
Process / Transaction Level Controls	The PROCESSES AND CONTROLS over financial reporting that are established with the operating Business Units and External Vendors (if contracts permit). These processes and controls usually comprise a significant portion of the COSO component – Control activities.
Process ID	The UNIQUE ID that identifies a process used in the internal control framework. The process ID may be a compound key that comprises of the Business Unit ID that operates the process and the Process ID. We strongly recommend that all process IDs be issued and controlled from the central SOX Department or other authorizing Department as this will assist in later stages of the entire framework's assessment.
Public Company Accounting Oversight Board (PCAOB)	The PCAOB is a regulatory body created by the Sarbanes-Oxley Act of 2002, which regulates audits of SEC registrants. Operating under the U.S. Securities and Exchange Commission, the PCAOB has the authority for registration, inspection, and discipline of firms auditing SEC registrants, and sets standards for public company audits.
Remediation Plan	An ACTION PLAN that outlines the steps by which a deficiency in the internal control framework will be corrected. The plan will include all steps, resources, costs and timelines.
Repository	See *SOX Repository*.
Risk Assessment	The identification and, where possible, the quantification of RISKS that have a direct or indirect impact on your company's financial reports and its related processes.
Routine Transaction	ROUTINE TRANSACTIONS are recurring financial activities reflected in the accounting records in the normal course of business (for example, sales, purchases, cash receipts, cash disbursements).
SAS 70	STATEMENT ON AUDITING STANDARDS (SAS) NO. 70, Service Organizations, is an internationally recognized auditing standard developed by the American Institute of Certified Public Accountants (AICPA). A SAS 70 examination signifies that a service organization has had its control objectives and control activities examined by an independent accounting and auditing firm. A formal report including the auditor's opinion is issued to the service organization at the conclusion of a SAS 70 examination. The report enables service organizations to demonstrate that they have adequate controls and safeguards when they host or process data belonging to their customers

Segregation of Duties The PROCESS OR RULE by which the separation of the management or execution of certain duties or of areas of responsibility is employed in order to prevent and reduce opportunities for unauthorized modification or misuse of the company's financial resources or assets..

Significant Account An ACCOUNT which directly contributes to a financial statement line that has been deemed to be significant in the company's financial reports. This account (and its related processes) will be required to be "*covered*" by the internal control framework.

Significant Account Control Coverage SIGNIFICANT ACCOUNT CONTROL COVERAGE – in this instance, we are referring to the Business Unit transaction level controls which should document the Significant Account and Process to which they apply. The controls received from a Business Unit are usually compared to the list assigned by the SOX Department at the end of each fiscal period. If the Business Unit did not "cover" or meet the requirement to implement a control(s) for specific significant accounts, the unit is usually required to correct this deficiency promptly.

Significant Deficiency PCAOB Auditing Standard 2 Paragraph 9 defines a significant deficiency as:

A SIGNIFICANT DEFICIENCY is a control deficiency, or combination of control deficiencies, that adversely affects the company's ability to initiate, authorize, record, process, or report external financial data reliably in accordance with generally accepted accounting principles such that there is more than a remote likelihood that a misstatement of the company's annual or interim financial statements that is more than inconsequential will not be prevented or detected.

Significant Process The processes which control the processing of transaction for a specific transaction type or account.

SOX Repository The unit within the SOX Department that is responsible for the secure storage of all SOX material. In most companies, this material is stored in a digital format. The access to the material should be restricted to the highest security levels within your company. Some companies buy specialized SOX systems.

The Repository is also responsible for providing the information for all analyses and reports or the preparation of these analyses and reports.

Standardized Control A STANDARDIZED CONTROL is one which has been designed and tested for use throughout your entire company.

The control is usually developed by a team and distributed throughout the organization for use by all Business Units. *These controls cannot be changed or altered in any way by the operating Business Units.*

The assessment of this control is based on a standard series of steps that is developed by the same design team.

Standardized Process A STANDARDIZED PROCESS is one which has been designed and tested for use throughout your entire company.

The process is usually developed by a team and distributed throughout the organization for use by all Business Units. *These processes cannot be changed or altered in any way by the operating Business Units.*

The assessment of this process is based on a standard series of steps that is developed by the same design team.

Walkthrough A Walkthrough is the review of a process from initiation (e.g. order entry) to end process (e.g. revenue recognition). In this review, a single, representative transaction is selected and is traced from the beginning to the end of the process to verify that the process and its related controls are accurately documented and that the controls are operating as designed.

Printed in the United States
48721LVS00003B/3-104